Contents

6 The Tuscan Coast: Livorno to Lazio 137

7 The Val d'Orcia, Valdichiana & Pitigliano 163

8 Perugia, Assisi & Northern Umbria 187

9 Orvieto & Southern Umbria 217

The Insider 237

Index 247

About the Authors

Donald Strachan is a London-based writer, editor and copywriter. He has written about European travel for the *Sunday Telegraph, Independent on Sunday, Sydney Morning Herald* and *Zest* magazine, and is co-author of Frommer's *The Balearics With Your Family* (2007). He lives in Hackney with his partner and two young daughters.

Stephen Keeling grew up in England, lived briefly in Latvia and spent 12 years as a financial journalist in Asia. Despite attempts to kick his gelato addiction, he has been to Italy many times – an incomparable knowledge of Tuscan Chinese restaurants formed while chaperoning a group of Vietnamese officials in 1994. Stephen has written travel guidebooks on Taiwan, Spain, Mexico and Puerto Rico, and currently lives in New York City.

Acknowledgements

First, thanks to Stephen, my co-author: right place, right time, right person. Professionally, thanks too to Adriana at ENIT and staff at APT and Pro Loco offices all over Tuscany and Umbria. Thanks to Anne for being an art professor and a great cook when I needed both, Phil for the papers, and Dominic for those books that arrived too late; to Mum and Dad for Umbria, Mary and Nuccio for kindness and Italy's best underground office, and Colin and Sue for a special place to write and a nudge in the direction of Pistoia. Most of all, to Lucia, Lili and Ruby without whom thousands of the words here wouldn't exist. Love you. (DS)

Special thanks to Karen Tomashavsky at the Museo di Storia della Scienza in Florence, my co-author Donald, Barbara Keeling for the computer, and as always, Tiffany Wu for all her help and support. (SK)

An Additional Note

Please be advised that travel information is subject to change at any time and this is especially true of prices. We therefore suggest that you write or call ahead for confirmation when making your travel plans. The authors, editors and publisher cannot be held responsible for experiences of readers while travelling. Your safety is important to us however, so we encourage you to stay alert and be aware of your surroundings.

Star Ratings, Icons & Abbreviations

Hotels, restaurants and attraction listings in this guide have been ranked for quality, value, service, amenities and special features using a star-rating system. Hotels, restaurants, attractions, shopping and nightlife are rated on a scale of zero stars (recommended) to three (exceptional). In addition to the star rating system, we also use 5 feature icons that point you to the great deals, in-the-know advice and unique experiences. Throughout the book, look for:

FIND	Special finds – those places only insiders know about
MOMENT	Special moments – those experiences that memories are made of
VALUE	Great values – where to get the best deals
OVERRATED	Places or experiences not worth your time or money
GREEN	Attractions promoting responsible tourism policies

The following abbreviations are used for credit cards:

AE	American Express
MC	Mastercard
V	Visa

A Note on Prices

Frommer's provides exact prices in each destination's local currency. As this book went to press, the rate of exchange was €1 = £0.72. Rates of exchange are constantly in flux; for up-to-the minute information, consult a currency-conversion website such as www.oanda.com/convert/classic. In the Family-friendly Accommodation section of this book we have used a price category system.

An Invitation to the Reader

In researching this book, we discovered many wonderful places – hotels, restaurants, shops and more. We're sure you'll find others. Please tell us about them, so we can share the information with your fellow travellers in upcoming editions. If you were disappointed with a recommendation, we'd love to know that too. Please email: frommers@wiley.co.uk or write to:

Frommer's Tuscany & Umbria with Your Family, 1st edition
John Wiley & Sons, Ltd
The Atrium
Southern Gate
Chichester
West Sussex, PO19 8SQ

Photo Credits

Cover Credit

Main Image: © Theodore Liasi / Alamy
Small Images (L-R):
© Brian Lawrence Images Ltd / PCL
© Tibor Bognor / Alamy
© Robert Harding Picture Library Ltd / Alamy
© Jon Arnold Images / Alamy
Back Cover: © Rod Edwards / TTL

Front Matter Credits

pi: © Theodore Liasi / Alamy; piii © Brian Lawrence Images Ltd / PCL; © Tibor Bognor / Alamy; © Robert Harding Picture Library Ltd / Alamy; © Jon Arnold Images / Alamy; piv: © Brian Lawrence Images Ltd / PCL; © Tibor Bognor / Alamy; © Robert Harding Picture Library Ltd / Alamy; © Jon Arnold Images / Alamy.

Inside Credits

© Chris Parker / Axiom: p197.
© Donald Strachan: p4, p10a, p10b, p11, p37, p42, p49, p51, p60, p68, p72, p75, p81, p84, p95, p110, p112, p122, p123, p136, p140, p148, p150, p154, p157, p161, p175, p176, p184, p191, p193, p199a, p199b, p202, p204, p207, p212, p217, p228, p231, p233.
© Lucia Santi: p1, p104, p147, p170.
Courtesy of Alamy: p127 (© Stock Italia); p129 (© Ian Aitken / John Warburton-Lee Photography); p187 (© Enzo Signorelli / CuboImages srl); p222 (© Walter Aerla / CuboImages srl); p237 (© John Ferro Sims).
Courtesy of Fototeca ENIT: p7b, p120, p169, p172, p224 (© Vito Arcomano); p98 (© Paola Ghirotti),
Courtesy of PCL: p53, p107 (© Brian Lawrence Images Ltd); p77 (© David Noble); p89 (© Edmund Nagele).
Courtesy of Photolibrary: p137 (© Cephas Picture Library Ltd); p180 (© bruno Morandi / Robert Harding Picture Library Ltd).
Courtesy of The Travel Library (TTL): p5 (© Mike Kipling); p7 (© Stuart Black); p163 (© Rod Edwards).

1 Family Highlights of Tuscany & Umbria

'Never an empty bed in Tuscany' is a phrase you often hear from expatriates living in this dreamiest corner of central Italy. Such is the epic scenery, the rustic food and iconic wines, and the everyday beauty, that if you live here, you're never short of a weekend guest. It's the same in Umbria. Urban, rural or beachfront, hill-town street café or rustic farmhouse, both regions have an unsophisticated, easy charm that welcomes you just as it leaves you in no doubt that this is a place apart. The lone cypress standing in the Val d'Orcia; the morning mists over the Vale of Spoleto; the sublime art and architecture of Renaissance Florence or medieval Siena – you could *only* be here.

So, how do you begin to get the best out of Tuscany and Umbria, now you're travelling as a family? You've doubtless spotted a few guidebooks to choose from. Some of them are great – we occasionally use them ourselves. But none tell you where in Pisa to feed a toddler who can't wait until 7.30pm for the restaurants to open. Or where to change a nappy close to Assisi's Basilica, how to entertain a bored teen in the Lunigiana and where to find a soft-play area near Florence's Duomo. We could go on. It's no longer enough for your guidebook to pinpoint all the frescoes and fine dining. You want to know all that *as well*, but first you need to locate a quality ice cream and a playground. Now. What you want most of all is for someone to have looked at Tuscany and Umbria with new eyes – along with at least one pair of young eyes – that have visited the area as parents, and spoken to countless families who live and work there. That's where we come in. Between us, we've lived, worked and travelled in every corner of both regions, to find places to take your children that aren't listed anywhere else. We've come up with tips, tricks and custom-made itineraries to help you experience the classic sights and tastes as a family. To help you enjoy together the very best of the culture and lifestyle of both Tuscany and Umbria.

Let's pause for a second. Don't think this is a book for the children – a guide to 'what youngsters can do in Tuscany and Umbria'. It isn't. A family holiday is about *all of you* having fun, which means three different kinds of days. First, *their* days: water parks, theme parks, turtle parks, animal parks, Pinocchio parks, all the child-centric entertainment you can find. It's here. Second, there are *your* days: some children are going to hate the Uffizi, we all know it, so you need to jump the queue and get round in two hours, or leave them with friends and family so you can do it properly. Do you want to dash off for a cultural afternoon, to taste Tuscany's finest wines, or for a candle-lit dinner, leaving the little ones with the grandparents? Keep reading, it's all here. Third are the best days of all – days when you're *all* doing something you love: hiking in the Maremma, canoeing on Lago Trasimeno, watching a Serie A football match, climbing Siena's tower, exploring tunnels under Orvieto or soaking up the sun on an Elban beach. Or (and don't laugh) you're in a temple of Renaissance art armed with some killer facts to help you make

14th-century frescoes interesting for everyone, however young. These sorts of days are the backbone of our book, so please read on.

Perhaps you have one more question: are Tuscany and Umbria really for *my* family? Don't believe (all) the hype: you certainly don't need to be rich to find exploration and inspiration here. With the right advice, it can be cheap to fly in, cheap to get about, cheap to eat out and cheap to stay. When you want to splash out, we'll suggest where and you can take it from there. Tuscany, in particular, isn't short of luxury hideouts, award-winning spas and unique rural retreats. Then there's the art. *All that art*. In truth, if you're not even *a tiny bit* interested in Renaissance art and architecture, you've picked the wrong destination. You can find all-inclusive complexes, great water parks and golf courses elsewhere, for less. You're paying a premium in Tuscany and Umbria to be close to this art, so we've chosen the best for you to sample and put it in context. If you don't know much about it yet, you're in the best place on earth to learn. Just reward yourselves with an ice cream afterwards.

Over the course of our lives, we've travelled the length of Italy. We've raised children, made friends and lived like Italians. Take it from us: you're about to embark on a tour of the very best bit. Enjoy!

BEST FAMILY EXPERIENCES

Best Outdoor Adventures With hiking, biking and canoeing trails for all ages and abilities, the **Parco Regionale della Maremma** is the number-one reason to base yourselves in south-western Tuscany. See p. 154. Get ready, get wet, go. Riding the rapids of the **Valnerina** is for everyone, aged 4 to 74. Just don't wear your favourite shirt. See p. 13. Zip-slides, Tibetan bridges, quads and mountain bike trails await you at the **Parco Avventura Fosdinovo**, in the Lunigiana. It isn't cheap, but where else can you have this much fun in a Tuscan tree? See p. 131. The whole of **Isola Polvese**, Lago Trasimeno's biggest island, is now a nature reserve and environmental education centre. There's room to roam and sights to see together. See p. 199.

Best Underground Worlds Get a feel for Etruscan life, and death, at the **Tomba della Quadriga Infernale** outside Sarteano. This recent discovery was painted 300 years before Christ and is at the heart of a network of Etruscan burial sites. See p. 178. They lay under the mud of Pisa's old harbour for two millennia, but now 11 Roman ships have been uncovered at the **Cantiere delle Navi Antiche di Pisa**. Watch the digging and restoration in action. See p. 115. Seeing all 1,200 of Orvieto's caves would take half a lifetime. A one-hour guided tour with **Orvieto Underground** takes in subterranean homes, water wells, ceramic ovens, pigeon coops, quarries, natural fridges and WW2 air-raid shelters. See p. 222.

Best Museums Half-Italian, half-Scot Frederick Stibbert probably didn't intend it, but his eccentric collection, now the **Museo Stibbert**, is a Florentine mini-mecca for the knights'n' castles, Harry Potter generation. Don't miss the medieval suits of armour. See p. 58. For a spot of science, including Galileo's instruments, Michelangelo's Compass and a medieval pharmacy, Florence's **Museo di Storia della Scienza** treats curious children of all ages. See p. 54.

Best Beaches There are 150 perfect beaches to choose from on Elba, so start planning now. The perfect crescents and fluorescent waters at **Fetovaia** and **Cavoli** could be the Seychelles; the rock pools at **Sant'Andrea** offer more for little explorers than sun, sand and pedaloes. See p. 148. Head for the massive sandy arc of the **Tombolo della Feniglia**, which joins the almost-island of Monte Argentario to the mainland. See p. 158.

Best for Footie Fans Tuscany has four Serie A teams, and they all welcome youngsters. The child-friendliest of the lot is little **Livorno**. A seat in their best stand will cost you €35 – your under-8s get in for €1. Come on 'the purples'. See p. 142. Followers of the rich and famous might prefer **Fiorentina**. See p. 63.

Best Bike Rides The tree-lined boulevards that crown **Lucca**'s mighty walls are a great way to see the city for young families – good and flat for cycling. See p. 121. The gentle gradients and quiet roads around **Lago Trasimeno** are ideal tracks for an afternoon in the saddle. See p. 200.

Best Ascents There isn't a view to match the 1,019m summit of Elba's **Monte Capanne** cable car. From Livorno to Lazio, Corsica to Capraia, Tuscany is laid out below on a turquoise carpet of Mediterranean Sea. See p. 149. There's one place the children will want to head the minute you reach Siena. The 388 steps of the medieval **Torre del Mangia**, the city's bell tower, end at a dizzying lookout above the Campo. See p. 81.

Fetovaia Beach, Elba

Piazza del Campo, Siena

EXPLORING TOGETHER

Best Hill-towns Italy's spiritual heart, **Assisi**, sits on its perfect perch above the Vale of Spoleto. See p. 201. To see **San Gimignano** at its best, stay overnight and wander the medieval heart as night falls. Rise early and catch the Collegiata in peace. See p. 88. **Volterra** is Tuscany's friendliest hill-town with fine art, good food and the region's best festival for children. See p. 92.

Undervisited Gems Your first sight of **Pitigliano**, sprouting from volcanic rock, is one that will linger long after you've left Tuscany. The town is a warren of twisted streets and gnarled staircases, with a preserved Jewish ghetto and plenty of outdoor Etruscan action. See p. 179. The 'Balcony of Umbria', **Montefalco** is a hill-town whose dozing nature conceals Umbria's finest wine and somewhere to see Renaissance painting without the jostling. See p. 225.

Best Castles Climb up to Cortona's **Fortezza Medicea Girifalco** to see four intact bastions and a keep, as well as unmatched views over the Valdichiana and Lago Trasimeno. See p. 166. Montalcino's **Fortezza** kept the Sienese flag flying for four years after the city's defeat by Florence. It's now the only place in Tuscany where you can scramble over medieval walls and taste one of the town's 208 Brunello wines, all at the same time. See p. 175.

Perfect Piazzas **Piazza del Campo**, the scallop-shaped setting for Siena's famous Palio race, is the heart of the city and an icon of medieval town-planning. Park yourself at a café as night falls and soak up the evening. See p. 81. Simple, serene and equally celebrated, Todi's **Piazza del Popolo** is Umbria's most majestic square. *Palazzi* of 13th-century vintage are complemented by a 12th-century Duomo that whispers architectural perfection. See p. 223.

JUST FOR CHILDREN

Best Animal Encounters For turtles and tortoises of every size and species, including a giant Sahel, **Carapax Turtle Sanctuary** is your place. It's focused entirely on children, with a playground, picnic area and plenty of environmental education. See p. 152. Get to know the secret night-time lives of wolves, owls and lynx on a moonlight visit to **Pistoia Zoo** – remember to book ahead. See p. 124.

Best Toddler Time-outs There's a world of magic waiting under Città di Castello, at the **Botteghe Artigiani di Silvio Bambini**. His miniature, moving high street, crafted from olive and oak, took 22 years to make – and not a bit gets lost in translation. See p. 24. When toddlers are tired of pounding the pavement, stop in at Florence's **Mondobimbo** play area for assorted things that bounce, squish and bang. And you can take the weight off your feet, too. See p. 62. There's enchantment, imagination and some intriguing design at Collodi's **Pinocchio Park**. Once the maze has been conquered, make for Painting Corner or a live show. See p. 125.

Older Ones Only For the grisly, gruesome and morbidly fascinating, head over Florence's Arno to **La Specola**. If the Room of Skeletons doesn't get the children, the dissected wax head and mock-ups of plague-infested Florence surely will. See p. 60. There are no models at **Le Mummie di Ferentillo**, in the crypt of Santo Stefano, just a grisly parade of mummified corpses in a ghoulish Umbrian setting. See p. 231. Visit Florence's **Palazzo Vecchio** in the company of celebrated 16th-century art historian Giorgio Vasari – this tour of the secret passageways and hidden rooms of Florence's city hall is in English – and you'll need to book ahead. See p. 51.

ART & ARCHITECTURE

Best Churches Western art was born at the glorious **Basilica di San Francesco** in Assisi. The Gothic Upper Church houses Giotto's 28-part fresco, *The Life of St Francis*. Downstairs, look out for more sublime Giotto, Simone Martini, Pietro Lorenzetti and Cimabue. See p. 202. Masaccio's magical *Scenes from the Life of St Peter*, in Florence's **Santa Maria del Carmine**, marked the next giant leap forward in painting perspective, realism and emotion. See p. 61. Arezzo is the home of Tuscany's most perfect frescoes: Piero della Francesca's **Legend of the True Cross** is a giant of Western art. See p. 98. Garish or glorious, there's nothing on the

Basilica di San Francesco, Assisi

planet quite like **Orvieto's Duomo**, and don't miss some gruesome interpretations of the *Last Judgement*. See p. 220.

Essential Paintings Start at Florence's **Uffizi** (p. 52) for Botticelli's *Birth of Venus* and Leonardo's *Adoration*. Siena's **Museo Civico** (p. 83) is a showcase for Simone Martini's *Maestà* and Ambrogio Lorenzetti's civic *Allegories*. Umbria's top gallery, the **Galleria Nazionale** in Perugia (p. 194) houses Perugino's moving *Adoration* and Piero della Francesca's *Annunciation*, painted in precise perspective. And don't forget Volterra's **Pinacoteca** (p. 93) for Rosso Fiorentino's *Deposition*, the first truly 'modern' work of Tuscan art.

Best Art Places with Children There's no hushed reverence and few crowds at Siena's **Santa Maria della Scala**, slowly transforming itself into a series of galleries, passageways and exhibition spaces, with tons of room to get thoroughly lost. Highlights include the spooky basement Museo Archeologico. See p. 84. The role of art in everyday religious life is brought home at Florence's **Museo di San Marco** – especially upstairs in Fra' Angelico's frescoed monks' cells. See p. 57.

Awe-inspiring Architecture There is no building in the world more easily recognisable than Pisa's 12th-century **Leaning**

The Leaning Tower, Pisa

Tower. Children need to be 8 or older to climb to the top. See p. 113. For sheer building expertise, Brunelleschi's dome of the Florentine **Duomo di Santa Maria del Fiore** is peerless. Admire it for free, climb inside it or haul yourselves up Giotto's bell tower for the best view of all. See p. 49. Spoleto's awe-inspiring **Ponte delle Torri**, 90m above the Tessino gorge, is impressive enough. Don't even ask how those Romans built an aqueduct before it. See p. 230.

THE BEST ACCOMMODATION

Best Urban Bases A rural view, two minutes from the centre of Spoleto? It can only be the **Hotel Gattapone**: family suites, panoramic windows and parking on your doorstep make a unique treat for older children. See p. 234. Yours for €2000 a week: the frescoed **Palazzo Antellesi** in Florence's Piazza Santa Croce has been converted into 13 apartments. Five minutes from the Uffizi, five from the Arno and barely more than five from everything you want to see in Florence. See p. 68.

Best Country Retreats Individually decorated rooms, a picturesque location handy for Pisa and Lucca, and scrambled eggs for breakfast: the **Hotel Villa Rinascimento** has all that at a price that won't bust the budget. See p. 134. The six apartments at **Agriturismo Al Gelso Bianco** could hardly be better sited, close to Florence, Chianti and the Sienese hill-towns. Ask for 'Ginestra' and your terrace looks right at San Gimignano. See p. 100. There are no views at the **Fattoria San Lorenzo**, just well-equipped, split-level mini-houses in a converted farm complex among quiet Maremman countryside. See p. 158.

Best Campsites Come for the views, stay for the services. The **Barco Reale**'s lofty perch on Monte Albano ensures panoramas from Prato to Livorno – and the site has activities during summer to keep your youngsters amused. See p. 133. Florence's **Campeggio Michelangelo** is packed all summer, with good reason. The rooftop views are far-reaching, the children get a playground and there's nowhere else in the city you can stay at this price. See p. 70.

THE BEST FOOD

Best Tuscan Treats Quality Tuscan cooking bang in the middle of a tourist town – you must be in Volterra's **Antica Osteria dei Poeti**. Dig in – see p. 106. Not a boar in sight at the Etruscan Coast's tastiest fish restaurant, **La Barcaccina** on San Vincenzo beach. While you're waiting for your seafood, kick off those shoes and build some sandcastles. See p. 162.

Fourteen for Free

You'll be surprised at how much you can see and do in Tuscany and Umbria for nothing.

- Drive through the mesmerising, cypress-studded landscape of **Le Crete Senesi** along the SS438, p. 88.
- Wander in the footsteps of St Francis on **Monte Subasio**, p. 204.
- Enter every **cathedral** in Tuscany and Umbria (except the one in Pisa).
- Explore an **Etruscan burial site** above the Valdichiana, p. 178.
- View fine Renaissance frescoes in **Spoleto**, p. 229, **Assisi**, p. 202, and **Gubbio**, p. 207.
- Soak yourselves in the 37°C **thermal springs** at Saturnia, p. 182.
- Experience the monastic calm of **Sant'Antimo**, p. 175 and **Monte Oliveto Maggiore**, p. 173.
- Stand for hours admiring Ghiberti's **Gates of Paradise** in Florence, p. 50.
- Meet the Tuscan wildlife at the **Parco Naturale di Cavriglia**, p. 95.
- Drink in the emerald-green **Val d'Orcia** behind Pienza's Duomo, p. 173.
- Process the ancient **Via Cava di San Giuseppe**, outside Pitigliano, p. 161.
- Enjoy museums like Pisa's **Piaggio**, p. 116, and Siena's **Natural History**, p. 85.
- See the magnificent monuments of Pisa's Campo, including the **Leaning Tower** – from the outside, p. 113.
- Sun yourselves on the best **beaches** of Elba, p. 148 and the Tuscan mainland, p. 143.

Best Umbrian Cooking Hanging hams, Montefalco wine and a dessert that uses only Perugina chocolate. You won't find a more Umbrian eatery than **Al Coccio**, in Magione's suburbs. See p. 216. If it's a touch of class you're after, book a spot on the terrace at Montefalco's **Coccorone**. Enjoy a quality menu and attentive service at a great price. See p. 235.

Best Bargain Bites It's as local as it comes at **La Botteghina**. There's no proper menu, just a succession of Livornese specialities made with whatever looked good at this morning's market. Don't miss the *baccalà* or *cacciucco*. See p. 161. Home cooking doesn't get any better than **Da Bussè** in the Lunigiana. A Ligurian influence is obvious – the *pesto* is Tuscany's tangiest. See p. 136. Cheap eats in

Florence? You must be joking? Not at **Trattoria da Rocco:** take a walk to the Mercato di Sant'Ambrogio for a local lunch, with mains €3–4. See p. 76. Like the barbecue you always dreamed about, the outdoor flamegrill at **La Stalla** is Umbria's best self-service, just outside Assisi. Grab a tablecloth and cutlery, find a table and prepare to be dazzled. See p. 214.

Best Ice Cream Stops Where else to start but the ice cream World Champions: **Gelateria 'di Piazza'** in San Gimignano. Their Crema di Santa Fina is made with saffron and really hits the spot. See p. 90. There's no shortage of choice in Florence, but **Vivoli** edges it. See p. 75. You'll find Umbria's best *gelato* in the unlikeliest of spots, by a busy junction in Spoleto. **Colder** is worth the trip. See p. 229.

Perfect Pizza

Basilica di San Francesco, Assisi

2 Planning a Trip to Tuscany & Umbria

TUSCANY & UMBRIA

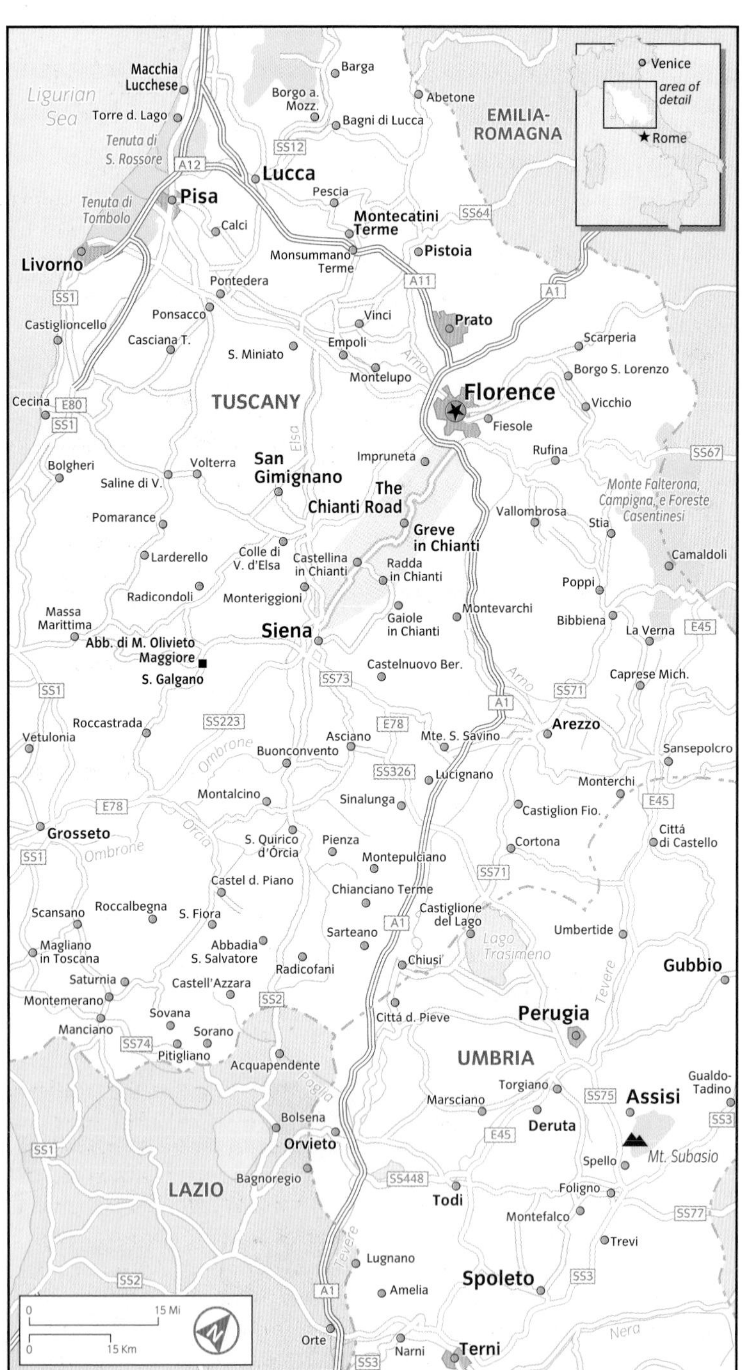

The key to a successful family holiday is planning. That doesn't mean you have to decide right now where to have lunch on day 11. But you'll certainly find that you get an enjoyable holiday, at an enjoyable price, if you do some initial groundwork from the comfort of your own home. Once you've arrived, your planning in advance means that everyone can hit the ground running.

One thing to remember about Italy is that '**family-friendly**' means just that. You'll find a welcome for your little ones in museums, galleries, restaurants and hotels – in fact just about everywhere you go. And don't fret about whether there's a children's menu or not in restaurants – waiting staff normally fall over themselves to help. A couple of weeks in Tuscany and Umbria and you will all be so relaxed that you won't want to come home ever again.

VISITOR & PLANNING INFORMATION

A bit of web research before the off helps separate the durum wheat from the chaff. **ENIT** (*Ente Nazionale Italiano per il Turismo*), the Italian Tourist Board, has a London office at 1 Princes Street, London W1B 2AY (*00800 482542*). It's the same freephone number for Ireland. Their English-language website (***www.enit.it*** or ***www.italiantouristboard.co.uk***) is a reasonable starting point.

In general, you'll find Italy fairly **web-savvy**. Every community, right down to the smallest *comune*, has an easily navigable site. Many are in English. For trip-planning purposes, start with the main *regione* tourist sites. For Tuscany, that's ***www.turismo.toscana.it***; for Umbria, ***www.umbria2000.it***. Especially useful are their events and festivals search engines. Plug your trip dates in to see what's on when you're there.

One level down, several *provincia* websites are worth checking. All are listed in the individual chapters that follow; among the best are ***www.terresiena.it*** and ***www.costadeglietruschi.it***.

Child-specific Websites

Specifically for children in Italy, ***www.bambinopoli.it*** is invaluable and informative. Also see ***www.deabirkett.com***, ***www.babygoes2.com*** and ***www.takethefamily.com***.

For Lone Parents

One organisation worth contacting if you're a lone parent travelling is the recently merged **One Parent Families / Gingerbread** (*0800 018 5026*, ***www.oneparentfamilies.org.uk***). There's tons of information on the site, including inspirational ideas for summer family fun and a fact sheet on holidaying as a lone parent.

Membership of the **Single Parent Travel Club** (*0870 2416210, www.sptc.org.uk*) costs £7.50/year. Be sure to ask your tour operator about single-parent discounts: camp specialists **Siblu** (*0870 2427777, www.siblu.com*) and **Canvas Holidays** (*0870 1917865, www.canvasholidays.co.uk*) have offered these in the past.

For Disabled Travellers

UK charity **Tourism For All** (*0845 1249971, www.holidaycare.org.uk*) produces a leaflet offering accessibility advice for disabled and elderly people travelling to Italy. It's available from their website and costs £3.50, but if you want to keep bang up-to-date, call their information line before you book. They also have online resources for anyone travelling with a disabled child. The **Owners Direct** (*01372 229330, www.ownersdirect.co.uk*) website allows you to search for accommodation by accessibility (*www.ownersdirect.co.uk/search-wheelchair-accommodation.asp*). **Accessatlast** (*01772 814 555, www.accessatlast.com*), the one-stop shop for accessible accommodation, also recommends property in Umbria between Perugia and Lago Trasimeno. **Accessible Italy** (*0378 941111, www.accessibleitaly.com*) specialise in English-speaking tours of Italy, including Siena, San Gimignano and Florence.

The national voluntary association representing disabled people in Italy is **AIAS** (*06 39731704/829, www.aiasnazionale.it*). Their Florence office (*055 3215145*) is at Via Leoncavallo 20. In **Spoleto** (*0743 48415*), in Umbria, you'll find them at Via XVI Marzo 1. If you have a query relating to train travel, call the **Trenitalia disabled helpline** on *199 303060*. They can also reserve equipped seats for you. **Co.In Sociale** (*06 7129011, www.coinsociale.it/tourism*) have a number of contacts for information about guides and tour packages.

Further invaluable websites for Umbria are *www.tourinumbria.org* and *www.assisiaccessibile.it*. The latter has detailed accessibility information on Assisi.

Throughout the book we've noted when an attraction has disabled access.

ENTRY REQUIREMENTS, CUSTOMS & BRINGING PETS

Passports & Visas

British and Irish citizens need only produce a valid **passport** or **national identity card** to be admitted to Italy. Either is acceptable. No visa is required. All other visitors must have a passport valid at least three months beyond the proposed stay. If your passport or identity card is stolen, report to your consulate (see p. 35) immediately.

Note that babies and children up to 16 not already on a parent or guardian's passport now need their own child passport. These last for five years (three for under-3s in Ireland). If your child is already on your passport they can continue this way until they turn 16, your passport runs out or they need to get their own.

Allow enough time before your trip to apply for a passport; six weeks or more during busy periods, like spring. Ensure that you have completed the form correctly, included the correct documentation and, most importantly, followed the strict regulations concerning photographs. These regularly hold up applications. For more information, contact the **United Kingdom Passport Service** (*0870 5210410, **www.ukpa.gov.uk***). Pick up application forms at your nearest passport office, any major post office or travel agencies. In **Ireland**, pick up an application form at any Garda station and most libraries. The Post Offices runs a **Passport Express** service, which enables you to have the application forms and photos checked before posting them. Call *1679 7600* or see ***www.foreignaffairs.gov.ie*** for more information.

Taking Your Pet

EU citizens can bring cats and dogs into Italy, as long as they have been issued with a **pet passport**, fitted with a **microchip** and **vaccinated** against rabies. Furry friends are not usually accepted at hotels or self-catering accommodation, so hire a villa if you can't bear to leave Fido at home. In any case, you'll have to ask the property owner for permission. See ***http://ec.europa.eu/food/animal/liveanimals/pets/index_en.htm*** for EU rules on the movement of animals; ***www.defra.gov.uk/animalh/quarantine/index.htm*** explains UK regulations on bringing your pet back home.

Customs

Coming into Italy, you can bring tobacco products and alcohol for your own use without limit, although you'll find them cheaper to buy at a supermarket in Italy than at the airport or in your local Sainsburys. If you're driving into Italy, you're unlikely even to be asked for your passport at the border, never mind to declare what you're carrying.

Coming home, you can bring any amount of goods for personal use, except new vehicles, mail-order purchases and more than 90 litres of wine, 10 litres of spirits, 110 litres of beer or 3,200 cigarettes. The rules for the UK and Ireland are almost identical. If in doubt, UK citizens should contact **HM Customs and Excise** (*0845 0109000, **www.hmrc.gov.uk***). In Ireland, download leaflet **PN1878** from the Revenue website (***www.revenue.ie***) or call *167 44050*.

What Things Cost in Tuscany & Umbria	Central Florence	Suburban Perugia
Set lunch at mid-priced restaurant	€12	€13
Bus fare (single)	€1.20	€0.90
1 litre milk in supermarket	€0.70	€1.05
½ litre still water in supermarket	€0.20	€0.17
1kg oranges	€1.55	€1.49
Small ice cream from *gelateria*	€1.70	€1.50
Packet of 32 nappies in supermarket	€8.79	€8.40
450g powdered infant milk in pharmacy	€12.50	€14.50
Espresso	€0.90	€0.80

MONEY

The Euro

Italy uses the **euro** (€). A euro is divided into 100 cents, and there are notes for €5–500 and coins for 1¢ to €2. At the time of writing, the euro–sterling exchange rate stood at €1.40 to £1, so conversion from one to another is relatively straightforward: two-thirds of the euro price gives you an approximate figure in pounds. For current rates and a handy converter, see ***www.xe.com***.

Credit & Debit Cards

Major shops, restaurants and hotels accept credit and debit cards. Although **Visa** and **Mastercard** are widely accepted, **American Express** and **Diners** are usually only taken at upscale places. In smaller shops and restaurants, and isolated towns, check whether cards are accepted before buying, as in many places they aren't. For lost or stolen cards, see p. 35.

If you intend to use your credit and debit cards abroad, let card providers know before you go away. This way they won't be suspicious when your cards are used abroad and refuse a withdrawal or cancel your card.

There's a **cashpoint** machine (*bancomat*) in pretty much every town; supermarkets have them as well as banks. You will be

TIP Keep Copies of Everything

Before you go, photocopy your passport, travellers' cheques, credit cards, itinerary and airline tickets. Carry one copy with you and leave a duplicate and your mobile number with someone back home.

Record the **emergency phone number** for each of your credit and debit cards. You'll probably find the number on the back of your card in minuscule print. Also see 'Credit Cards', p. 35.

TIP Without Breaking the Bank

- Opt for an agriturismo or a campsite rather than a hotel. That's one easy way to keep a tab on spending. Just check what kind of kitchen facilities your place has: some are limited to two electric rings and a microwave. When shopping, avoid supermarkets in resorts and tourist areas, and head to bigger stores on the outskirts of town.
- **Eating out** can be expensive, but there's no need to avoid it just because you're budgeting. Instead, visit at lunchtime and take a *menù turistico*. Avoid restaurants right on the main piazza or tourist drag: you wouldn't eat in Leicester Square, so skip the equivalent. Try and **eat DIY** once a day: buy bread, salami and a bottle of water from a supermarket and find a picnic spot.
- **Nappies** are pricey. If you're only visiting for a few days, bring your own. Otherwise, note that the small packs on sale in resort supermarkets are expensive, so opt for a bumper-sized bag. And never buy baby supplies in the pharmacy: always from a supermarket.
- **Free entertainment** is out there, especially if you time your holiday right. Ask at the tourist office for information on local festivals, and join in the celebrations without spending a penny. Also see 'Fourteen for free', p. 9.
- **Plan day trips to Florence** instead of staying there; that's the golden rule of Tuscany on a budget.

charged a minimum **withdrawal fee** each time you withdraw with your credit or debit card. Some debit card providers also impose a flat **transaction fee** every time you use your card. And on top of all that, most card issuers charge an **EU loading fee**, up to 2.75%, on every transaction. You'll make significant savings if you visit **Moneysupermarket** (✆ *0845 3455708, www.moneysupermarket.com*) and apply for a credit card with a **zero loading** rate. The **MoneySavingExpert** website (*www.moneysavingexpert.com*) is an invaluable online resource for this.

It is also advisable to **take more than one card** with you, in case one gets lost or damaged. If you're making a major purchase (over £100), remember that **Section 75 consumer protection** applies even abroad if you pay with a credit card: your card company will refund you if something goes wrong with your purchase.

Travellers' Cheques

Travellers' cheques are almost a thing of the past, given the abundance of cashpoints. If you do decide to carry them, bear in mind that banks have limited opening hours. Keep a record of the **serial numbers** in case of loss or theft. They can be cashed in Italian banks, big hotels and cambios (exchanges). Dealing with banks in Italy is slow and bureaucratic and they close for long lunches.

WHEN TO GO & WHAT TO PACK

Italy is a fabulous destination all year – you don't need hot weather to enjoy a visit. However, if you want to see what the country has to offer rather than jostle with crowds, **avoid July and especially August** (*le ferie*, holiday month). This peak season (and the priciest for hotels) is also the **hottest**. Florence in 37°C with a couple of toddlers can be challenging. Furthermore, family-run shops and restaurants away from tourist hotspots often close for all of August. Winter opening hours for almost everything is shorter. Seaside resorts are likely to be deserted and/or mostly shut.

Both Tuscany and Umbria have distinct seasons, so pack appropriate clothes. You're unlikely to need more than shorts and short-sleeved tops in **summer**, as long as you aren't planning to eat anywhere posh, nor are spending time in the Apennines, which can be wet and chilly almost anytime. Don't forget that you are expected to dress respectfully, with shoulders and legs covered, in all churches and cathedrals.

Florence is surrounded by hills and so can be cold and damp in **winter**. Elsewhere temperatures can be chilly, but rarely bitter away from the mountains. Spring is long and temperate almost everywhere, and usually warm by the coast. Most **rain** falls in the autumn. Look up the weather online before you go: for Umbria, check ***www.italy-weather-and-maps.com/weather/UMB*** and for Tuscany, ***www.italy-weather-and-maps.com/weather/TOS***.

A far bigger problem than weather is the **crowds**. Although the countryside absorbs peak-season hordes quite comfortably, Siena and especially Florence do not. Prepare yourselves for **queuing** everywhere.

Packing Your Car

If you're all travelling by **car**, keep the following handy:

❶ A cool box with drinks, snacks and fruit

TIP Baby Stuff

The following familiar baby brands are available in Tuscan and Umbrian supermarkets: **Huggies** and **Pampers** nappies; **Johnson's** for wipes and washing products; **Aptamil** and (in specialist baby shops) **Hipp Organic** for powdered and liquid milk. Reliable local baby food brands include Plasmon, Mellin and Milupa. If your little ones are wedded to certain products, **British Corner Shop** (*01454 228870*, ***http://britishcornershop.co.uk***) or ***www.tinytotsaway.com*** will ship them to your destination, at a price.

Devout Tuscany

What with the mesmerising scenery and rural idyll of a Tuscan holiday, there's a side that's easily missed. Every town and village, even clubs and societies, have their own **patron saint**. If you happen to be in town at the right time, you may chance upon Tuscans at prayer. Cities like Florence have several dates in the calendar: the place goes nuts for St John on 24th June, but lesser known locals St Zenobius (25th May) and St Antoninus (10th May) are also marked. Pisa pulls out all the stops for St Ranieri (see p. 112) on 17th June, whereas St Catherine of Siena (29th April; see p. 87) is one of Italy's most revered. San Gimignano shuts down for its namesake's feast on 31st January, and again on 12th March for St Fina (see p. 91). Other fairytale hill-towns celebrate their patrons in spring and summer: Agnes in Montepulciano on 20th April, Volterra's St Justus on 5th June and Arezzo's St Donatus on 7th August. But the most represented saint in Tuscan art isn't a local at all. St Sebastian is depicted in San Gimignano's Collegiata (p. 91), Siena's Palazzo Pubblico (p. 83) and just about everywhere else. He's the patron saint of **plagues**.

2. Window shades for the sun
3. Your child's favourite music or talking books
4. A first-aid kit
5. A box of wet wipes
6. Blankets
7. Plastic bags for motion sickness
8. A change of clothes for everyone
9. A mobile phone for emergencies
10. A list of car games from the RAC website (***www.rac.co.uk/web/knowhow/going_on_a_journey/games***)

Children's Kit

Beach tents When the sun shines, it really does shine, so take care not to get your little ones **burnt**. Although a traditional parasol can be bought cheaply from a resort souvenir shop, a beach tent is more adaptable.

Swimsuits Protective swimsuits are a good idea for children who won't stay still. Zip them up in a suit with **UV protection**, and they can carry on with their sandcastle building.

Lightweight pushchairs Fancy fashionable pushchairs soon become a burden in town: bring a **lightweight buggy** with a narrow wheelbase.

Portable highchairs As a rule, few restaurants provide highchairs, so bring one with you. Lightweight options include the compact 'Handbag Highchair' (a loop of fabric that secures your baby to the chair), the foldable

Handysitt toddler seat, and the Early Years' inflatable booster.

All the above are sold at **www.bloomingmarvellous.co.uk**. Another online site worth bookmarking is **www.kiddicare.com**.

Public Holidays

Offices and shops in Italy are closed on: **1st January, 6th January** (Epiphany, *La Befana*), **Easter Sunday** (***Pasqua***), **Easter Monday** (***Pasquetta***), **25th April** (Liberation Day, *La Liberazione),* **1st May** (Labour Day, *Festa del Lavoro)* **15th August** (Assumption, *Ferragosto*), **1st November** (All Saints' Day, *Tutti i Santi*), **8th December** (Immaculate Conception, *L'Immacolata*), **25th December** (Christmas Day, *Natale*) and **26th December** (*Santo Stefano*).

Italians are hooked on their long holiday, the '*quindici giorni*', around *Ferragosto*. Most family businesses and often entire town centres close away from tourist areas.

Child-friendly Events

One thing central Italy isn't short of is **festivals**. Even small towns have them on a regular basis. They can be great fun for families – and they're mostly free. Remember that **parking** will become difficult and hotels **expensive** and/or full around *festa* time. If you have very young children, or yours are frightened by crowds, stay away from the big festivals.

Some of the best are listed below (see relevant chapters for full details), but small village *festas* are fun too. Ask at the **local tourist office** or check the calendar on its website.

February
Carnevale Aretino Orciolaia, Arezzo, p. 96.
Carnevale, Viareggio, p. 127.

March
Torciata di San Giuseppe, Pitigliano, p. 180.

April
Coloriamo I Cieli, Castiglione-del-Lago, p. 198.

May
Festa del Grillo, Florence, p. 43.
Festa dei Ceri, Gubbio, p. 207.

June
Calcio Storico, Florence, p. 43.
Giostra del Saracino, Arezzo, p. 96.
Festa di San Ranieri, Pisa, p. 112.
Gioco del Ponte, Pisa, p. 112.
Spoleto Festival, p. 204.
Infiorate di Spello, p. 205.

July
Palio, Siena, p. 80.

August
Palio, Siena, p. 80.
Volterra AD1398, p. 93.
Bravio delle Botti, Montepulciano, p. 168.

September
Festa del Rificolonia, Florence, p. 46.
Giostra del Saracino, Arezzo, p. 96.
Luminaria di Santa Croce, Lucca, p. 120.

Calcio! The Football Season

Alongside Catholicism, Italy's other religion is football. A trip to an Italian football game is a fantastic experience. It's surprisingly easy to get tickets, too. The season runs from late August to mid-May, with one game played on Saturday evening (the anticipo), most on Sunday afternoons, and one on Sunday evening (the posticipio). Like England, the Italian league is split into four divisions: Serie A, B, C1 and C2. Currently, Florence, Siena, Empoli and Livorno have teams in Serie A. Italian ticket agencies worth trying are **TicketOne** (***www.ticketone.it***) and **Booking Show** (*899 030822, **www.bookingshow.com***). From the UK, try **Football Encounters** (*0870 7605556, **www.footballencounters.co.uk***) for Fiorentina tickets, although they're quite expensive. Or book them yourself. Each club has their own selling arrangements and generally it's cheaper than buying tickets for an English Premiership or major SPL game. For Fiorentina, see p. 63; for Livorno, p. 142. If you're taking children, ask for a *tribuna tranquilla* (a quiet stand): you don't want to end up sitting with the *ultras*.

October

Sagra del Torde, Montalcino, p. 174.

Eurochocolate, Perugia, p. 190.

INSURANCE & HEALTH

Travel Insurance

Travellers to Italy need to carry their **European Health Insurance Card** (EHIC), which replaced the E111 form, as proof of entitlement to free/reduced-cost medical treatment abroad. The easiest way to apply for a card is online (***www.ehic.org.uk***), call *0845 6062030* or get a form from a post office. Remember that EHIC forms only cover *necessary* medical treatment, so they are not replacements for travel insurance. When choosing travel insurance, read the small print of your home or credit card insurance carefully to check whether it covers you for lost cards, luggage, cancelled tickets or medical expenses. If not, opt for an **annual multi-trip policy** if you travel abroad at least twice a year.

Moneysupermarket (***www.moneysupermarket.com***) compares prices and coverage across a bewildering range.

Health

Take copies of **prescriptions** in case a family member loses his/her medicine or it runs out. Note the **generic name**, in case local pharmacists are unfamiliar with the brand. Remember to take an extra pair of contact lenses or prescription glasses.

If your child has an illness that needs swift and accurate treatment (like epilepsy, diabetes, asthma or a food or sting allergy),

MedicAlert (***www.medicalert.org.uk***) provides bracelets or necklaces engraved with an ID number and details of the medical condition. The number of a 24-hour emergency line is also engraved on the disc; this accepts reverse charge calls to access specific medical details from anywhere in the world and in over 100 languages.

For general advice on travelling with children, read *Your Child Abroad: A Travel Health Guide* (Bradt, £10.95).

TRAVELLING SAFELY WITH CHILDREN

Italy is a safe destination for children, especially away from the crowds. When you're walking through any town, you'll spot front doors left ajar while owners have popped out to chat to a neighbour. But **common sense** is still required. Make sure you lock cars and apartments. Don't leave valuables in sight in your car: leave them in a safe at your hotel or apartment reception. In resorts, don't leave your belongings in view by a pool or on the beach. Obviously, make sure you have adequate travel insurance (see p. 21) in case of theft.

Pickpockets and bag snatching are a problem around popular tourist attractions in big cities, particularly in Florence and Pisa. Beware groups of youngsters crowding around you as hands slip into your pockets. Mobiles and iPods are obvious targets. **Zebra crossings** don't mean what you think: wait until drivers have seen you and slowed before stepping into the road. Likewise in pedestrian zones (*zone pedonali*), watch for vehicles at all times.

On the **beach**, however shallow the water, do not let small children swim alone.

THE 21ST-CENTURY TRAVELLER

Mobile Phones

Your phone will switch from a British or Irish to an Italian network automatically on arrival, as

TIP **i-Kids**

If you're worried about your children wandering off in a city, or want to give them the freedom of the campsite, get a **GPS-based i-Kids handset** (***www.i-kids.net***). If your mobile has WAP and GPRS capabilities, you can track their movements and send them text messages. Each handset has an alarm button that dials your mobile when pressed, and can store up to three other numbers. Pre-set a radius beyond which your children are not to go: if they roam too far, you'll get a text message. The handset costs £99.99 from **mobiles2go** (*0844 8009133*, ***www.mobiles2go.com***). An 18-month contract costs £15.75 per month.

long as it is set up for **international roaming**. Call charges are higher than at home, and you pay to **receive calls** even if they divert to voicemail. To avoid shelling out for calls you don't answer, disable voicemail before you depart. Receiving text messages is free, although you pay more to reply.

For regular travellers to Italy, or for a long stay, it's worthwhile purchasing an **Italian pay-as-you-go SIM**. The phone shop will need to photocopy your passport. The SIM should cost €5–10 and your Italian number will have lower call charges, including to home. Make sure you've **unlocked** your handset before leaving: any local phone shop will do it for about a fiver. The major Italian networks are **TIM**, **Vodafone**, **3** and **Wind**.

You can also buy a global pay-as-you-go SIM in the UK from **Double Zero Double Four** (☎ *0870 9500044*, ***www.0044.co.uk***) for £29.99, including delivery and free unlocking if you have a Nokia phone. It's better value buying a SIM in Italy.

The Internet

Internet cafés are relatively common, but prices and the speed of service vary considerably. Under Italian **anti-terrorism laws**, every Internet café must photocopy the passport of non-Italian nationals and log their usage, so come prepared. To retrieve your email, use a **web-based email account**, or link your current email address to one. If you don't have webmail, get it from Yahoo (***www.yahoo.com***), Hotmail (***www.hotmail.com***) or various other companies – it's free.

If you're bringing your own laptop, the number of places with **WiFi** (wireless fidelity) access is small but growing. Some **campsites** have hotspots. Prices are generally reasonable: **Tin.it** (☎ *803380* or *070 5281020*, ***http://tin.alice.it***), for example, charges €2.95 per hour or €40 for seven days' unlimited access. You might find downloading a global hotspot locator like **JiWire** (***www.jiwire.com***) useful.

Getting There

By Plane For **Florence**, see Chapter 3. For **Pisa**, see Chapter 5. For **Perugia**, see Chapter 8.

By Car If you're packing the people-carrier to drive to Tuscany, two overnight stops en route make the journey comfortable. Florence is 1300km from Calais; Perugia is **1550km**. For a great free route planner, including advice on cost-effective travel, see the **ViaMichelin** website (***www.viamichelin.com***). **Ibis** motels (***www.ibishotel.com***) are hard to beat for overnight family stops. They're usually cheaper over the weekend.

Most UK **car insurance** policies include 30–90 days abroad without the need to apply for a Green Card, but check with your insurer. And don't leave home without appropriate breakdown cover from the AA, RAC or someone similar.

TIP Happy Flying with Your Children

- Introduce first-time flyers to likely **scenarios** (check-in, security, the safety talk, a bumpy ride, different noises) by playing 'let's go to the airport'.
- Read your toddler the 'Going on a Plane' chapter from *The Little Book of First Experiences* (Usborne, £5.99) before you go.
- Check with the airline that they provide bolsters or **seats for under-2s**.
- Listen to the safety announcements. Read the safety card and clock the nearest exits, the lifejackets and oxygen masks.
- Pack water, snacks and a few **toys** in your hand luggage.
- Make sure your child's seatbelt remains fastened: turbulence can occur at any time.
- Sit your child by the window or between two parents: it's harder for them to wander off.
- Read ***www.TravellingWithChildren.co.uk*** before you go.

Towing a car from Chianti to Cardiff can be *very* expensive. Make sure you pack your vehicle registration document (**Form V5**), insurance policy and **driving licence** (both parts). Roadside *documenti* checks are common.

Budget for the **road tolls** in France; you'll save money if you go around them through Belgium and Germany, although the quality of roadside picnic areas is markedly poorer. In **Switzerland**, you need to make a one-off payment of SFr.40 (about £16.50) at the border for a *vignetta* to use the motorway network; you'll be fined if caught without one.

If you enter Italy through the **Grand St Bernard tunnel** (***www.sitrasb.it***) south of Sion, your return ticket (€29.70) is valid for a month. Return tickets through the **Mont Blanc tunnel** (***www.tunnelmb.com***) from France are only valid for a week, so you'll need two singles (€31.90 each). The **Fréjus Tunnel** (***www.sftrf.fr***) linking Chambéry and Turin is the same: you'll need two singles at €31.90. The most scenic motorway route passes through the **St Gotthard Tunnel** in Switzerland and crosses into Italy via Lugano and Como. It's also free. There are mountain passes (Simplon, Petit St Bernard, Grand St Bernard), but these are slower and closed from late autumn to spring due to snow.

Note petrol is cheaper in **Luxembourg** and **Switzerland**, so with creative route-finding you can avoid tolls and refuel for less. Diesel is cheaper in Italy than in the UK. At many garages in Italy, you'll get a discount if you fill up yourself (*fai da te*).

By Train If you're flexible on dates and times, you may be able to get from London to Florence, via Eurostar (3 hours) and a sleeper (12 hours) from Paris, for just over £200. This is with the lowest overnight class (six-berth sleeper) and a lot of luck on availability. Contact **RailChoice** (☎ *0870 1657300, www.railchoice.co.uk*).

By Bus If you're brave enough to attempt to reach Tuscany by coach, there's one weekly **Eurolines** (☎ *08705 808080, www.nationalexpress.com/eurolines*) departure to Florence from London's Victoria coach station. The journey takes 28 hours with a 2-hour stopover in Paris and a half hour in Milan. Prices start at €71 with no child reductions.

By Package Tour You'll find a rundown of **tour operators** with packages suited to families on p. 244.

Getting Around

By Car Italians drive on the **right** and you'll need to develop a little patience with their on-road etiquette. *Autostrade* are motorways, denoted by green signs and a number prefaced with an A, like the Milan–Naples **A1**, which bisects Tuscany. *Strade statali* are state roads, and usually have two lanes. Their route numbers are prefaced with an **SS** or an **S**. Don't get hung up on the numbers, though: unlike *autostrade*, SS roads don't always have them on display; you'll just see blue signs listing destinations by name. If you happen to be on an **SP** (*strada provinciale*) road and cross a provincial border, the number changes anyway. **Unleaded petrol** is *benzina senza piombo*; **diesel** is *gasolio*. Most filling stations are closed on Sunday, but some have a pump fitted with a machine that takes notes or cards.

You pay by the kilometre to use motorways, but prices are nowhere near those in France. The **Autostrade per l'Italia** website (☎ *840 042121, www.autostrade.it*) has a toll calculator and also provides weather forecasts and traffic updates. Milan to Florence, for example, is €16. Verona to Siena costs €12.70. If you have Internet access, it's worth checking **QuattroRoute** (*www.quattroruote.it/infotrafic/index.cfm*) before you set off. There's a handy traffic-light system that pinpoints bad traffic **jams**. Despite a plague of roadworks (*cantiere*), you'll generally make good progress on the motorway as long as you stay away from the Florence ring-road (*tangenziale*). Journeys on minor roads can take an age.

If you need to stop to refuel (the children, not the car), you'll find the quality of Italian **service stations** a cut above what you're used to. The food's almost deli-quality, and healthy. Look for the **Autogrill** sign. If you want to get detailed on the planning front, there's a map of all their locations at *www.autogrill.it*. Note, the drill for ordering hot drinks at the bar is to **pay first**: take your receipt (*scontrino*) to the bar and repeat your order.

Driving Rules

Don't drink and drive: the legal UK blood alcohol limit is 0.8

mg; in Italy it's 0.5 mg. Besides the danger, **imprisonment** is a regular punishment. Seat belts are compulsory. Under new EU law, children under 4 must have a suitable car seat or booster, whilst those between 4 and 12 can't travel in the front unless restrained (exactly how depends on the size of your child; see ***www.childcarseats.org.uk***). Road signs are similar enough to the UK for you to work them out as you go. *Senso unico* means you're in a one-way street. A *zona pedonale* is a pedestrian zone. Speed limits are as follows: motorway, 130km/h; dual carriageway, 110km/h; trunk road, 90km/h (sometimes 70km/h); town, 50km/h. In fog, the limit is 50km/h whatever the road. There's obviously no crime in central Italy, because everyone in a police uniform is standing on the side of a country road with a **speed gun**: you have been warned.

It's compulsory to carry a **warning triangle**, a **visibility vest** and **spare headlight bulbs**. If you break down, you must put on the vest before getting out the car and erect the triangle just up the road from where you stop. Check all this kit is in a hire car before you drive off. The use of mobile phones in cars is prohibited unless they are fitted with speaker devices or used with headphones.

If **fined** for a minor contravention, you pay on the spot. Get a receipt.

Car Hire

If you're renting a car, remember both parts of your driving licence. You must have had a full licence for two years. When booking and picking up your hire car, you'll also need your **passport** and a **credit card**. Insurance on all vehicles is compulsory, but check the excess and what's not covered. You're sometimes better **booking everything in advance** from home, then you can offer a polite '*No, grazie*' to all the other stuff they'll inevitably try and flog you. **Holiday Autos** (***www.holidayautos.co.uk***) are reliable and competitive. The independent broker **AutoReservation** (*☎ 08704 203096*, ***www.autoreservation.com***) offers sizeable discounts on rentals from the big players. **Insurance4carhire.com** (*☎ 020 70126300*) does exactly what you think it does: it's an annual policy to reimburse nasty excesses and starts at £49.

Parking

To park your car, find a *parcheggio* (car park) or park on the street. **White lines** indicate free public spaces; **blue lines** mean you have to pay, usually reinforced with a *sosta a pagamento* sign. Find a meter, punch in how long you want to park, pay and stick the ticket somewhere visible in your car. If you park in an area marked *parcheggio con disco orario* look for the cardboard parking disc in your hire car's glove compartment or buy one at a petrol station. Dial up the time of your arrival and display it on the dashboard. How long you're allowed will be marked clearly on the sign. Never park in **yellow spaces**: they're for residents or businesses.

By Train Italy's national train network is comfortable, regular and reliable, if often late. It's also **good value**, fast and easy to navigate. If you are intending to use the train, visit the **Trenitalia** website (***www.trenitalia.it***) before you leave home to check routes, timetables and fares.

There's little difference between first and second class: keep your money. Outside rush hours, you're sure to get a seat. However, on faster routes between cities, you need to **book** to sit together. If all you're doing is dotting about a region, you'll generally use **R** (*Regionale*) trains, which stop at all main stations. For longer journeys, aim for an **ES** (*Eurostar*) or **IC** (*Intercity*) train, as these are faster and not much more expensive.

When buying a ticket, ask for either *andata* (one-way) or *andata e ritorno* (return). Two singles cost the same as a return, so if you're not sure of your plans, buy a **single**. Not every train is the same price: for an ES or IC, ask for your ticket *con supplemento rapido* (with a fast supplement) to avoid on-board penalty charges; you'll also be allocated a seat. Most importantly **stamp your ticket in the yellow box** on the platform (*convalidare*) before boarding. It's not unknown for tourists to get fined for unstamped tickets.

The Man in Seat Sixty-One (***www.seat61.com***) dispenses invaluable advice for European rail travel.

By Bus Regional buses are called *pullman*, although *autobus*, the term for a city bus, is sometimes used. It's not easy getting hold of a timetable for local buses; the best option is often to **download** them from the company websites (see below). News-stands or tobacconists (*tabacchi*) and local bars usually sell bus tickets. It's **more expensive** to buy them on the bus. Remember to stamp them using the yellow machine on board.

The following bus companies are useful:

APM, Perugia. *075 506781*, ***www.apmperugia.it***.

Some Driving Times

Florence to Siena	1 hour
Florence to Perugia	2¼ hours
Pisa to Florence	1 hour
Pisa to Grosseto	1¼ hours
Perugia to Orvieto	1½ hours
Perugia to Terni	1¼ hours

ATL, Elba/Livorno. 0565 914392, *www.atl.livorno.it*.

ATAF, Florence. 800 424500, *www.ataf.net*.

CPT, Pisa. 050 505511, *www.cpt.pisa.it*.

LFI, Arezzo. 0575 39881, *www.lfi.it*.

RAMA, Grosseto. 0564 475111, *www.griforama.it*.

SITA, Florence. 055 214721, *www.sitabus.it*.

TRAIN, Siena. 0577 204111, *www.trainspa.it*.

By Ferry For Livorno to **Capraia**, see p. 141. For Piombino to **Elba**, p. 147. For information on the ferry to **Isola Giglio**, see p. 157. If you're heading to Sardinia or Corsica by ferry, your first port of call should be the **Toremar** website: *www.toremar.it*.

By Taxi If you're concerned about being ripped off by local drivers, or just like to have everything sorted before you leave, book your **airport taxi** in advance. **Taxi Transfers** (08700 111717, ***www.taxitransfers.co.uk***) and **Holiday Taxis** (0870 444 1880, ***www.holidaytaxis.com***) offer this service. Frankly, though, it's cheaper to jump in an airport cab when you arrive.

The only city where you're likely to need a taxi while you're here is **Florence**: call 055 4242.

On Foot There's plenty of good **walking** all over Tuscany and Umbria. Not all of it is child-friendly, though. By the seventh Chianti winery, most toddlers are reaching their limit. You'll find one or two gentle routes recommended in the main chapters.

By Bike Although renting a bike in central Florence amounts to madness, in some cities and towns two wheels are the best way to get you and the family round the sights. For **Lucca**, see p. 121; for Lago Trasimeno, p. 196; and for the Florence periphery, p. 64.

ACCOMMODATION

Hotels

If you plan to book a hotel yourself, spend a bit of time on **research**. Make sure the area you choose has the right amenities, and the accommodation suits you and the children. See if it has a website and study the photos with your sceptical head on. If your Italian is up to it, call them yourself: you might get a deal. All the hotels listed by this guide are family-friendly – as is most of Italy. General websites like **Expedia** (0871 2260808, ***www.expedia.co.uk***), **Travelocity** (0870 2733273, ***www.travelocity.co.uk***), **eBookers** (0871 2235000, ***www.ebookers.com***) and **Hotels.com** (0871 2000171, ***www.hotels.com***) all provide the basic drill: a fast, efficient booking service, with regular deals and offers. **Venere** (☎ *00800 83637300*, ***www.venere.com***) is good on Tuscany and Umbria.

The screenscraper service at **TravelSupermarket** (***www.travelsupermarket.com***) allows real-time comparisons of room prices at hundreds of online resellers. Just plug in your dates and what level of luxury you're looking for and they fire back the best online rates. Although there are thousands of places to stay, remember major tourist spots like Florence get **very full** during July and (especially) **August**, and in the weeks around **Easter**. If you're going to splash out on a top-of-the-range place, take five minutes to check it hasn't been slated at **TripAdvisor** (***www.tripadvisor.com***). Always take a copy of your **reservation confirmation** with you: mistakes happen.

If your budget stretches to a bit of luxury, **The Hotel Guru** (***www.thehotelguru.com)***, recommends top 10 lists for Florence, the Tuscan countryside, Tuscan towns and Umbria. **Charming Small Hotels** (***www.charmingsmallhotels.co.uk***) recommends several more, and also publishes a couple of handbooks covering the region. Check out Alistair Sawday's **Special Places to Stay**, Italy edition or look online (***www.sawdays.co.uk***) for recommendations with a green emphasis. Boutique website **Mr and Mrs Smith** (***www.mrandmrssmith.com***) has a small number of Tuscan offerings in the mega-pricey bracket. Similarly style-conscious ***www.i-escape.com*** has properties in Florence and rural Tuscany searchable by child-friendliness.

Although we've focused throughout the book on unique places to stay, popular **chains** provide a great alternative, especially for tight budgets, short stops en route and cities. Family-friendly **Ibis** (***www.ibishotel.com***) has two well-priced motels near Florence. One notch up, **Best Western** (☎ *0800 393130*, ☎ *1800 709101* in Ireland. ***www.bestwestern.com***) runs hotels all over Italy. Children go free in parents' rooms, and at breakfast, and there's all the baby kit you'll ever need at **Novotel** (☎ *055 308338*, ***www.novotel.com***). There is one just outside Florence. There's a rundown of family **tour operators** serving the region on p. 244.

INSIDER TIP

If you're staying in southern Tuscany, it's worth knowing that Article 151 of the law governing *alberghi* in the Province of Grosseto forbids you from putting anything in your **minibar** that wasn't there when you arrived. Honestly.

You might come across some new **vocabulary** on your hotel-hunt. An *albergo* is the old name, sometimes translated as 'inn'. *Locanda* once meant an inn or carriage stop, although it's now often used to refer to a place with charm or (delusions of) grandeur. A *pensione* is a guesthouse: these are often the cheapest and most cheerful, usually perfect for youngsters. There are also a number of cracking youth hotels (*ostelli*) with family rooms. These vary in size, but are economical and a great way to make friends. There's a list at the **Associazione Italiana Alberghi per la Gioventù** website, ***www.ostellionline.org***. To obtain a Youth Hostel Association card check ***www.yha.org.uk*** or call *0870 7708868* in the UK. Family membership is £22.95.

Agriturismi

For a taste of rural Tuscany, staying and eating in an *agriturismo* (a converted farmhouse) can be a fantastic family experience. The **Agriturism in Tuscany** website (***www.agriturismo.regione.toscana.it***) allows you to search for accommodation by province or town. Look out for the *Agriturismo e vacanze in campagna* guide published annually by the Touring Club Italiano (€20); you'll find it in most good Italian bookshops. For further information, check the **Agriturist Toscana** (*055 287838*, ***www.agriturist.it***) website. You'll find news, offers and itineraries in Italian. Also worth a look before you book are **Turismo Verde Toscana** (*055 20022*, ***www.turismoverde.it***) and **Terranostra** (*055 3245011*, ***www.terranostra.it***). The **AgriturismoOnLine** website (*075 8619693*, ***www.agriturismoonline.com***) allows you to search by accommodation type and province for places to stay.

Self-catering

If you're in a large group, or fancy renting a villa, apartment or house independently, join the pan-European **Homelidays** (***www.homelidays.com***) network. Their versatile website allows you to search for properties by location, price range, facilities like pools and air conditioning, accommodation type and size, and disabled access. You can even specify up to 50 required local amenities like golf, amusement parks or wine tours. They'll email you when a property matching your criteria becomes available. It's free to join, and they currently list 1,500 properties in Tuscany and Umbria. **Owners Direct** (*01372 229330*, ***www.ownersdirect.co.uk***), **Holiday-Rentals.co.uk** (*020 87435577*, ***www.holiday-rentals.co.uk***) and **Holiday Lettings** (*01865 201444*. ***www.holidaylettings.co.uk***) have similarly impressive ranges. The **Slow Travel Network** (***www.slowtrav.com***) has exhaustive reviews of properties and places in Tuscany. There are, of course, plenty of **tour operators** offering upmarket villas. See p. 244.

Camping & Mobile Homes

Happy campers will find lots of places to pitch up, and a number of sites also rent out camping gear. Start with the **Federazione Italiana Campeggiatori** (*055 882391*, ***www.federcampeggio.it***).

TIP A Cheap Hotels Checklist

- Ask about special rates and other **discounts**: Dial the hotel directly to ask the price of a room and push for a *sconto* (discount). Ask if children stay free in the room (and clarify at what age they becomes an adult). If not, is there a family rate?
- Seek deals: See what price the hotel is offering and check if any **Internet** sites have it cheaper. Many hotels offer Internet-only discounts, or supply rooms to ***www.lastminute.com*** or ***www.expedia.co.uk*** at lower rates.
- Ask for a **long-stay discount** if you're planning to stay least five nights. You might get one – but only if you ask.
- Avoid excess charges and **hidden costs**: When you book a room, ask whether the hotel charges for parking. Use your mobile or prepaid phone cards instead of dialling direct from rooms. Forget the minibar. Finally, ask about additional charges (balcony, view, cot, air conditioning and so on). It all adds up.
- Book an **apartment**: A kitchen allows you to shop and cook your own meals. This is a big money saver, especially for long stays.
- **Avoid staying in Florence**: you can visit on a daily basis to see the sights.

Other useful websites for comparing facilities are ***www.easycamping.it***, ***www.camping.it*** and ***www.campeggi.com***. If you're a serious camping family, or planning a longer tour of Tuscany and Umbria, we recommend you buy a copy of **Alan Rogers' Guide: Italy 2008** (£8.99).

EATING & DRINKING

The day starts with *colazione* (breakfast). *Pranzo* (lunch) and *cena* (dinner) consist of *antipasti* (appetisers), *primo* (first course) of pasta, soup or risotto, and a *secondo* (main course) of meat or fish, accompanied by a *contorno* (side dish) of veggies, finished off with *dolce* (dessert) or *formaggio* (cheese) and a *caffè* (coffee). You don't have to order the lot: a *primo* at lunch is usually enough; at dinner, an *antipasto* and *secondo* does the trick. For a taste of some **Tuscan and Umbrian specialities**, see p. 244.

Don't get too hung up on special menus for youngsters. The children's menu is usually anything they want, including stuff not on offer to you. At the very least, staff will cook up a tomato or meat sauce with pasta. And there's always pizzerias: we haven't listed too many in later sections, but as a general rule **walk two streets back** from the main piazza and you're safe with a pizza anywhere.

A Wine Label

It would take a book at least the size of this one to explain the

I'll Have the White One, Please

If you think that white ice cream is just *vanilla*, think again. **Vaniglia** is just the start, and tastes strongly of vanilla. **Crema** is creamy white (sometimes egg-yolky) without the vanilla flavour and **Crema Fiorentina** is yellow with a slight liquorice tang. **Fiordilatte** ('flower of milk') is bright white and milky. **Stracciatella** is (usually) *fiordilatte* with veins or chunks of chocolate through it, whereas **Panna Cotta** ('cooked cream') is based on the sweet, rich Italian dessert, with a slightly toasted flavour. **Crema di Riso** is another bright-white concoction, not unlike cold rice pudding. For other great ice cream ideas, see p. 75.

byzantine **Italian wine laws** and how they apply to Tuscany and Umbria. To keep things simple, here are some words to look out for:

Indicazione Geografica Tipica (IGT) a guarantee of grape variety and place of origin. Some of Tuscany's best wines are sold with IGT status.

Denominazione di Origine Controllata (DOC) the basic classification for a good wine, which has to conform to yield rules and quality checks.

Denominazione di Origine Controllata e Garantita (DOCG) Italy's best wines, which have to conform to the same checks as DOC wines and more.

Imbottigliato all origine bottled where it was made, usually a good sign.

Riserva a special, aged selection.

Brunello di Montalcino outstanding DOCG wine from the hills around Montalcino, made entirely from the Sangiovese grape. A good bottle will set you back around €4.

Rosso di Montalcino what people on regular budgets buy if they want a Montalcino wine.

Vino Nobile di Montepulciano quality DOCG wine from the hills east of Montepulciano.

Chianti Classico red from the *('classico')* Chianti zone: a staple Tuscan wine the world over.

Sagrantino di Montefalco Umbria's best DOCG wine, a velvety red that matches wild boar like a dream.

Vin Santo almost yellow, sweet white wine, traditionally aged under the tiles of Renaissance *palazzi*.

'Super Tuscans' you won't see these words on a label, but if someone offers you a glass of **Sassicaia**, **Tignanello** or **Ornellaia**, say yes. As long as you're not paying.

INSIDER TIP

If you stand at a bar – *al banco* – you'll be charged the minimum for your drinks, ice cream and panini. If you sit down, you incur a cover charge and heftier prices for the same stuff. Sit outside and you'll pay even more.

GETTING CHILDREN INTERESTED IN TUSCANY & UMBRIA

Before You Go

Here are some ideas to help get your children fired up for free before you leave home:

- Talk to their school about getting an **Italian penpal.**
- Get some Italy holiday brochures and cut out pictures to make a **collage**. When you're away, try and spot images from the collage
- Cook **Tuscan food** together using the recipes at ***www.tuscanrecipes.com***. For Italian food in general, try the BBC Food website (***www.bbc.co.uk/food***).
- Involve them in **planning**. Set realistic expectations: you won't get round every church or every important artwork.
- Encourage them to **pack drawing pads and crayons**: galleries and churches don't mind a child sitting quietly and scrawling, as long as it is not on the priceless art.

Holiday Reading

For You

The sheer number of **Tuscany travelogues** is overwhelming. Any bookshop worth its onions will have half a dozen. Isabella Dusi's ***Vanilla Beans and Brodo*** (Simon & Schuster, £7.99), set in Montalcino, stands out from a mawkish crowd. Iris Origo's ***War in the Val d'Orcia: 1943–44*** (Allen & Busby, £8.99) paints a grittier picture. You'll pick up plenty about Tuscany by packing Tim Parks' ***A Season with Verona*** (Vintage, £6.99), even though it hardly mentions the place and is (or appears to be) mainly about football. Older teens used to adult themes will love it. Along the same lines, Luigi Barzini's ***The Italians*** (Penguin, £10.99) remains a 40-year-old classic.

To get your tastebuds warmed up before you go, Pino Luongo's seasonal cookery book ***Simply Tuscan*** (Pavilion, £10.75) repays the investment. ***The Silver Spoon*** (Phaidon, £25), more encyclopaedia than cookbook, has enough Tuscan recipes to keep you busy. James Lasdun's ***Walking and Eating in Tuscany and Umbria*** (Penguin, £9.99) combines the two things Tuscans do best. Some of the walks are a bit long for young'uns, but you can easily shorten them. It's better on Tuscany than Umbria. There are also ***Sunflower*** walking guides

Know Your Apse from Your Nave

Apse The enclosed space behind the main altar
Basilica Originally a Roman public hall, but now an important church without a bishopric
Campanile The bell tower of a church
Cappella A chapel, a dedicated religious space created off the aisles or transepts of a church
Chiostro The cloisters, internal roofed walkways found in monasteries
Duomo Another word for *cattedrale*, i.e. the cathedral
Fresco A picture painted on damp plaster
Lunette The arched space between the walls and a vaulted ceiling
Nave The central aisle of a church leading from the main door to the altar
Sacristy The room where the priest's garments and sacred bits-and-pieces are (or were) kept
Transept The cross-arms of a church, running at 90° to the nave

to ***Tuscany*** (Sunflower Books, £10.99) and ***Umbria and the Marches*** (£10.99).

For wine lovers, Hugh Johnson's ***Tuscany and Its Wines*** (Mitchell Beazley, £16.99) is worth the money, as is his ***World Atlas of Wine*** (Mitchell Beazley, £35). Either is an irreplacable companion to Tuscan wine-tourism. David D Busch's ***Digital Travel Photography: Digital Field Guide*** (Wiley, £13.99) is essential kit for keen snappers. Art-fiends should start with ***Renaissance Art: A Very Short Introduction*** (Oxford, £6.99) before graduating to Giorgio Vasari's classic ***Lives of the Artists*** (Oxford, €8.99), published in 1550.

If it's fiction you're after, the tensions and pretensions of EM Forsters' two Tuscan tales, ***A Room with a View*** and ***Where Angels Fear to Tread***, are set in Florence and San Gimignano respectively. Boccaccio's ***The Decameron*** (Oxford, £9.99) is the Florentine classic, but pack your toothbrush. It's a long old journey. Ditto Dante's seminal ***Divine Comedy***, in three volumes.

For the Children

Children of all ages should read (or be read) the classic Tuscan story, ***Pinocchio*** by Carlo Lorenzini, especially if you're heading to Pinocchio Park (p. 125). Try and get the version before Disney got its hands on it. With really young ones, the film will do fine.

Toddlers will enjoy ***Vulca the Etruscan*** (British Museum Press), a fun picture book about one boy, his dog and an Etruscan necropolis. It's out of print, but you should be able to pick up a cheap copy at Amazon's

Marketplace (***www.amazon.co.uk***). Older primary children into art and history will enjoy ***Perugino's Path*** by Nancy L Clouse, an illustrated book about the Umbrian painter. For readers in the Harry Potter-ish age group, try Georgia's fantastical adventures in the *Stravaganza* series: Mary Hoffman's ***Stravaganza: City of Flowers*** (Bloomsbury, £6.99), is set in Florence, and ***Stravaganza: City of Stars*** (£6.99) in Siena.

FAST FACTS: TUSCANY & UMBRIA

Alcohol There is no **minimum age** for drinking in Italy and no restrictions on where you can buy alcohol.

Babysitting See individual accommodation entries for places that offer babysitting services.

Breastfeeding Breastfeeding in public is acceptable, but you may get stared at, especially if you're feeding an older infant. Brazen it out, or find an out-of-the-way spot.

Business Hours Regular hours are 9am–1pm and 4–7.30pm, or thereabouts. **Banking hours** are shorter: 8.30am–1.30pm and 2.35–3.35pm, Monday to Friday.

Chemists Look for the *farmacia* sign and the green cross. There is usually one chemist open late and on a Sunday. There should be a list of where is open in the window of every *farmacia*. It's also a good idea to take a first-aid course yourself; there's a **CD-ROM** (£24.99) developed in collaboration with St John's Ambulance: see ***www.firstaidforkids.com***.

Consulates The **British Consulate** is in Florence, at Lungarno Corsini 2 (*055 284133*, ***www.britishembassy.gov.uk***). It's open 9am–1pm and 2–5pm Monday to Friday. **Irish citizens** should call their embassy in Rome (*06 6979121*, ***www.ambasciata-irlanda.it***).

Credit Cards For lost or stolen cards, make sure you have your emergency number handy (see p. 16). Make a note of it and keep it separately. The main ones are: **American Express** *+44 1273 620555;* **Barclaycard** *+44 1604 230230;* **MasterCard** *800 870866* (an Italian number).

Electricity Italy uses 220V, 50Hz. Power sockets have two or three holes. Buy a two-pin **European adaptor** at home.

Emergencies For **police**, call *113*. For the **carabinieri**, call *112*. For the **fire brigade**, call *115*. In a **medical** emergency, call *118*.

Legal Assistance The Italian section on the British Embassy website (***www.britain.it***) has a list of lawyers; click 'Services for Britons in Italy' then 'If things go wrong'. Your travel insurance company can also advise.

Maps The plastic *Rough Guide Map: Tuscany 1:200,000* (£5.99) has the distinct advantage of holding together when others are falling apart, and the distinct disadvantage of excluding Umbria. A decent driver's map of the whole area is Michelin's 1:400,000 *563: Toscana, Umbria.* For walkers, Kompass 1:50,000 maps have the detail you need.

Newspapers Florence's nominally national rag is *La Nazione*, read throughout Tuscany but rarely elsewhere. By the coast you're more likely to see *Il Tirreno*; in Umbria, the *Corriere dell'Umbria*. The closest Italy has to national newspapers – *La Repubblica* (Roman, centre-left), *La Stampa* (Milanese, rightish with a business bias) and *Corriere della Sera* (Milanese, centre-right) – are all widely available, as is the iconic pink sports paper, *La Gazzetta dello Sport*.

Post It costs 65¢ to send home a postcard (or letter up to 20g) by *posta prioritaria*. Stamps can be bought in *tabacchi* and post offices. Postboxes are red and usually attached to walls.

Smoking Italy banned smoking in all bars, restaurants and offices in 2005.

Telephone Public telephones are plentiful, some take credit cards and have instructions in English, but most use *schede telefoniche*, available from *tabacchi* and newsstands. To call an Italian number from the UK, dial 00; then 39; then the area code; and finally the number. To call home from Italy, first dial 00; then the country code (UK 44, Ireland 353); then the area code (dropping the 0 it begins with); then the number. If you're looking for a number within Italy, dial ☎ *176* for numbers in Europe, and ☎ *1790* for numbers outside Europe. If you need operator assistance to make a call, dial ☎ *1720044* to reach BT in the UK or ☎ *1720353* for Ireland.

Time Zone GMT+1 hour in winter; BST+1 hour in summer.

Tipping Check if service is included in the bill. Otherwise 10–15% is the norm, but by no means compulsory. Don't tip **bad service**, but let staff know why.

Toilets & Baby Change There are few public toilets, so you're best off making a small purchase at a bar or café and using theirs. Museums and galleries often have toilets, but baby-changing facilities are few and far between. Large bars may only have a fold-down changing table, so carry a **changing mat** with you.

Water Nobody in Italy drinks tap water, even though it's perfectly safe. Still water is *acqua senza gaz* or *naturale*, whereas sparkling water is *acqua frizzante*.

3 Florence

Deservedly one of the world's most visited cities, Florence ★★ (Firenze in Italian) can be the highlight of a family trip to Tuscany, if you do it right. Architecturally it retains a severe medieval character, and though parts of it are staggeringly beautiful – Florence's Duomo is one of the most striking in Italy – there's one thing that draws the hordes: art. Florence *was* the **Renaissance**, south of the Alps at least. This blossoming of classical ideals, painting and sculpture in the 15th century changed the world. The great Renaissance leaders Botticelli and Michelangelo created some of their most inspired work here; Leonardo da Vinci spent his formative years in the city. The Uffizi is Europe's greatest gallery, dripping with masterpieces.

The best way to get the most out of your time in Florence is to plan what you want to see in advance. The city is crammed with artwork, history and great buildings, so accept that you're not going to see everything. And visiting Florence isn't plain sailing. The streets stream with people, it's hard to get around with toddlers and it's more expensive than anywhere else in Tuscany. But don't be put off: missing Florence would be a big mistake. The *centro storico* is compact and pedestrianised in parts, there are plenty of parks, weird museums, markets and ice cream opportunities to amuse even the youngest visitors. With a bit of forward thinking, you will get to enjoy Florence's cultural heavyweights with no problem. The purpose of this chapter is to help you to plan ahead for a successful visit *in famiglia* – we've highlighted must-sees and included ideas to make your holiday go like a dream.

ESSENTIALS

Getting There

By Air Most visitors fly to **Pisa's Galileo Galilei airport** (☎ *050 849300, **www.pisa-airport.com***), 95km west of the city and an hour away by train. **British Airways** (☎ *0870 8509850, **www.ba.com***) flies from London Gatwick and Manchester; **Ryanair** (☎ *0871 2460000, **www.ryanair.com***) from Bournemouth, East Midlands, London Stansted, Glasgow and Liverpool in the UK, plus Dublin in Ireland. **easyJet** flies (☎ *0905 8210905, **www.easyjet.com***) from Bristol; **Jet2** (☎ *0871 2261737, **www.jet2.com***) and **Thomson** (☎ *0870 1900737, **www.thomsonfly.com***) both operate services from UK regional airports in summer. **Alitalia** (☎ *0870 5448259, **www.alitalia.com***) has domestic flights from Rome and Milan.

Shuttle buses operated by **Terravision** (☎ *06 32120011, **www.terravision.eu***) depart from the front of the airport terminal every hour to Florence's **Santa Maria Novella** station (70 minutes). It costs €8 one-way (buy tickets from the booth in the airport arrivals hall). The train is a cheaper (€5) but slower option

Children's Top Attractions in Florence

- Climb the **Duomo** for incomparable views over the city, p. 49.
- Fast-track to see Botticelli, Michelangelo and Leonardo in the **Uffizi**, p. 52.
- Compare ***David*** in the Accademia with its two replicas, p. 57.
- Taste some of the world's best **ice cream**, p. 75.
- Unleash budding scientists in the **Museo di Storia della Scienza**, p. 54.
- Wander the city walls to **Piazzale Michelangelo**, p. 61.
- Explore the grottoes and gardens of the **Giardino di Boboli**, p. 61.
- Get medieval with the armour at **Museo Stibbert**, p. 58.
- Go back in time with a tour of the **Palazzo Vecchio** led by Cosimo de' Medici, p. 51.
- Munch the morning away at **Mercato Centrale**, p. 73.

(70–100 minutes): there are seven direct services between 6.40am and 10.20pm. Alternatively, trains connect the airport to Pisa Centrale (6 min) every 30 minutes for regular services to Florence (1 hour).

Florence Peretola (Amerigo Vespucci) airport (☎ *055 3061300. www.aeroporto.firenze.it*) is just 5km north-west of the city centre, and **Meridiana** (☎ *020 78392222. www.meridiana.it*) operates regular flights from the UK (London Gatwick). The **Vola in Bus** (☎ *800 570530. www.ataf.net*) runs into the city every half-hour between 6am and 11.30pm, and from 5.30am to 11pm in the other direction (€4.50; 30 minutes), terminating at the SITA bus station (see p. 40) near Santa Maria Novella train station. Buy tickets on the bus or at machines in the terminal. **Taxis** should cost €16–20 and take 20 minutes.

By Car Florence has excellent road connections with the rest of Italy, but visiting by car can be a headache. Traffic is intimidating, and parking is hard to find and expensive. If you're a hiring a car to tour Tuscany, start or end your holiday in Florence, and do the city without it. If driving from the UK, consider tackling the city via day-trips from elsewhere. It's best to arrange car rental before you arrive to get the best rates (see p. 26), though most major rental companies have offices in Florence (see 'Fast Facts: Florence', below).

If you do visit Florence by car, head for a car park and leave it there – driving around the city is pointless. Some hotels have garages, or can at least point you in the direction of the nearest one: ask in advance. **Firenze Parcheggi** (*www.firenzeparcheggi.it*) runs all eight official city car parks: the most

TIP Free Parking!

If you don't have too much luggage or buggies, park for free at Piazzale Michelangelo (see p. 61), just south of the river Arno, and then walk or take bus 12 or 13 into the centre. Watch out for scams: there are **no charges**, even if the friendly local guiding you into a space asks for some money. The *piazzale* is easy to reach: from the A1 *autostrada*, take the **Firenze-Certosa** exit and head north along Via Senese (towards *centro*). The *piazzale* is signposted once you get into the city; if you go through the Porta Romana you've missed it.

convenient are the 24-hour one under Santa Maria Novella **station** (€3 per hour) and **Parterre** behind Piazza Libertà north of the centre, at Via Madonna della Tosse 9 (*055 5001994*. €1.50 per hour, €18 for 24 hours). To find them approach Florence from the north and follow signs to the *centro* – you'll see parking signs as you approach the centre.

By Bus Long-distance **buses** to Florence are operated by various companies, most with terminals around Santa Maria Novella station. The main **SITA** (long-haul *055 214721;* local *800 373760.* ***www.sitabus.it***) terminal is on Via Santa Caterina da Siena, off Piazza della Stazione. SITA operates regular services from **Arezzo, Perugia, Siena** and **Volterra. TRAIN** (*0577 204246.* ***www.trainspa.it***) services to **Siena** also depart from here. It's €6.50 to Siena with either company (every 15–30 minutes).

By Train Florence lies on the main north–south high-speed rail (*892021.* ***www.trenitalia.it***) line with fast services from **Bologna** (€11.50), **Milan** (€27), **Rome** (€26.50) and **Venice** (€23.50). Local trains connect with **Pisa** (€5.40) and **Arezzo** (€5.40). For **Siena**, take the bus. Trains arrive at **Santa Maria Novella**, the main station, a short walk west of the Duomo. The ticket office is open 5.45am–10pm, or use the 24-hour machines inside the station.

Visitor Information

The main **tourist office** is at Via Cavour 1r, just north of the Duomo (*055 290832.* ***www.firenzeturismo.it***). It's open 8.30am–6.30pm Mon–Sat, 8.30am–1.30pm Sun. Of the others scattered across the city, the most convenient is just off Piazza Santa Croce at Borgo Santa Croce 29r (*055 2340444*): it's open 9am–5pm Mon–Sat, 9am–2pm Sun. Opposite the **train station** at Piazza della Stazione 4 (*055 212245*) hours are 8.30am–7pm Mon–Sat, 8.30am–2pm Sun.

Numerous **websites** offer visitor information for Florence. Try ***www.firenze.net*** and ***www.yourwaytoflorence.com***. When in the tourist office, grab a copy of **The Florentine** (***www.theflorentine.net***), a bi-weekly

English-language news and listings magazine.

The City in Brief

The **river Arno** bisects Florence east to west, with most sights lying to the north around the old centre (*centro storico*), while the district south of the river, **Oltrarno**, has some great sights of its own. The two areas are linked by eight bridges, most famously the **Ponte Vecchio** (see p. 59). At the heart of the *centro storico* lies **Piazza del Duomo**, home to the city's cathedral; a short walk away along Via dei Calzaiuoli is **Piazza della Signoria** and the **Galleria degli Uffizi** (see p. 52). North of the Duomo lie the markets of **San Lorenzo**, while **San Marco** lies beyond this, attracting crowds to the **Accademia** to see Michelangelo's *David*, and also for niche museums that appeal to children. South-east of the Duomo is **Santa Croce**, while **Oltrarno** across the river boasts the **Giardino di Boboli** and the classic view from **Piazzale Michelangelo**.

Ponte Vecchio: A Florence Timeline

59 BC Florence (Florentia) is founded by Julius Caesar, as a settlement for army veterans
552–1115 City ruled by the Goths, Lombards and finally the Franks
1115 Florence granted independent status within the Holy Roman Empire
1348 Black Death kills half the city's population
1406 Florence conquers Pisa
1469–92 Rule of Medici patriarch Lorenzo il Magnifico – the golden age of Renaissance
1494 Extremist monk Fra' Girolamo Savonarola helps drives the Medici from the city and takes control
1498 Savonarola burned at the stake for heresy; Florence becomes a republic until 1512, when the Medici return
1555–57 Florence takes control of Siena
1737 The last of the Medici dukes dies; Florence passes to the French House of Lorraine until 1859
1860 Florence joins the new state of Italy, becoming capital 1865–70
1944 Retreating Germans spare just one of Florence's bridges: the Ponte Vecchio
1966 Great Arno Flood; the river rises 6m and destroys priceless works of art
1993 Car bomb damages the Uffizi and kills five
2004 Fiorentina football club make a triumphant return to Serie A after years in the doldrums

Ponte Vecchio

Getting Around

Most visitors tour Florence **on foot**, and although distances aren't great, the walking can be tiring with pushchairs or young children. **Local buses** are a useful alternative. Orange **ATAF** (℡ *800 424500. **www.ataf.net***) buses have plenty of space and pushchair access. Buy tickets from automatic machines, shops and *tabacchi* all over the city, or the main ATAF information office just outside Santa Maria Novella (7.15am–7.45pm daily). Tickets are valid for unlimited travel within 70 minutes (€1.20), 24 hour (€5) or 3 days (€12). The **Biglietto Multiplo** provides four 70-minute tickets

National Curriculum

The mention of anything to do with school is likely to elicit howls of protest from youngsters, but almost everywhere you go in Florence can give your children a leg-up. The UK's **National Curriculum** has an **Art and Design** component, which suggests visiting galleries for all Key Stages: in Key Stage 1 (5–7 years) the emphasis is getting children to focus on shapes, colours and textures; in Key Stage 2 (7–11 years) to build awareness of the roles and purposes of art in different times and cultures. In Key Stage 3 and 4 (over 11s), there are modules on *Italian Renaissance Painting*, *Italian Architecture* and *Mannerism in Italy* – Florence is at the core of all three, and the artistic sights of **San Gimignano** (p. 88), **Arezzo** (p. 96) and **Assisi** (p. 201) are relevant too. Note also that Florence's excellent **Museo di Storia della Scienza** (p. 54) hosts regular school visits from the UK and Ireland.

TIP Hop On, Hop Off

A hassle-free way to get around the city is on a double-decker tourist bus, operated by UK-based **City Sightseeing** (UK 01708 866000. ***www.city-sightseeing.com/florence.htm***). It operates two different routes with over 15 stops around the *centro storico*. Route **A** (City Route) makes a loop from Santa Maria Novella station to Piazzale Michelangelo (50 minutes) while **B** (Fiesole Route) starts at Porta San Frediano and heads out to Fiesole (105 minutes). Tickets (€20, €10 child 5–15, free under-5s) are valid for 24 hours on both routes. Bus stops are clearly marked on the street – start anywhere. Buses run daily: in spring and summer every 30 minutes; every hour in autumn and winter.

for €4.50 or 10 for €10. Always validate your ticket in the yellow machines on board – you'll be fined otherwise. You can buy tickets on the bus but there's **no change** and it's €2 for a single. Several useful routes start outside Santa Maria Novella station: route **13** runs clockwise to Piazzale Michelangelo, **12** gets there by a less scenic route, while **7** takes you straight to Piazza San Marco and on to **Fiesole**.

The smaller electric **bussini ecologici** run through the centre and are handy if the children get tired: route **A** starts at the train station and runs past the Duomo and Piazza della Signoria before heading north of Santa Croce, while **D** runs from the train station to Ponte Vespucci and along the south bank of the Arno in a loop that includes Palazzo Pitti.

Taxis are metered but relatively expensive, from €8 up for short trips. In practice it's tough to hail one in the street, so make for a central rank or call **Radio Taxi** on *055 4242*, *055 4798*, or *055 4390*. Major **ranks** are found in Piazza Santa Croce, Piazza del Duomo, Piazza della Republica, Piazza San Marco and Piazza Santa Maria Novella.

Family-friendly Florentine Festivals

The **Scoppio del Carro** (Explosion of the Cart) takes place on Easter Sunday; this sees a cartload of fireworks pulled to the Duomo by six white oxen and ignited by a mechanical dove. Held in the Parco delle Cascine on the first Sunday after Ascension Day (40 days after Easter), the **Festa del Grillo** ★ (Festival of Crickets) sees hundreds of crickets sold in wooden cages; they are released *en masse* after a parade. The **Festa di San Giovanni** (St John's Day, 24th June) celebrates Florence's patron saint, with a massive fireworks display at Piazzale Michelangelo, and the first game of **Calcio Storico** ★★, medieval football. The *calcio* is a chaotic three-match, week-long series held in Piazza Santa Croce and Piazza della Signoria, with teams representing the four ancient city districts. The winning team

CENTRAL FLORENCE

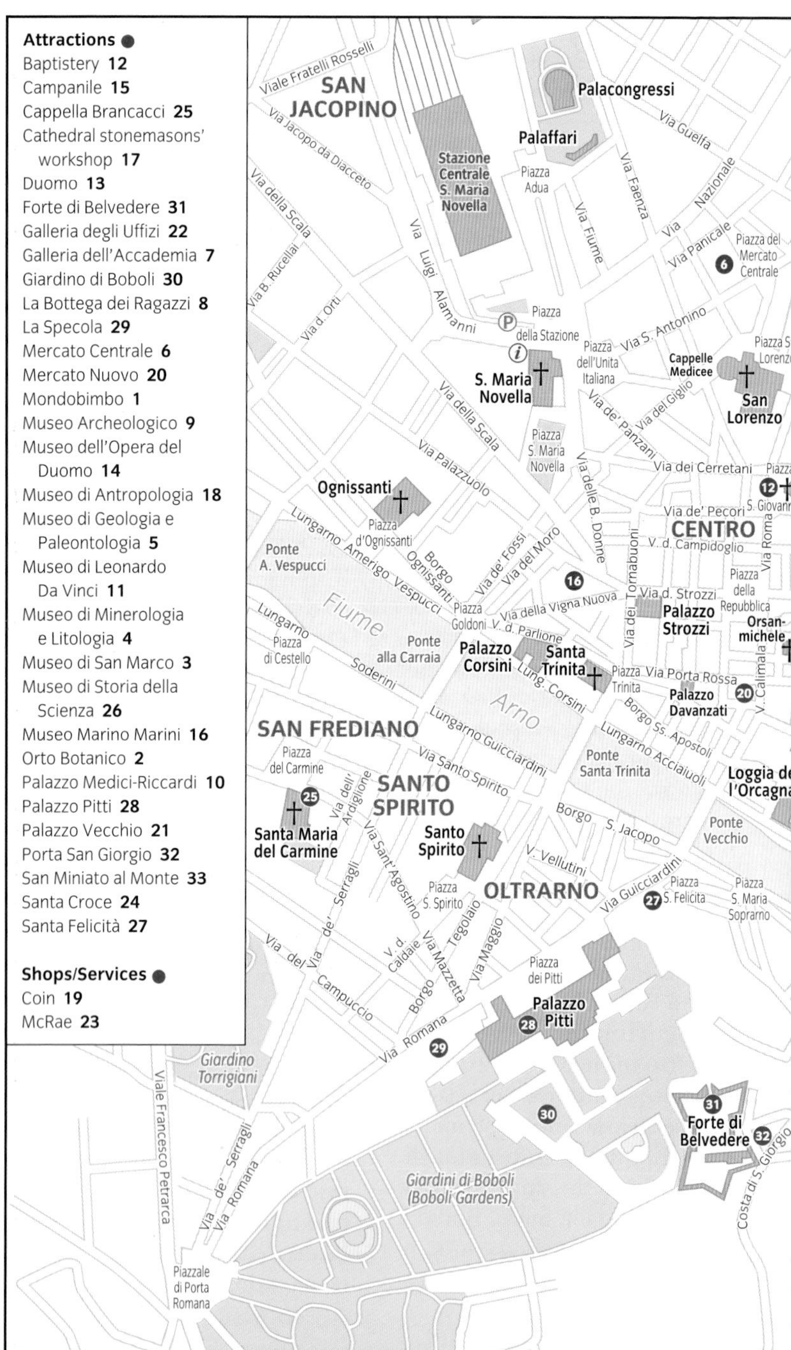

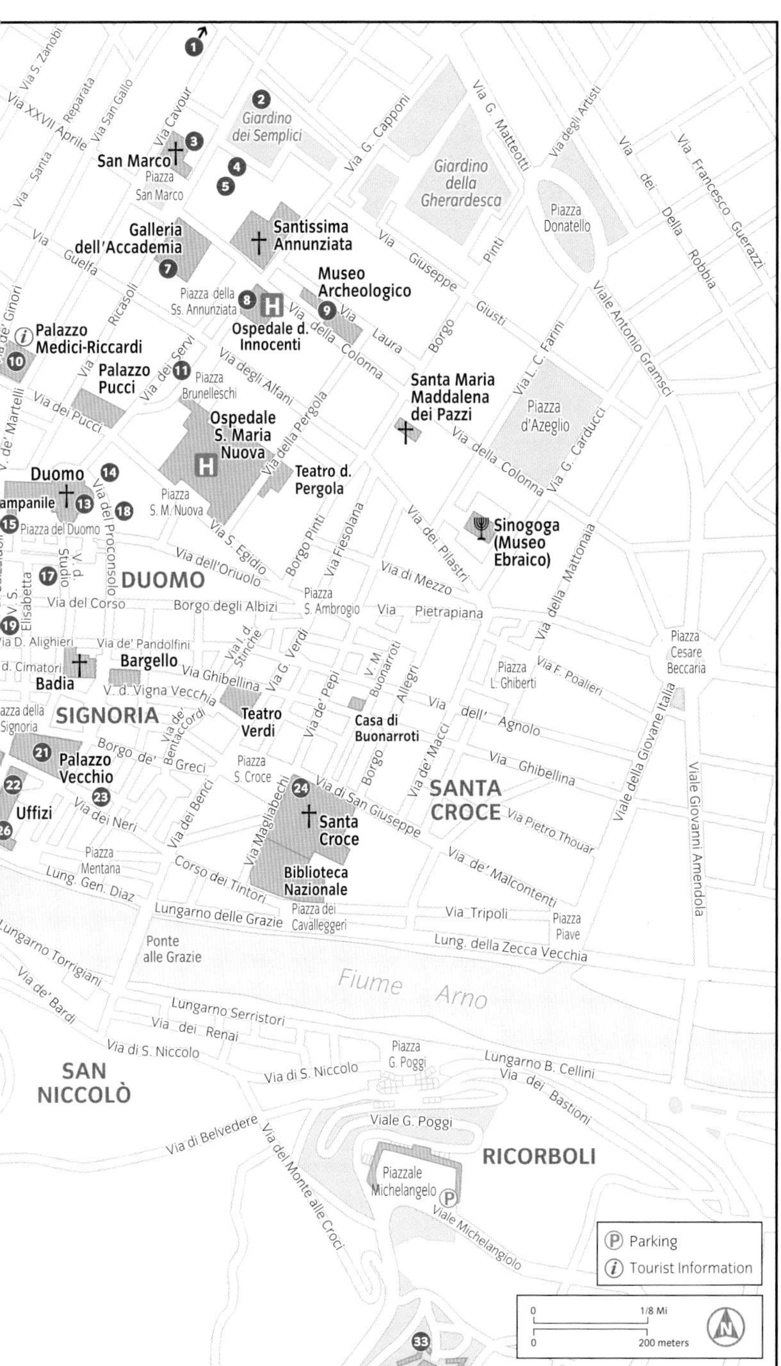
Giardino dei Semplici
San Marco
Piazza San Marco
Galleria dell'Accademia
Santissima Annunziata
Giardino della Gherardesca
Piazza Donatello
Museo Archeologico
Piazza della Ss. Annunziata
Ospedale d. Innocenti
Palazzo Medici-Riccardi
Palazzo Pucci
Piazza Brunelleschi
Santa Maria Maddalena dei Pazzi
Piazza d'Azeglio
Ospedale S. Maria Nuova
Duomo
Campanile
Piazza del Duomo
Piazza S. M. Nuova
Teatro d. Pergola
Sinogoga (Museo Ebraico)
DUOMO
Piazza S. Ambrogio
Piazza Cesare Beccaria
Bargello
Badia
Piazza L. Ghiberti
SIGNORIA
Teatro Verdi
Casa di Buonarroti
Palazzo Vecchio
Piazza S. Croce
SANTA CROCE
Uffizi
Santa Croce
Piazza Mentana
Biblioteca Nazionale
Piazza dei Cavalleggeri
Piazza Piave
Ponte alle Grazie
Fiume Arno
Piazza G. Poggi
SAN NICCOLÒ
RICORBOLI
Piazzale Michelangelo
Via S. Zanobi
Via XXVII Aprile
Via S. Reparata
Via San Gallo
Via Cavour
Via Santa
Via Guelfa
Via Ricasoli
Via G. Capponi
Via G. Matteotti
Via degli Artisti
Via dei Della Robbia
Via Francesco Guerazzi
Via Giuseppe Giusti
Via Pinti
Via della Colonna
Via Laura
Borgo Pinti
Viale Antonio Gramsci
Via L. C. Farini
Via de' Ginori
Via dei Servi
Via degli Alfani
Via dei Pucci
Via de' Martelli
Via della Pergola
Via G. Carducci
Via del Proconsolo
Via S. Egidio
Via dell'Oriuolo
Via Fiesolana
Via dei Pilastri
Via di Mezzo
Via della Mattonaia
V. d. Studio
V. S. Elisabetta
Via del Corso
Borgo degli Albizi
Via Pietrapiana
Via D. Alighieri
Via de' Pandolfini
Via I. d. Stinche
Via G. Verdi
V. M. Buonarroti
Via Allegri
Via d. Cimatori
Via Ghibellina
V. d. Vigna Vecchia
Via F. Poalieri
Via dell' Agnolo
Via de' Bentaccordi
Via de' Pepi
Piazza della Signoria
Borgo de' Greci
Borgo Allegri
Via de' Macci
Viale della Giovane Italia
Viale Giovanni Amendola
Via dei Neri
Via dei Benci
Via Magliabechi
Via di San Giuseppe
Via Pietro Thouar
Via de' Malcontenti
Lung. Gen. Diaz
Corso dei Tintori
Lungarno delle Grazie
Via Tripoli
Lung. della Zecca Vecchia
Lungarno Torrigiani
Via de' Bardi
Lungarno Serristori
Via dei Renai
Via di S. Niccolo
Lungarno B. Cellini
Via dei Bastioni
Viale G. Poggi
Via di Belvedere
Via del Monte alle Croci
Viale Michelangiolo
Parking
Tourist Information
1/8 Mi
200 meters

receives a calf to roast at a raucous street party. The **Festa della Rificolona** ★ (Virgin's Birthday, 7th September) is marked by a colourful procession of children to Piazza Santissima Annunziata, each carrying a paper lantern with a candle inside, followed by the inevitable boisterous street parties.

FAST FACTS: FLORENCE

American Express The office is at Via Dante Alighieri 22r (*055 50981*), open 9am–5.30pm Mon–Fri, 9am–12.30pm Sat.

Car Rental **Avis**, Borgo Ognissanti 128r, *055 2398826;* **Europcar**, Borgo Ognissanti 53r, *055 290437/8;* **Excelsior**, Via Lulli 76, *055 3215397;* **Hertz**, Via Maso Finiguerra 33r, *055 282260;* **Thrifty**, Borgo Ognissanti 134r, *055 287161.* See also p. 26.

Chemists You can find 24-hour chemists inside the **train station** (Farmacia Santa Maria Novella), at Piazza San Giovanni 20r, and at **Farmacia Molteni**, Via dei Calzaiuoli 7r. Pharmacies are scattered all over the centre, usually open 8.30am–1pm and 4–8pm, Mon–Sat.

Consulates The **UK Consulate** is at Lungarno Corsini 2 (*055 284133.* ***www.britain.it***). Citizens of **Ireland** should contact their embassy in Rome (*06 6979121*).

Currency Exchange You'll find **cashpoints** and *offici di cambio* (exchange booths) throughout the centre, while major banks can be found around **Piazza della Repubblica**. Opening hours are usually 8.30am–1.30pm and 2.35–3.35pm Mon–Fri.

Dentists & Doctors For English-speaking doctors contact the 24 hour **Tourist Medical Service** on *055 475411* (***www.medicalservice.firenze.it***). Their clinic is at Via Lorenzo il Magnifico 59 (11am–midday and 5–6pm, Mon–Fri, 11am–midday, Sat). Consultations cost at least €50.

Emergencies For **fire** call *115;* for an **ambulance** or first-aid call *118;* for a general emergency or **police**, call *113;* for road assistance or **breakdowns**, call *116.*

Hospitals The main one in central Florence is **Ospedale Santa Maria Nuova**, at Piazza Santa Maria Nuova 1 (*055 27581*) with a 24-hour casualty. The **Associazione Volontari Ospedalieri** (*055 4250126*) provides 24-hour translators for medical emergencies.

Internet Access There are numerous Internet cafés scattered all over Florence, and you must show **photo ID** before accessing the web. **Internet Train** (***www.internettrain.it***) has 10 outlets including Via Porta Rossa 38r (9.30am–midnight Mon–Sat, 10am–midnight Sun), Via de'Benci 36r (9.30am–1am Mon–Fri, 10am–1am Sat, midday–1am Sun) and Piazza Stazione 14 (under the road,

TIP Baby Changing & Breastfeeding

Changing nappies on the go in Florence can be a challenge as toilets are small. Italian mums bring their own changing mats. The best public lavatories are at Via Filippina, just east of Palazzo Vecchio. **Coin** department store at Via dei Calzaiuoli 56r (see p. 65) has a **baby room** and toilet on the second floor and the **Prénatal** store at Via Brunelleschi 22r (see p. 65) has a similar facility. You might have to pretend to buy something, but staff are sympathetic. Florentine women tend not to **breastfeed** in public, but with a million foreigners in town, you won't raise many eyebrows. The tourist office at Via Cavour is happy for mothers to feed inside, while the baby rooms at the shops mentioned above are also good spots. The new cathedral visitor centre will have baby rooms. Restaurants and cafés are usually happy to **warm bottles** (*riscaldare, per favore*).

8.30am–7.30pm Mon–Fri, 9am–8pm Sat, midday–8pm Sun). Prices are €1 for 10 minutes, €2.70 for 30 minutes and €4.30 for 1 hour. Under-26s get a discount.

Lost Property Property handed to the police or railway police gets taken to the city office on Via Circondaria (☎ 055 3283942); open 9am–midday Mon–Wed, Fri–Sat.

Police Call ☎ 112 or ☎ 113 in emergencies. Report **lost passports** or thefts at the *Questura*, Via Zara 2 (☎ 055 49771), open 8am–8pm daily; translators are usually available until 2pm. You'll have to fill in a form (*denuncia*) if you intend to claim.

Post The main **post office** is at Via Pellicceria 8, near Piazza della Repubblica, open 8.15am–7pm Mon–Sat. You can buy stamps (*francobolli*) at tobacconist stores (*tabacchi*), identified outside by a white 'T' on a blue background.

Safety Florence is a **safe** city for families, though it attracts pickpockets and bag-snatchers, *scippatori*, who tend to operate in large **crowds** of tourists. Don't flash expensive jewellery, cameras, watches and bags as you walk around, and wear money in a pouch or belt. Carry bags across your shoulders: it makes them harder to grab. If you're **parking** in the city, never leave anything of value inside. Avoid the area around the **train station** and **Parco delle Cascine** at night.

Toilets There are 11 public toilets in the centre, open every day (usually 60¢). The most convenient are located **behind the Bargello** at the top of Via Filippina (10am–6pm 1 Oct–20 Mar; 9am–7pm 21 Mar–30 Sept); in the **tourist office** at Borgo Santa Croce 29r (10am–5pm); the **subway** at Santa Maria Novella (8am–8pm) and inside the station itself; plus Via dell' Ariento 14, near the **Mercato Centrale** (7am–2pm and 3–7.30pm).

SEEING FLORENCE

Florence has a history that goes back to the Romans, but most of what you see today is evidence of its **Golden Age**: the late-medieval and Renaissance periods when its merchants and bankers, particularly the **Medici** family, made it one of Europe's largest and richest cities. Their cash, combined with a flowering of artistic genius, created an awesome legacy of painting, sculpture and architecture. In addition to the main sights, there's a huge amount that appeals to children too.

A lot of the fantastic art in Tuscany and Umbria is biblical in subject. It's worth swotting up on the main themes in advance; they appear again and again. Engage children by asking them to spot these stories: **David and Goliath** (see p. 57), the **Annunciation** (Archangel Gabriel tells Mary she is to conceive God's son), the **Adoration of the Magi** (three kings bring gifts to the infant Jesus), the **Last Supper** (*Cenacolo* in Italian, Christ's last meal with his disciples), the **Crucifixion**, the **Deposition** (Jesus is taken down from the Cross), the **Assumption** (Mary dies and passes into Heaven), and the **Last Judgement** (the world ends and we all get our just reward).

Piazza del Duomo

If you have only a short time in Florence, head straight for **Piazza del Duomo** ★★★, the spiritual heart of the city. This bustling square is dominated by the exotic cathedral and **Brunelleschi**'s awe-inspiring dome. Aspiring builders can peek into the cathedral **stonemason's workshop**, just south of the piazza at Via della Studio 23a.

TIP Beating the Queues

Children aren't patient, especially in the heat, so we advise that you reserve popular gallery tickets in advance. All state-owned **Firenze Musei** attractions (***www.firenzemusei.it***) sell pre-booked tickets. Queues at the **Galleria degli Uffizi** and **Galleria dell'Accademia** can be horrific.

For the **Uffizi,** reserve tickets opposite the gallery entrance or use the booking line (same number for all museums), ✆ *055 294883*, 8.30am–6.30pm Mon–Fri, 8.30am–12.30pm Sat. There are English-speaking operators and a €3 booking fee. You'll be given a set time and asked to collect your ticket before entry. This won't get you out of queuing, but it will install you at the back of a much shorter one.

Admission to all state-owned museums is **free** for EU citizens under 18 and over 65 (show passports). Many are closed on **Mondays** and none accepts credit cards at the door. Last entry is usually 30 minutes before closing.

Brunelleschi's Dome

Duomo (Cattedrale di Santa Maria del Fiore) ★★

AGES 9 AND UP

*Piazza del Duomo. ☎ 055 2302885. **www.duomofirenze.it**. Bus: 1, 3.*

With its mesmerising 19th-century marble exterior, the Duomo is the grandest and greatest structure in Florence. Construction took most of the 14th century, and by 1418 all was complete save the dome and façade. In stepped Filippo Brunelleschi, who started the landmark dome project in 1423, only to die before its completion in the 1460s.

Climbing the dome ★★ is the highlight of Florence for most children, and it pays to do this first (through a separate entrance on the north side of the cathedral); there will be long **queues** unless you get there early. The views are magnificent and the clamber to the top lots of fun (warning: there are 463 steps). The first section ends at a narrow gallery that skirts the base of the dome, with a vertigo-inspiring drop down to the nave and where you can eyeball Vasari's massive **fresco** of the *Last Judgement*, plastered around the dome. The final ascent is within the shell of the dome, up to the base of the white marble lantern for a panorama across the red rooftops of the city.

If there's a huge queue to get inside the cathedral itself, you can comfortably skip it, but there are one or two interesting artworks. Top of the list is Michelino's *Dante Exploring the Divine Comedy*, with its mountain of purgatory on the left (topped by Adam and Eve) and a portrayal of the dome itself on the right. Red-robed Dante is portrayed in the middle, outside the city walls.

An alternative **climb** provides a different city perspective and a close-up of Brunelleschi's dome. The **Campanile** ★, the cathedral's bell tower, was started by Giotto in 1334 and finished by Andrea Pisano and Francesco Talenti several years later. The Campanile is slightly shorter at 84.7m high, but with 414 steps to the viewing area (no lift), still quite a hike. It's open 8.30am–7.30pm daily, and costs €6 (under-6s free). When queues to climb the dome crawl around the block, there's often no one waiting here.

***Cathedral open** 10am–5pm Mon–Fri, closes 4pm Thu; 10am–4.45pm Sat; 1.30pm–4.45pm Sun; closes 3.30pm first Sat of month. **Adm** free. **Dome open** 8.30am–7pm Mon–Fri;*

8.30am–5.40pm Sat; closes 4pm first Sat of month. ***Adm*** *€6, free under-6s.* ***Amenities*** *disabled access (cathedral only), English, shop.*

Baptistery AGES 5 AND UP

Piazza San Giovanni. 055 2302885.

Next door to the Duomo, the Baptistery is the oldest building in Florence, with its origins in the Dark Ages. Today the crowds come to wonder at its magical **bronze doors** ★★, the 'Gates of Paradise' cast by **Lorenzo Ghiberti** in the 15th century (these are reproductions – the originals are in the **Museo dell'Opera**, Piazza del Duomo 9, *055 2302885*), and the stunning mosaic **ceiling** ★ inside. Focus on the details: the main vault depicts *Christ in Judgement*, flanked by images of Paradise and a particularly lurid vision of hell. The devil chomps away on a sinner, surrounded by demons and with serpents erupting from his horny head. Dante pops up again: he's hooded in black, and being led through hell by Virgil, to the left of Lucifer.

Open *midday–6.30pm Mon–Sat, 8.30am–1.30pm Sun.* ***Adm*** *€3, free under-6s.* ***Amenities*** *disabled access, English.*

INSIDER TIP

One way to really see Florentine art, especially in places like the Baptistery when the mosaics are way above your head, is to bring **binoculars**. It's easier to pick out the details that make the frescoes so absorbing: serpents, demons, angels and assorted products of the Renaissance imagination.

Museo di Antropologia FIND

AGES 8 AND UP

Via del Proconsolo 12. 055 2396449. ***www.msn.unifi.it****.*

This odd anthropology museum is one of Florence's less visited gems, its dusty collection of traditional garments and artefacts from tribal cultures hiding truly remarkable finds. The highlights are the **Peruvian mummies** ★, petrified remains of Incas buried near Cuzco 500 years ago. Although most children will find this grimly fascinating, you might feel it's not suitable for smaller ones: the skulls, some still with scraps of hair, are a bit gruesome, and there are small babies wrapped in cloth and rope. Don't miss the pygmy bows and arrows in Sala 4, the Inuit jacket made from whale stomach and the multi-coloured feathers in the Amazon section.

Open *9am–1pm Mon, Tue, Thu, Fri, Sun; 9am–5pm Sat.* ***Adm*** *€4, €2 6–21s.* ***Amenities*** *shop.*

Around Piazza della Signoria

Gateway to the Uffizi and the secular heart of the city, **Piazza della Signoria** ★★ is crammed with tourists and ringed with magnificent sculpture. At the heart of the piazza stands the austere **Palazzo Vecchio**. Look for the reproduction of Michelangelo's **David** (p. 57), the **Fountain of Neptune** (Roman god of the sea) and the supercilious image of Medici duke **Cosimo I** (1587–94). In

TIP Size Matters

When the Duomo was completed in the 1460s, it was the largest church in the world, holding the title until the completion of St Peter's in Rome in 1626. It's now the fourth largest.

Neptune, Piazza della Signora

the piazza's arcaded **Loggia dei Lanzi** ★, don't miss Giambologna's marble 1584 *Rape of the Sabine Women*: it marks the point when Florentine art abandoned drama in favour of melodrama. Cellini's brilliant bronze **Perseus** ★ (1554), holding aloft Medusa's head, falls the other side of the good-taste line.

INSIDER TIP

If you're looking for a specific art picture that you've seen on your visit, try the **news-stand** in the north-west corner of the piazza. He has 5,000 postcard images and will try to find what you're after.

You might also want to stroll along Via Calimaruzza to the **Mercato Nuovo**, for souvenir shops and the bronze boar known as **Il Porcellino** ★. Children can clamber over it and, for luck, try to get a coin to fall from its mouth into a grille below its head. Coins go to local children's homes. The market is open 9am–7pm daily mid-February to mid-November; 9am–5pm Tuesday to Saturday mid-November to mid-February.

Palazzo Vecchio ★★

AGES 8 AND UP

Piazza della Signoria. 055 2768465.

Dominating the piazza with its striking tower, the old **city hall** is primarily an art museum, although part of it still houses the city council. It dates from 1299 and was extended by the Medici in the 1540s. Though its core collections are rather dry, the ground-breaking **Emozioni da Museo** ★★★ (arranged in cooperation with the Musei di Ragazzi; see 'The Children's Museum', below) makes this one of the most rewarding attractions in the city for children. In addition to interactive workshops held throughout the palace, like **fresco painting** (30 minutes), costumed guides lead groups on animated tours of the

FUN FACT Big Whitey

The Neptune statue in the Piazza della Signoria is known as il Biancone, 'Big Whitey', an allusion to its white marble and large size. The statue has been vandalised six times, most recently in 2005 when a hand was snapped off by drunken revellers, allegedly by accident.

building. Most of these are held in Italian, but there are excellent **English** options: a tour led by an actor dressed as Giorgio Vasari, the painter and architect who helped redesign the *palazzo* in the 1550s, takes in secret passageways (*percorsi segreti*) normally closed to visitors (10am and 11.30am Tue and Thu, 3.30pm and 5pm Fri and Sat, 10.30am and midday Sun; €8, €5.50 ages 18–25, €2 children 8–17, €22 family).

'An Invitation to Cosimo's Court' (11am and 3pm Mon and Wed, 10am, 11.30am, 3pm, 4.30pm Sat and Sun; same prices) involves a visit to the Medici apartments followed by an audience with Cosimo de' Medici or his Spanish wife, Eleonora. For both tours **book in advance** (*055 2768224*), and children must be 8 or older.

Open *9am–6pm daily, closes 1pm Thu.* ***Adm*** *€6, €4.50 18–25s, €2 children 3–17, €14/16 family (5 people).* ***Amenities*** *English, shop.*

Galleria degli Uffizi ★★★

AGES 7 AND UP

Piazzale degli Uffizi 6. 055 2388651. ***www.uffizi.firenze.it.***

The finest gallery in Italy, the **Uffizi** (the word means 'offices') was established by Vasari in 1560 for his patron, Cosimo I de' Medici. The artwork here is mind-blowing, but there are few concessions made for children. The usual advice is to make a tour of the first 15 rooms, dedicated to the Renaissance, but if you have youngsters and don't expect to come back, concentrate on the most famous paintings.

The works of **Botticelli** are collected in Rooms 10–14, with **Primavera (Allegory of Spring)** ★★ and **The Birth of Venus** ★★★ his most famous. Both were painted in the 1480s; they're colourful and stimulating, and easy to appreciate. *Primavera* depicts Venus in the centre, the goddess of love, surrounded by classical figures such as Flora (goddess of spring) embraced by the West Wind. Botticelli may have used local beauty Simonetta Vespucci as his model for Flora, and again in *Birth of Venus*, where the goddess of love floats on a scallop shell rising from the ocean.

Paintings by **Leonardo da Vinci** are shown in Room 15. The **Annunciation** ★★ (1475) is one of his greatest works, showing meticulous attention to detail, and there is an unfinished sketch of the **Adoration of the**

Galleria degli Uffizi

Magi ★★★, sporting the most entrancing angels ever painted.

Don't miss Room 18, the octagonal **Tribuna**, which holds classical sculpture. The circular **Doni Tondo** ★ (1508) in Room 25 is one of Michelangelo's most masterful combinations of paint and sculpture, depicting the Holy Family. Room 26 has a collection of **Raphael**'s work, especially **Pope Leo X** with **Cardinals Giulio de'Medici** and **Luigi de'Rossi** ★★. His depictions of this dodgy-looking party are magical.

Check out Venetian master **Titian** in Room 28 for his outstanding **Knight of Malta** ★★ and sensual nude **Venus of Urbino** ★★.

The later galleries contain magnificent work from outside Florence. Rembrandt's **Self Portrait as an Old Man** ★ in Room 44 is a melancholy depiction of one of the world's greatest painters. **Caravaggio**, who dropped dead in the Tuscan Maremma (see p. 157), is found in Room 43, although he's outshone by Artemisia Gentileschi's (yes, a woman) grisly depiction of **Judith Slaying Holofernes** ★.

Open *8.15am–6.50pm (until 10pm Tue Jul–Sep) Tue–Sun.* ***Adm*** *€6.50, €3.25 18–25s.* ***Amenities*** *café, disabled access, English, shop.*

TIP The Children's Museum

The **Museo Ragazzi di Firenze** ★★★ (*055 2768224.* ***www.museoragazzi.it***) is based at the Palazzo Vecchio: it's an association that organises workshops and events for children. The key ones are held at the **Palazzo Vecchio** (see above), but some are organised at other museums. Most are in Italian, but it's worth checking ahead or visiting the desk inside the Palazzo Vecchio entrance (no need to pay).

The Big Three

Three of Italy's most celebrated Renaissance painters spent formative years in Florence. **Sandro Botticelli** (1444–1510) was the son of a Florentine tanner and spent most of his life in the city, where his enigmatic work ranged from early Renaissance to sombre, almost modern expressionism. His paintings exhibit a rare beauty – unlike Michelangelo, he could paint women, even if they all seem to resemble Cate Blanchett. He was a sensitive soul, a bit of an eccentric, and ended life as a pauper, virtually forgotten. **Leonardo da Vinci** (1452–1519), a great friend of Botticelli (although he disliked his work), was born in Vinci (p. 126), the illegitimate son of a peasant girl and Florentine lawyer. He moved here at 12 and spent his early career in Florence before settling in Milan. Da Vinci was good-looking and self-confident, an intellectual force; his diagrams of machines and mechanical devices are as impressive as his paintings. He was also a bit of dandy. Da Vinci detested the outstanding talent of the High Renaissance, **Michelangelo Buonarotti** (1475–1564), who was born in Caprese, south of the city and grew up in Florence among impoverished gentry. He was too obsessed with God for science-minded Leo. At 26 Michelangelo was commissioned to create *David*. He moved to Rome in 1505, where he frescoed the Sistine Chapel, and left Florence forever in the 1530s. Ruggedly handsome, he was an awkward man with a volatile temperament: his flat nose was broken in a fight.

Museo di Storia della Scienza

★★ **AGES 5 AND UP**

Piazza dei Giudici 1. 055 265311. www.imss.fi.it.

This enlightening **science museum** is a trove of fascinating instruments, giant spheres and telescopes, formerly the private collections of the ruling Medici and Lorraine families, in an evocative setting straight out of Hogwarts. Helpful English-speaking guides are on hand to offer explanations and demonstrate the more elaborate machines: children are encouraged to guess what will happen, and then work out why.

Highlights on the first floor include **Michelangelo's compass** in room 1 and **Galileo**'s middle finger is preserved in glass in room 4. The telescope room (5) is another favourite, with Galileo's lens (with which he discovered the four moons of Jupiter), an ornate 'ladies telescope' and some walking-stick binoculars. On the second floor look out for the Frankenstein-like electrostatic generators in room 14 and the medieval pharmacy (room 19), set up like an apothecary on Diagon Alley complete with Dragon's Blood.

The museum runs an excellent programme of **educational**

activities for schools in English, but nothing as yet for families. If you speak Italian, the 'Weekends at the Museum' (€7.50, €5 children 7–18, free under-7s) on Saturdays 3.30–5pm are highly recommended: children get to interact with a performer dressed as Galileo as he describes his greatest theories and experiments. It's also worth taking a look at the small shop on site for replicas of **Galileo's compass** (with CD, €25).

Open *9.30am–4.30pm Mon, Wed–Fri, 9.30am–12.30pm Tue and Sat; until 4.30pm Sat and 10am–12.30pm 2nd Sun of month 1st Oct–31st May.* ***Adm*** *€6.50, €4 children 7–18.* ***Amenities*** *disabled access, English, shop.*

INSIDER TIP

Stately **Piazza della Repubblica**, a few blocks west of Piazza della Signoria, is known for upmarket cafés, and has an old-fashioned **merry-go-round** in the middle. It's open 10am–8pm daily; €1 for children, €1.50 for adults, €5 for six rides.

Museo Marino Marini FIND

AGES 5 AND UP

Piazza San Pancrazio. 055 219432. www.museomarinomarini.it.

This innovative gallery displays over 180 works by Marino Marini (1901–80), the celebrated Pistoiese sculptor whose abstract themes of horse and rider dominate the collection. It's the space as much as the work that appeals to children. The restored church has a warren of castle-like walkways and passages, all great fun to explore. The basement is devoted to hands-on **activities for children** ★ and at the weekends the museum runs interactive art programmes for families (€4 per person), in Italian only. In high season ask in advance about English speakers.

Open *10am–5pm Mon, Wed–Sat, closes 1pm Sun; closed Aug.* ***Adm*** *€4.* ***Amenities*** *disabled access, shop.*

Santa Croce ★ AGES 7 AND UP

Piazza Santa Croce 16. 055 244619. www.santacroce.firenze.it.

Just east of Piazza della Signoria, Piazza Santa Croce is best known for its Gothic **church**, a stone edifice constructed for the Franciscans around 1294, with a soaring timbered ceiling and several **frescoes**. Giotto's damaged **Life of St Francis** ★ is inside the Cappella Bardi, right of the altar; at the end of the same transept, his student Taddeo Gaddi steals the show with exquisite **Scenes from the Life of the Virgin** ★, painted between 1332 and 1338.

It's the **buried Renaissance celebrities** that hold the appeal for older children. **Michelangelo**'s body was brought here from Rome in 1574, 10 years after his death; his ludicrously ornate tomb was designed by Vasari. Next-door is the neoclassical monument to **Dante**, who died in 1321 and is buried in Ravenna. Further up the aisle is the relatively simple white tomb of the writer **Machiavelli** (he died in 1527), while **Galileo** is buried on the other side of the nave in

Museums & Galleries

Tuscany and Umbria house the most inspirational collections of art and history on the planet, and experiencing them together will be a highlight of your holiday. With a little planning, you'll get even youngsters mesmerised. You'll find plenty of ideas scattered throughout, but don't discount museum or gallery **audioguides** – you might be surprised just how much a mature child can glean from them. Otherwise:

Get arty Take drawing materials to the museum – few will object to your youngster quietly scribbling – and set goals like finding specific paintings, or the work of the most famous painters (see 'The Big Three', p. 54).

Get cameras Cheap or disposable cameras can be a great way to engage the children. Check photography is allowed first, and then get them to snap what they like best to reproduce back at home, or in the hotel that night. They can recreate statues or ancient pottery with modelling clay, if you've got room in the suitcase.

Get creative with treasure trails With a bit of preparation, you can knock up a list of 10 or more 'best things to see' to create your own treasure trail, and get each child to tick them off. Multicoloured clipboards are a good idea. If you don't have time for that, visit the gift shop first, buy postcards and use those instead. You can also get them to keep a record of how many times characters (Mary, David) or scenes (Assumption, Last Supper) appear, and chat about how they differ (see p. 48).

Be focused With young children make sure you limit your time in galleries to small doses, focusing on something that your child finds appealing: period dresses or dolls; paintings of animals, battles, or ships; even ancient weapons and tools.

another elaborate number topped with a statue of the great scientist (died 1642); one hand holds a telescope while the other hovers over a globe. As you leave via the cloister, pause by Donatello's 1433 **Annunciation** ★.

Open *9.30am–5.30pm Mon–Sat, 1–5.30pm Sun.* ***Adm*** *€5, €3 children 11–18.* ***Amenities*** *disabled access, English, shop.*

San Marco & Around

If you're walking up to San Marco along Via Cavour, Benozzo Gozzoli's painted chapel inside the Palazzo Medici-Riccardi (*055 2760340.* ***www.palazzo-medici.it***), at no 3, has an innovation designed to appeal to technophile teens. Downstairs in 'Lorenzo's Workshop' (on the right inside Michelozzo's courtyard) are two giant screens showing the fresco cycle. Stand on the hotspot in front of them and you can scroll forward and back, or single out areas of the images to hear detailed commentary about – all with a wave of your finger. It's

David, Goliath & Michelangelo

David's clash with Goliath is one of the most memorable tales in the Old Testament. Humble David slew the Philistine champion, a feared warrior and giant, with a single stone from his sling, and went on to replace Saul as king of a united Israel. Jump forward 2,000 years to 15th-century Florence, where David was regarded as a symbol of the city's independent Republican status: little Florence standing proud against the tyrannical bullies of the Papacy and the Holy Roman Empire. Florentine nobles took to commissioning sculptures of their hero: Donatello's bronze *David*, made for Cosimo de' Medici in 1430, was one of the first to evoke the humanist Renaissance style. It's in the **Bargello Museum** (Via del Proconsulo 4. 055 2388606) along with Andrea Verrocchio's *David* (1476). In 1501 Michelangelo was commissioned to create yet another *David* – unveiled in Piazza della Signoria in 1504. It was moved to the Accademia in 1873.

Don't miss the two **replicas**, one in Piazza della Signoria, the other in Piazzale Michelangelo. See if the children can spot any differences.

one giant **virtual video game** where you direct the Procession of the Magi. The palazzo is open 9am–7pm Thursday to Tuesday; entry is €5, €3.50 6–12s.

Galleria dell'Accademia

AGES 7 AND UP

Via Ricasoli 58–60. 055 2388609.

Each year, thousands of people visit the Accademia to see one thing: Michelangelo's 1504 statue of **David** ★★★. The sculpture is truly sublime and worth every euro (see 'David, Goliath & Michelangelo', below). It's over 4m tall, and took four days, ropes, winches, 40 men and a wooden cage to move it from the artist's studio into Piazza della Signoria. Locals immediately dubbed it *Il Gigante* (the giant). When it was transported to the Accademia, special tracks were laid so that the statue could be moved by rail truck.

Older children will appreciate the spectacle and reverence accorded the statue. The gallery also contains the **Four Slaves** (or '*Prisoners*'), unfinished expressive figures by Michelangelo, still bearing the rough chisel marks of the master.

Open *8.15am–6.50pm Tue–Sun.*
Adm *€6.50, €3.25 18–25s.*
Amenities *disabled access, English (audioguide, €4.65), shop.*

Museo di San Marco ★

AGES 5 AND UP

Piazza San Marco 3. 055 2388608.

Housed in the former Dominican convent of San Marco, next to the church, is a museum packed with exquisite frescoes by **Fra' Angelico**. His **Annunciation** ★ on the first-floor wall is what most come to see; even better is his **Deposition** ★★ in the old hospice, on the right by the entrance. Quite novel for youngsters are the 44 frescoed **monks' cells** upstairs. Squeeze inside to view the paintings, and imagine months spent in silent contemplation. Zealous monk Savonarola, who ruled Florence between 1494 and 1498, had a cell here. At the other end are large VIP cells once occupied by the convent's founder, Cosimo de' Medici.

This is a pleasant art spot to visit with a **buggy**.

Open *8.15am–1.20pm Tue–Fri, until 6.20pm Sat, 8.15am–1.20pm 1st, 3rd and 5th Mon of month, 8.15am–6.20pm 2nd and 4th Sun of month.* ***Adm*** *€4, €2 18–25s.* ***Amenities*** *disabled access, shop.*

Museo di Storia Naturale

AGES 5 AND UP

Via La Pira 4. 055 2756209. ***www.unifi.it/msn****.*

Florence's natural history museum is actually an umbrella organisation for a series of five related collections, all excellent for young children: the **anthropology** (see p. 50) and **zoology** (see p. 60) collections are located elsewhere, but nip into the University of Florence and you'll find two absorbing sections: the **Museo di Minerologia e Litologia** (*055 2757537*) and **Museo di Geologia e Paleontologia** (*055 2757536*).

The mineral museum has a vast collection of precious pieces collected by the Medici dukes, a treasure trove for aspiring gemmologists. As well as almost every type of mineral and crystal, diamonds, rubies, sapphires and opals are displayed on snuff-boxes, cups and vases – there's even a dog's head in purple quartz. The geology museum is perfect for children who love fossils, one of the largest collections in the world. There are a handful of dinosaur and mammoth skeletons on display. It's also worth popping into the **Orto Botanico** (*055 2757402*), around the corner at Via Micheli 3 if you fancy a break in the sun.

Open *9am–1pm Mon, Tue, Thu, Fri, Sun; 9am–5pm Sat.* ***Adm*** *€4, €2 children 6–14, €10 family; all museums €6/4.* ***Amenities*** *disabled access.*

Museo Stibbert ★★ FIND

AGES 5 AND UP

Via Stibbert 26. 055 486049. ***www.museostibbert.it****. Bus: 4.*

This unusual museum is a trek north of the centre, but if any of your children are into castles, knights or Harry Potter, they'll love it. Set in an opulent villa once owned by half-Italian, half-Scot Frederick Stibbert (1838–1906), the rooms are a blend of exotic castle décor and ornate Baroque, but it's Stibbert's eccentric collection of **weaponry** that stands out: lances, swords, pikes and muskets, as well as numerous suits of European, Japanese, Middle Eastern and Arabic armour. You have to tour the museum as part of an **escorted group** (maximum 20 people) – groups leave every 30 minutes and take at least an

Leo in San Lorenzo

If you can't make it to Leo's birthplace Vinci (see p. 126), Florence has two **Leonardo da Vinci museums** of its own. **Le Macchine di Leonardo da Vinci** at Via Cavour 21 is open 9.30am–7.30pm daily; it costs €5, €4 for children aged 6–18. At the **Museo di Leonardo da Vinci** ★ (*055 282966. **www.mostredileonardo.com***), at Via dei Servi 66/68r, youngsters are encouraged to touch the machines and see how they work, including the armoured tank and his ground-breaking flying machines. It's open 10.30am–6.30pm daily and costs €6, €5 for children aged 6–18. Elsewhere around San Lorenzo, the bustling street market, and Europe's largest covered food hall, the **Mercato Centrale** (see p. 64), are great spots to wander.

hour. You get several minutes in each room to wander around alone. There's plenty of space inside but some steps, and so it's tricky with a **pushchair**.

The **Museo di Ragazzi** organises weekly tours of the museum by costumed guides (see p. 53) including Turkish sultan Suleiman the Magnificent (who laid siege to Vienna in the 1530s), although these tours are almost always in Italian: check at the Palazzo Vecchio for English visits.

Open *10am–2pm Mon–Wed, until 6pm Fri–Sun.* ***Adm*** *€6, €4 child 3–12.* ***Amenities*** *café, English, picnic area, shop.*

Oltrarno

Oltrarno, the only part of the old city south of the **Arno**, is best approached by walking across **Ponte Vecchio** ★★. The bridge is a Florentine icon and a firm family favourite (a bridge with shops on it!), a medieval legacy groaning with crowds taking in the views and gold stores. The current bridge was built in 1345, and was the spared by the retreating German Army in 1944. Look at the shops on the bridge and walk down the banks of the Arno either side for better views – and there are top **ice cream stops** at both ends (see p. 75).

FUN FACT **Shhhhh!**

The enclosed corridor that runs along the top of Ponte Vecchio is part of the **Corridoio Vasariano**, a private passageway linking Palazzo Vecchio to Palazzo Pitti. Medici Duke Cosimo I found the idea of mixing with the hoi polloi on the way to work rather distressing, and so commissioned Vasari to design his secret VIP route in 1565. It's sometimes possible to **walk** the corridor – check at the ticket desk inside the Uffizi.

Palazzo Pitti AGES 7 AND UP

*Piazza Pitti 1. 055 2388611. **www. palazzopitti.it**. Bus: 11, 36, 37, B.*

Built in the 15th century for the Pitti family, the largest palace in Florence was acquired by the Medici in 1549 and today acts as an umbrella for eight museums and the **Giardino di Boboli** (see below). The most expensive section is dedicated to the lavish art collection (**Galleria Palatina**), particularly works by **Raphael**. The **Galleria del Costume** ★ (*055 2388763*) has a selection of dresses and robes from the 1700s to today, while the **Museo degli Argenti** has a vast collection of silverware plus all manner of exotic jewellery and decorative items. The rather dry **Museo delle Porcellane** stands inside the Bóboli gardens, and the **Museo delle Carrozze** (Carriage Museum) is likely to remain closed for some time.

***Open** 8.15am–3.30pm daily Jan–Feb, Nov–Dec; closes 5.30pm Mar, 6.30pm Apr–May, and Sep–Oct, 7.30pm Jun–Aug. **Adm** (Galleria Palatina, Appartamenti Reali and Galleria d'Arte Moderna) €11.50, €5.75 18–25s. **Adm** (Galleria del Costume, Museo degli Argenti and Giardino di Boboli) 6, €3 18–25s. **Amenities** disabled access, English, shop.*

Museo La Specola ★

AGES 8 AND UP

Via Romana 17. 055 2288251.

The zoological section of the **Museo di Storia Naturale** (see p. 54) specialises in morbid fascination, and so is definitely **unsuitable for younger children**. Highlights include the 'Room of the Skeletons', a collection of dinosaurs and extinct stuffed animals: the Tasmanian Tiger (Thylacine), Great Auk and Passenger Pigeon. The 600 models of human arms, legs, cadavers and organs in the **Cere Anatomiche** are, alas, extremely lifelike. The final room is particularly **grisly**: three tableaux created by Gaetano Zumbo for Cosimo III depicting Florence during the Plague, embellished with rats, rotting flesh and heaps of the dead. To top it off, there's a dissected wax head in the centre of the room. Nice.

Boboli's Isolotto

***Open** 9am–1pm Mon, Tue, Thu, Fri and Sun, until 5pm Sat. **Adm** €4, €2 child 6–14, €10 family. **Amenities** disabled access.*

Giardino di Boboli ★★ ALL AGES

Piazza Pitti. ☎ 055 2651816.

The **Boboli Gardens**, laid out in the 16th century just behind Palazzo Pitti, are a great place for the children to let off steam. Although picnics are discouraged, it's easy to find a secluded spot to munch in peace. There's plenty to see and explore, with elaborate grottoes, ponds and statues all over the place. The most famous is the Mannerist **Grotta Grande** ★, crammed with ostentatious statuary including replicas of Michelangelo's *Four Slaves*. Don't miss the **Fontana di Bacco** close by, with a fat dwarf sitting on a giant turtle. He was Morgante, a jester at the Medici court. Other highlights include the little fountain-spattered island of **Isolotto**, in a pond full of huge goldfish, and an ancient Egyptian obelisk.

A couple of **short, sharp gradients** and pebbled walkways make the Boboli tricky for buggy-pushers.

***Open** 8.15am–3.30pm daily Nov–Feb; until 4.30pm Mar; until 5.30pm Apr, May, Sep, Oct; until 6.30pm Jun and Aug. **Adm** €6, €3 18–25s. **Amenities** café, disabled access, English.*

Piazzale Michelangelo ALL AGES

You know those classic rooftop-and-dome **views** ★★★ of Florence you see *everywhere*? They're snapped from this piazza-cum-car-park on the southern edge of Oltrarno, lined with touristy stalls and a couple of good cafés. It's also the home of another huge copy of Michelangelo's *David*, looking out across the city. The best way to reach the square is to walk up from the river or along the city walls (see below), although bus 13 and City Sightseeing bus A also stop here. Behind the square, and a steep walk away, is the ancient Romanesque **Basilica di San Miniato al Monte** ★, surrounded by a flamboyant cemetery that's more city-of-the-dead than straightforward graveyard.

Cappella Brancacci ★★

AGES 12 AND UP

Santa Maria del Carmine, Piazza del Carmine. ☎ 055 2382195.

To understand the core of what the **Renaissance** was about, visit Oltrarno's **Brancacci Chapel**. The images here, painted between 1424 and 1428, stand on the cusp of the new artistic age. Compare the two representations of Adam and Eve up high at the entrance to the chapel. The one on the right, painted by **Masolino**, is a beautifully realised but template image of the couple. Do they *really* look tempted? **Masaccio**'s depiction of the **Expulsion from Eden** ★★★, meanwhile, is raw with realism and despair. Anyone familiar with Edvard Munch's *The Scream* will recognise Eve's expression. Masaccio was the most studied (and copied) artist between Giotto and Michelangelo; had he not died aged just 27, his name would be much more familiar.

Most of the chapel interior was frescoed by Masolino and

Masaccio with *Scenes from the Life of St Peter*, but it was completed by **Filippino Lippi**. See if you can tell who did what – or grab one of the handy cheat cards (in English). If you're passing by early in the day, **book** your timed entrance slot (you get 15 minutes).

Open *10am–4.30pm Mon–Sat, 1–4.30pm Sun.* ***Adm*** *€4, free under-6s.* ***Amenities*** *English, shop.*

West of the Centre

Museo della Matematica ★

FIND AGES 6 AND UP

Giardino di Archimede, Via S. Bartolo a Cintoia 19a. 055 7879594. ***www.archimede.ms****. Bus: 1A.*

This excellent **interactive museum** makes a worthy break from Renaissance art, although it's a long trek from the centre. Housed in a contemporary building, it has three sections: 'Beyond the Compass: the geometry of curves' explores the mathematics of everyday objects, while 'Pythagoras and his Theorem' sheds light on his great equation through puzzles and games. 'A Bridge over the Mediterranean' is an historical exhibition about Pisan mathematician Leonardo Fibonacci and the transfer of maths from the Islamic world to medieval Europe.

The museum runs **guided tours in English** for groups (minimum 12 people, €5) and 'Mathematical Sundays' on the first Sunday of the month between October and May: workshops for children (aged 6 and up) with topics ranging from ancient maths to origami. If you call ahead, English speakers are usually available.

Open *9am–1pm Mon–Fri, 3–7pm Sun, closed Aug.* ***Adm*** *€5, €3 per person for families.* ***Amenities*** *disabled access, parking, picnic area, shop.*

ENTERTAINMENT & ACTIVITIES

Play Areas FIND

If you're travelling with children under 10 and need a break from sightseeing, head out to **Mondobimbo** ★ (behind Piazza della Libertà. *055 5532946*), open 10am–12.30pm and 3–7.30pm daily. For €5 your child gets a supervised indoor play area with bouncy castles, a toddlers-only zone and plenty of games and slides. There are snacks and seats for dozing parents, and the owners speak English.

Florence has several indoor play areas specially designed for youngsters known as **Ludoteche**, although most outside the centre are targeted at local children. The best for English-speakers is **La Bottega dei Ragazzi** ★ at Via de Fibbai 2 (*055 2478386*), by Piazza Santissima Annunziata. It's free and open 9am–1pm and 3–7pm Monday to Saturday. Creative workshops and activities for children aged 3–11 in English include art, Florentine history and children's rights. Call two days in advance to book: prices are €10 for 6–11s, €5 for 3–5s (they need 10 children for an event).

La Viola: Fiorentina

Despite recent problems with crowd violence, Italy's *Serie A* remains one of the most exciting **football** leagues in the world. The Florence team is **Fiorentina**, known as *La Viola* for its violet-coloured shirts. They usually play alternate Sundays at the Stadio Comunale Artemio Franchi, Campo di Marte. To get there from Santa Maria Novella, take a train (one stop) to Campo di Marti (5 minutes) or bus **52** on matchdays (30 minutes). Italians do take their children to games, but even though Fiorentina has a decent safety record, it's rare to see children under 8. Check with the tourist office about the visiting teams, as some games (like those against **Juventus** and **Empoli**) can be feisty.

For tickets, go to **Chiosco degli Sportivi** (*055 292363*) at Via degli Anselmi 1, a booth just off Piazza della Repubblica. It's open 10am–7.30pm Tuesday to Saturday, 10am–12.30pm Sunday during the season: ask for the main **Nervi** stand and get a *distinti*, a numbered seat. Tickets cost upwards of €20. There's not much food at the ground, so bring snacks. For merchandise, check out ***www.fiorentinastore.com*** or head to **Ale' Viola** at Via del Corso 69r, where small Fiorentina shirts go for €10.

Cycling

Although there's little joy in pedalling round the crowded *centro*

A Walk Along the Walls

If your children still have energy after a trip to the Boboli, up the dose of fresh air by walking along the southern edge of the old walls to **Piazzale Michelangelo** (see above). It's a quiet part of the city, with fine views and lanes lined with olive trees. From the back of the Boboli, signs lead around the solid-looking **Forte di Belvedere** (a star-shaped fortress dating from 1590 open for exhibitions only), and along the narrow lane on the other side: here signs point down the hill to Giardino Bardini, but turn right instead to **Porta San Giorgio**, the old gate. From the gate follow the road downhill to the left (Via di Belvedere), along the base of the impressive walls. It's not busy, but watch out for the occasional speeding Fiat. At the bottom of the hill (Porta San Miniato) turn right until you come to the steps on the left (Via San Salvatore al Monte) – it's a short but steep climb up here past the **Rose Garden** (open May–Jun only) to the *piazzale* where ice cream awaits at **Ristorante Michelangelo** (open 7am–2am; €2–4).

storico, Florence is developing an ambitious network of **peripheral cycle routes** that offer a welcome break from sightseeing for active families; route maps are available at the tourist office. Among the best is the **Ciclopista dell'Arno**, 11.7km along the banks of the river. There are eight **Punti Biciclette** (bike points) around the city, where you can hire bikes for €8 per day or €1.50 per hour. You must leave a photocopy of your passport and return cycles before closing time. The most central is in front of the train station at Piazza della Stazione (☎ *055 6505295*). It's open 7.30am–7pm Monday to Saturday, and also 9am–7pm on summer Sundays.

For trips farther afield, **Florence by Bike**, at Via San Zanobi 120r (☎ *055 488992*. ***www.florencebybike.it***), arranges cycle tours in English or rentals only from €2.70 per hour to €14 per day. Note that wearing a **cycle helmet** is obligatory, though plenty of locals don't bother.

Go to the Park

The largest park in Florence is the **Parco delle Cascine**, along the northern bank of the river Arno west of the centre. You can picnic here, play on the **swings and slides** or take a dip in the **swimming pool** (Le Pavioniere, Viale della Catena 2. ☎ *055 362233*). It's safe during the day, but don't linger after **dark**.

Fiesole

If you plan to stay in Florence for a while (or are making the city your base), **Fiesole** ★ offers a welcome change of pace and an escape from the crowds. The village lies 300m up in the hills north of the city, with scintillating views, a decent Roman and Etruscan museum, and a great walk back down the hill if you're travelling by bus (no. **7** from Santa Maria Novella station, 20 minutes). The helpful **tourist office** is at Via Portigiani 3 (☎ *055 598720*. ***www.comune.fiesole.fi.it***). It's open 9am–6pm Monday–Saturday, 10am–1pm and 2–6pm Sunday March–October; 9am–5pm Monday–Saturday and 10am–4pm Sunday otherwise.

SHOPPING

San Lorenzo street market is the place to pick up touristy goods and souvenir T-shirts for youngsters, while the **Mercato Centrale** ★ is a wonderland of Tuscan food (see below). The **Cascine market** in the Parco delle Cascine is the biggest in

TIP The Red & the Black

Somewhat eccentrically, Florence's central streets have two separate sequences of numbers, red (suffixed 'r') and black (no suffix). Work out which you want and ignore all others.

Florence, held every Tuesday morning with hundreds of stalls selling clothes and shoes.

Gucci

Via de' Tornabuoni 73r. 055 2645432. ***www.gucci.com****.*

Gucci was founded in Florence in 1921, and this is its flagship store. Fun for older children to take a peek but maybe not to buy – unless you have bags of money...

Open *3–7pm Mon, 10am–7pm Tue–Sat.* ***Credit*** *AmEx, MC, V.* ***Amenities*** *disabled access.*

Coin

Via dei Calzaiuoli 56r. 055 280531. ***www.coin.it****.*

The city's top department store has a strong children's section and a baby room.

Open *10am–8pm Mon–Sat, 11am–8pm Sun.* ***Credit*** *AmEx, MC, V.* ***Amenities*** *disabled access.*

Prénatal

Via Brunelleschi 22r. 055 213006. ***www.prenatal.com****.*

Dedicated to all things *bambini* (think Mothercare in the UK), with a good selection of clothes and pushchairs, bottles, crayons and baby books (Italian only).

Open *10am–7.30pm Tue–Sat, 3.30–7.30pm Sun–Mon.* ***Credit*** *AmEx, MC, V.* ***Amenities*** *disabled access.*

La Città del Sole

Via dei Cimatori 21r. 055 2776372. ***www.cittadelsole.it****.*

Old-fashioned toy store, selling wooden puzzles, board games, puppets, science kits and (crucially) bubbles (*bolle*).

Open *3.30–7.30pm Mon, 10am–2pm and 3–7.30pm Tue–Sat.* ***Credit*** *AmEx, MC, V.* ***Amenities*** *disabled access.*

McRae

Via de' Neri 32r. 055 2382456. ***www.mcraebooks.com/shop****.*

The best place for English-language books in the city, with an excellent selection of children's literature as well as local history, art and culture, and Italian cooking.

Open *9am–7.30pm daily.* ***Credit*** *AmEx, MC, V.* ***Amenities*** *disabled access.*

Alice's Masks ★

Via Faenza 72r. 055 287370. ***www.alicemasks.com****.*

Established by master craftsman Agostino Dessi and his daughter Alice, this wonderful little shop is crammed with hand-made, papier-mâché masks in Venetian *Carnevale* and *Commedia dell'arte* styles.

Open *9am–1pm, 3.30–7.30pm Mon–Sat.* ***Credit*** *AmEx, MC, V.* ***Amenities*** *disabled access.*

FAMILY-FRIENDLY ACCOMMODATION

Staying in Florence is generally **expensive**, and although there are good-value, family-friendly hotels dotted around the city, it's worth considering an **apartment**

FLORENCE ACCOMMODATION & DINING

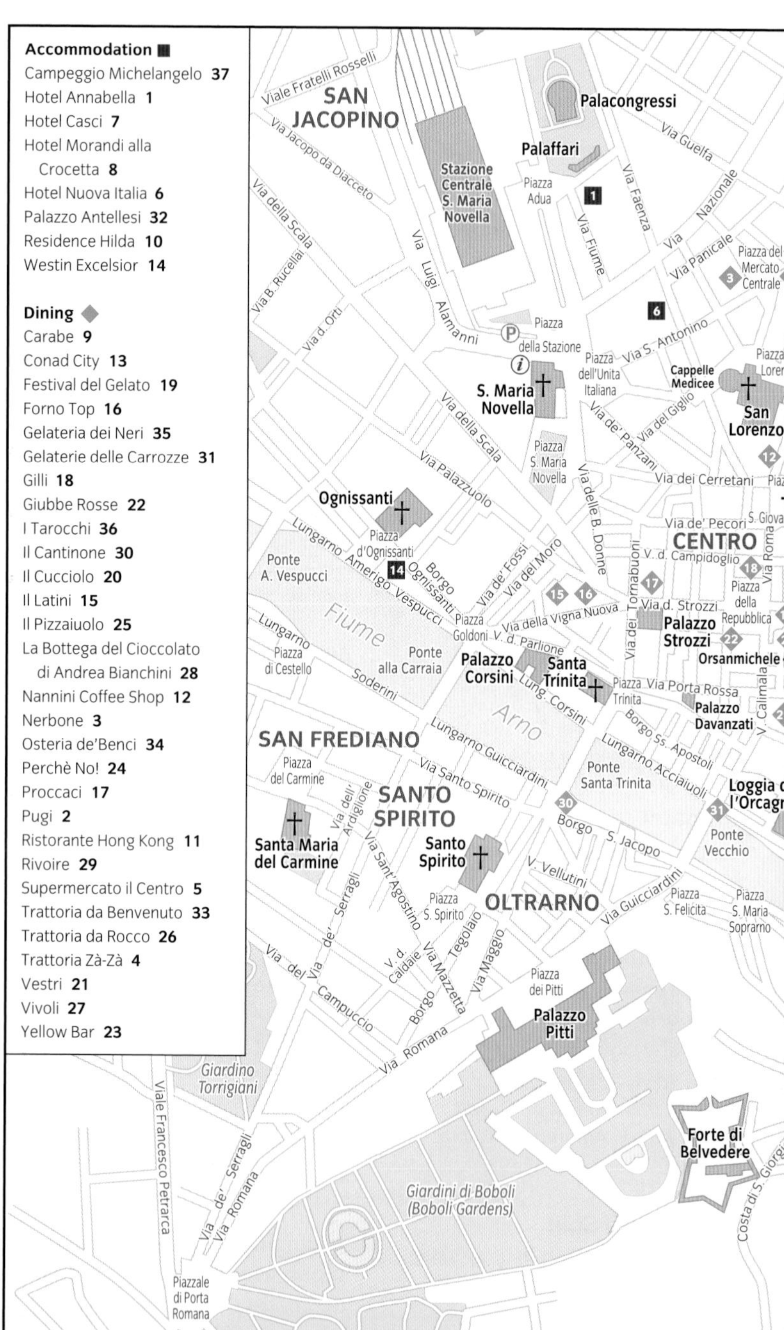

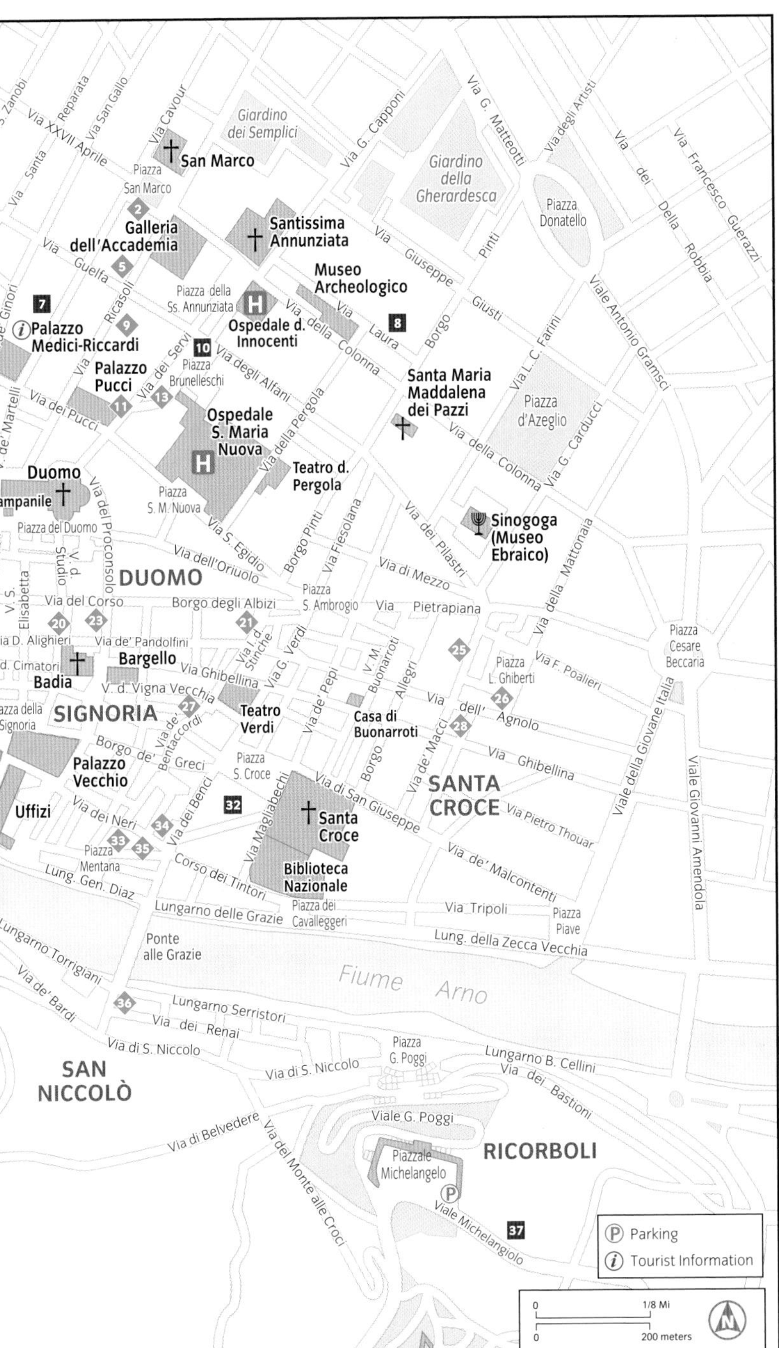

San Marco
Piazza San Marco
Galleria dell'Accademia
Santissima Annunziata
Museo Archeologico
Giardino dei Semplici
Giardino della Gherardesca
Piazza Donatello
Piazza della Ss. Annunziata
Ospedale d. Innocenti
Palazzo Medici-Riccardi
Palazzo Pucci
Piazza Brunelleschi
Ospedale S. Maria Nuova
Santa Maria Maddalena dei Pazzi
Piazza d'Azeglio
Teatro d. Pergola
Duomo
Campanile
Piazza del Duomo
Piazza S. M. Nuova
Sinogoga (Museo Ebraico)
DUOMO
Piazza S. Ambrogio
Piazza Cesare Beccaria
Bargello
Badia
SIGNORIA
Piazza della Signoria
Teatro Verdi
Casa di Buonarroti
Piazza L. Ghiberti
Palazzo Vecchio
Uffizi
Piazza S. Croce
Santa Croce
SANTA CROCE
Biblioteca Nazionale
Piazza Mentana
Piazza dei Cavalleggeri
Piazza Piave
Ponte alle Grazie
Fiume Arno
Piazza G. Poggi
SAN NICCOLÒ
RICORBOLI
Piazzale Michelangelo
Via Cavour
Via San Gallo
Via Santa Reparata
Via XXVII Aprile
Via Guelfa
Via Ricasoli
Via dei Servi
Via degli Alfani
Via della Colonna
Via Laura
Via G. Capponi
Via G. Matteotti
Via degli Artisti
Via dei Della Robbia
Via Francesco Guerazzi
Via Giuseppe Giusti
Borgo Pinti
Viale Antonio Gramsci
Via L. C. Farini
Via G. Carducci
Via dei Pucci
Via de' Martelli
Via della Pergola
Via del Proconsolo
Via S. Egidio
Via dell'Oriuolo
Via Fiesolana
Via dei Pilastri
Via di Mezzo
Via della Mattonaia
V. d. Studio
Via del Corso
Borgo degli Albizi
Via Pietrapiana
Via D. Alighieri
Via de' Pandolfini
Via d. Cimatori
Via Ghibellina
Via I. d. Stinche
Via G. Verdi
Via de' Pepi
V. M. Buonarroti
Via Allegri
Via F. Poalieri
Via dell' Agnolo
V. d. Vigna Vecchia
Via de' Bentaccordi
Borgo de' Greci
Via de' Macci
Borgo Allegri
Viale della Giovane Italia
Viale Giovanni Amendola
Via dei Neri
Via dei Benci
Via Magliabechi
Via di San Giuseppe
Via Pietro Thouar
Via de' Malcontenti
Corso dei Tintori
Lung. Gen. Diaz
Lungarno delle Grazie
Via Tripoli
Lung. della Zecca Vecchia
Lungarno Torrigiani
Via de' Bardi
Lungarno Serristori
Via dei Renai
Via di S. Niccolo
Lungarno B. Cellini
Via dei Bastioni
Viale G. Poggi
Via di Belvedere
Via del Monte alle Croci
Viale Michelangiolo
Parking
Tourist Information
0 1/8 Mi
0 200 meters

rental. You'll get a proper kitchen, more space, usually with separate rooms for the children, and cheaper rates the longer you stay. Reputable online agents include ***www.florenceand abroad.com*** and ***www.windowson tuscany.com***. Whichever type of accommodation you choose, remember to make **bookings well in advance** for summer arrivals.

EXPENSIVE

Palazzo Antellesi ★★★ FIND

*Piazza Santa Croce 21–22. 055 244456. **www.palazzoantellesi.com**.*

These magnificent apartments occupy a 16th-century frescoed *palazzo* right on Piazza Santa Croce. Perfect for families, the largest apartment sleeps seven–eight people, the smallest three–four, all with fully-equipped kitchens. Each has an individual name and price, and must be booked in advance. The **Donatello** suite is ideal for large families or groups: arranged around an inner courtyard on the second floor, you also get a small terrace and spacious dining room with a table for 12, 3 bedrooms and 3 bathrooms. Essentially, the key benefits are the same whichever apartment you choose: more space than a hotel, and the chance to decide when you eat (in a city when most restaurants open around 7.30pm). All feature tall windows and tasteful furniture in period style: frescoed ceilings, wooden beams, antique chairs and plenty of potted plants.

***Apartments** 13 (sleep 3–8). **Rates** €2000–5000 per week. **Amenities** babysitting, gym, parking (16). **In apartment** A/C, fridge, Internet access, safe, sat TV.*

Residence Hilda ★★ FIND

*Via dei Servi 40. 055 288021. **www.residencehilda.it**.*

These elegant rental apartments have a great location near the Duomo, and although the rooms lack historic charm, they

Palazzo Antellesi

make up for it with smart, **modern** facilities. The benefits for families are considerable: all 12 have spacious living areas with a double or twin sofa-bed, large bathrooms, fully equipped kitchens with microwave, and double bedroom (the suite deluxe also comes with super cool flat-screen TVs hanging from the wall). Each is decorated in warm colours, with clean white walls and wood floors.

Apartments *12.* ***Rates*** *Doubles €190–230, family rooms/suites €280–350. Cots and highchairs free. Extra bed €30, under-12s €20.* ***Credit*** *AmEx, MC, V.* ***Amenities*** *babysitting, disabled access, private garage.* ***In room*** *A/C, fridge, Internet access, safe, sat TV.*

Westin Excelsior ★

Piazza Ognissanti 3. ☎ 055 264201. ***www.westin.com/excelsiorflorence.***

Among several luxurious hotels in Florence, the Westin offers the most perks for families. The sumptuous furnishings, first-class service, and wall-to-wall marble interiors are certainly impressive, and the hotel also runs the **Westin Kids Club** (ages 3–12). Your children get a bag stuffed with goodies like a world map, games and colouring set; parents get an infant safety kit that includes first-aid gear and toys. The hotel's 'Discovery Room' also organises regular child activities. Check the website for low-season family offers, which usually include free buffet breakfasts for under-17s, free beds for children sharing with their parents and a 50% discount if they want their own room.

Rooms *171.* ***Rates*** *Doubles €350–700, junior suites €1100–1300. Cots free.* ***Credit*** *AmEx, MC, V.* ***Amenities*** *babysitting, bar, children's club, disabled access, gym, parking (30), restaurant with children's menu.* ***In room*** *A/C, fridge, Internet access, safe, sat TV.*

MODERATE

Hotel Morandi alla Crocetta ★

Via Laura 50. ☎ 055 2344747. ***www.hotelmorandi.it.***

This charming hotel was once a convent. Its characterful rooms are now tastefully furnished with a blend of antique and modern styles – Persian rugs, religious relics, alcoves and wooden beams add to the historic feel. Larger rooms are perfect for a family of four (with extra space for a cot); aim for one that has a **patio**, with table, chairs and plants to add a homey feel. The hotel welcomes young children, and will even supply books and furry toys on arrival if asked in advance. Note that triples are officially for three, but if a child is small enough to share a bed with parents, that doesn't count: a €40–75 saving for a family of four.

Rooms *10.* ***Rates*** *Double €177–220, triple €220–295, quad €260–370. Cots €20. Breakfast €11.* ***Credit*** *AmEx, MC, V.* ***Amenities*** *babysitting, disabled access, parking (€16).* ***In room*** *A/C, fridge, safe, sat TV.*

INEXPENSIVE

Hotel Annabella

Via Fiume 17. 055 281877. ***www.hotelannabella.it****.*

One of the most family-friendly hotels in the city, the Annabella is run by the English-speaking Vittoria family and set within an attractive, early 20th-century building near the station. Doubles and triples are large; all have wooden floors, comfortable beds and clean bathrooms, with simple but attractive furnishings and sometimes writing desks. Children under 2 stay for free with their parents (in a double room), and children under 13 receive a 30% discount. Pets are welcome, and you can have a balcony if requested in advance. All rooms are **non-smoking**.

Rooms *15.* ***Rates*** *Double €60–185, triple €75–225. Cots free. Breakfast 5–10.* ***Credit*** *AmEx, MC, V.* ***Amenities*** *babysitting, bar, disabled access, parking (€20–25).* ***In room*** *A/C, sat TV.*

Hotel Casci

Via Cavour 13. 055 211686. ***www.hotelcasci.com****.*

This 15th-century *palazzo* is great value, especially outside high season, with spacious triples and quads – most very quiet. It was owned by the composer Rossini in the 19th century, and rich frescoes are visible on the ceilings. All rooms are clean and simply decorated with tiled floors and comfortable beds. The most spacious are at the rear and can accommodate four–five people. Watch out for special offers: in low season they sometimes supply one free museum ticket each if you stay three nights or more.

Rooms *26.* ***Rates*** *Double €100–150, triple €130–190, quad €160–230. Breakfast included.* ***Credit*** *AmEx, MC, V.* ***Amenities*** *babysitting, bar, disabled access, parking (€25, valet, 15 car park).* ***In room*** *A/C, fridge, safe, sat TV.*

Hotel Nuova Italia ★

Via Faenza 26. 055 287508. ***www.hotel-nuovaitalia.com****.*

This lovely hotel has been running since 1920, and is today managed by the friendly Viti family. Another great deal, there are 10 spacious, comfortable triples, 5 of which can be converted easily into quads. In low season, families of four only pay for three. Rooms are pleasantly decorated with carpets, paintings and period furniture, but you'll most appreciate the small size of the hotel: the staff are attentive and helpful, providing all sorts of **family tips**. Eileen (from Canada) and Luciano Viti have children of their own and so can field virtually any query you have (in the unlikely event the answer isn't in this book).

Rooms *20.* ***Rates*** *Double €75–119, triple €109–129, breakfast included. Cots free.* ***Credit*** *AmEx, MC, V.* ***Amenities*** *babysitting, parking (€20).* ***In room*** *A/C, safe, shower only, sat TV.*

Campeggio Michelangelo ★★

Viale Michelangelo 80 (behind Piazzale Michelangelo). 055 6811977. ***www.ecvacanze.it/ing/michelangelohome.asp****.*

Making a base at the city's favourite **campsite** is still a popular option for families visiting Florence, for good reason. Views from the wooded fringe are stupendous. It's set in the pleasant surroundings of gardens and olive trees, a short bus ride (numbers 12 or 13) from the centre; unsurprisingly, it's packed in high season. Renting relatively comfortable two- or three-bed tents, with firm camp beds that come with sheets and pillows, is more expensive than pitching your own or parking a camper. There's also a children's **playground**, and the restaurant 50m down the road (10% discount with camp pass) has a tennis court and football field to rent.

Open camping *(sleeps 1000).* ***Rates*** *Adults €8.90–9.90, children 2–12 4.50–4.90, pitch €11.70–12, car €5.50, rental tents (mixed) €24.40–25.40 (private) €43.90–44.90.* ***Credit*** *MC, V.* ***Amenities*** *bar, Internet access, laundry, parking, restaurant, safe, shower only, supermarket.*

FAMILY-FRIENDLY DINING

Florentine cuisine is among the best in Italy, although tourism has made bargains elusive. Most restaurants open solely for lunch and dinner, which means **eating late**: we've noted some exceptions below. There are several snack places open all afternoon, and in good weather, a few picnic options, too.

If the children are screaming for **MacD's** and there's no dissuading them, there are invariably busy outlets inside Santa Maria Novella station, just outside on Piazza della Stazione and at Via Cavour 61r near the tourist office.

Snacks, Cafés & Food-on-the-Go

Florence is packed with cafés and snack bars, ranging from the elegant and expensive to cheap-and-simple pizza-slice parlours. Top of the heap are the posh cafés that ring Piazza della Repubblica, expensive but worth at least one trip for the experience: **Gilli** ★ is the oldest, established in 1733 with an opulent interior and terrace, best visited for its sublime hot chocolate (€6) in five flavours. Slightly less pretentious, **Giubbe Rosse** across the piazza at no. 14 has tables outside and similar prices; ditto **Rivoire** in Piazza della Signoria.

For an earthy snack experience, make for **Pugi** ★, famed for its *schiacciata alla Fiorentina*, sweetish flatbread made with olive oil. The branch at Piazza San Marco 9b is open 7.45am–8pm Monday to Friday, closing 2.15pm Saturday. Take a ticket and wait for your number to be called. **Forno Top** at Via della Spada 23r is another no-nonsense bakery serving *schiacciata* (€1–1.20), as well as *focaccia* (€1.55) and pizza (€2). It's open 7.30am–1.30pm and 5–7.30pm Monday to Saturday.

Nannini at Via Borgo San Lorenzo 7r is a branch of Siena's celebrated café, famed for *Panforte* cake (open 7.30am–8pm daily), while **Procacci** ★ at Via de'Tornabuoni 64r is best known for drool-worthy *tartufati*, truffle-butter rolls (€1.60); it's open 10.30am–8pm Monday to Saturday, but closed August. Children also love **Il Cucciolo**, Via del Corso 25r, for *bomboloni*: plain, cream or choc-filled doughnuts (80¢) made upstairs and tossed down a tube, still piping hot; their fresh mini pizzas (€2.90) are also good on the move. It's closed Sundays.

Restaurants

Near the Duomo & Piazza della Signoria

Trattoria da Benvenuto VALUE TUSCAN

Via de Neri 47/Via Della Mosca 16r. *055 214833.*

This no-frills restaurant is the closest thing you'll get to a traditional neighbourhood diner in the centre of the city, serving hearty portions of Tuscan food at long wooden tables in cosy surroundings. The best dishes are old favourites ravioli and gnocchi, but the *simpatico* staff are used to serving children and happily whip up plain spaghetti with tomato sauce on demand. The English menu offers plenty of other dishes like roast chicken, pork and no end of pasta (€5–6).

***Open** 12.30–3pm and 7pm–10.30pm Mon–Tue and Thu–Sat. **Main courses** €6–7.*

Ristorante Hong Kong CHINESE

Via dei Servi 35r. *055 2398235.* ***www.ristorantehongkong.com.***

Tired of Italian food? It might seem like sacrilege, but it happens, especially with easily bored youngsters to feed. If

Rivoire, Piazza della Signoria

TIP Pack a Picnic Treat

The indoor Mercato Centrale ★ is chock-full of Tuscan specialties, multi-coloured pastas, bread, cheese and meats downstairs, with fruit and vegetables upstairs as well as nuts, wine, ready made sandwiches, and food stalls; it's open 7am–2pm Monday to Saturday and 4–8pm Saturday in winter.

There are several **supermarkets** close to the *centro storico*: **Supermercato il Centro** has five branches, including Via Ricasoli 109r opposite the Accademia, Via Donizetti 64 and Via dei Ginori 41r (all 8am–8pm Monday to Saturday, 10am–7pm Sunday). **Conad City** has a branch at Via dei Servi 56, open 8.30am–8pm Monday to Saturday.

The most exotic **chocolate** shop in Florence is **La Bottega del Cioccolato di Andrea Bianchini** ★ at Via de'Macci 50 (10am–midday and 4–7.30pm Tuesday to Saturday), with a small but exquisite range of handmade chocolates. For more chocolate and superb **hot chocolate** closer to the centre, try **Vestri**, Borgo degli Albizi 11r.

you're touring Tuscany, Florence provides a welcome opportunity for a change of cuisine. This nominally Cantonese restaurant knocks out favourites from all over China, with a slight but discernable Italian bias (compare the presentation with what you'd get at home). The tables are Italian in style, but with plenty of space for six to share. Food is excellent: succulent spring rolls, dumplings and a vast range of noodle and rice-based dishes. The sizzling plates of beef with pepper are a good choice, and you can't go wrong with pork dishes.

Open *midday–2.30pm and 7.30pm–midnight daily.* ***Main courses*** *€6–12.* ***Credit*** *AmEx, MC, V.* ***Amenities*** *reservations accepted.*

Yellow Bar ★ AMERICAN DINER

Via del Proconsole 39r. ☎ 055 211766.

This American-style restaurant is a great option for children for two reasons. First, its tasty hamburgers and pizzas (€6.50–7.50) provide another break from the predominantly Italian restaurants in town. More importantly, it's **open all day**. The food's all served in a diner-like hall with comfy seating and wooden tables for four – and it still knocks out a decent selection of pastas, like home-made spaghetti with prawns. It gets packed with students in the evenings.

Open *12.30pm–2am daily.* ***Main courses*** *€6–10.* ***Credit*** *AmEx, MC, V.* ***Amenities*** *reservations accepted.*

Near Santa Maria Novella

Nerbone ★ FLORENTINE LUNCH

Mercato Centrale (Via dell'Ariento entrance, stand 292). ☎ 055 219949.

One of several no-nonsense snack bars inside the Mercato Centrale, this stall was established in 1872 and serves the best *bagnato* (boiled-beef sandwich in gravy, €2.50) in town. It makes a tasty, convenient lunch stop for families, but is a little adventurous at the same time. If the *bagnato* looks fatty, there are plenty of other good-value pasta and sandwich options on offer, from €5.50. Just five tables stand opposite the stall, so get here before the rush (12.30pm) if you want to sit. If it's too busy, try **Pork's**, a few stalls along.

Open *7am–2pm Mon–Sat, closed 2 weeks in Aug.* ***Main courses*** *€3–7.*

Trattoria Zà-Zà ★★ ITALIAN

Piazza del Mercato Centrale 26r. 055 215411. ***www.trattoriazaza.it.***

Named after the sound a bee makes – 'buzz' in Italian – this is one of the most family-friendly eateries in the city, with the added attraction of being **open all day**. There are no special menus for children, but staff are used to handling finicky youngsters, and will cook up any pasta they fancy. It has a terrace outside, with wooden tables for four, and some that seat six, and a cosy, rustic atmosphere inside – check out the photos of the restaurant's 'famous' patrons on the walls to see if you recognise any. The *menù turistico* is good value at €15: you get *penne* or ravioli as a *primo*, followed by a choice of solid *secondi* like roast chicken or veal with tomato-stewed beans. Try the *migliaccio* (chestnut torte) for dessert, super-refreshing in summer.

Open *11am–midnight Mon–Sat, closed Aug.* ***Main courses*** *€10–12.* ***Credit*** *AmEx, MC, V.* ***Amenities*** *reservations accepted.*

Il Latini ★ TUSCAN

Via del Palchetti 6r. 055 210916. ***www.illatini.com.*** *Off Via della Vigna Nuova.*

Opened in 1950, this is one of the most popular tourist haunts in Florence, but an essential experience nevertheless. Children will love the cellar-like surroundings, hams hanging from the ceiling and bustling atmosphere. Everyone is thrust together on long communal tables where large portions of Tuscan favourites are delivered with gusto. The menu is short and focused, with just a handful of main dishes, rarely costing more than €15 – you'll get a *primo* for €5–7. It's all good, but the ravioli always wins rave reviews and the *bistecca* is a safe bet for main.

Open *12.30–2pm and 7.30–10.30pm Tue–Sun, closed 15 days in Aug.* ***Main courses*** *€10–20.* ***Credit*** *AmEx, MC, V.* ***Amenities*** *reservations accepted.*

Near Santa Croce

Il Pizzaiuolo ★ GOURMAET PIZZA

Via de' Macci 113r. 055 241171.

If you fancy a special pizza night, this is the place to come – the only Neapolitan pizzeria in the city. Legend has it that pizza was created on the streets of Naples in the 18th century: the *Margherita* is named after a Queen of Savoy, who visited the city in 1869 and loved pizza topped with basil, mozzarella and tomatoes (it reminded her of the new *tricolore* Italian flag). Honouring this tradition, pizzas here are the real deal, and tables

Ice Cream Heaven

Italy gave the world pasta, pizza and the cappuccino, but it's the creation of **gelato** in the 16th century that has proved its most addictive export for *bambini*. As a general rule, signs proclaiming *produzione propria* (home-made) are an indication of quality. Cones range from a standard €1.50 to €8 for *un gigante*.

Vivoli ★★★ Via Isole delle Stinche 7r. ☎ 055 292334. ***www.vivoli.it***. Often claimed to be the best in Italy – and confident enough about its wares to ban cones. Make a pilgrimage at least once to say you've been. ***Open*** *9am–1am Tue–Sun, closed Aug and Jan–early Feb.*

Festival del Gelato ★★ Via del Corso 75r. Almost as good as Vivoli, and in a better location between the Duomo and Uffizi, with 70 extraordinary flavours. ***Open*** *8am–1am summer, 11am–1am winter, Tue–Sun.*

Ice Cream Heaven - Festival del Gelato

Carabe ★★ Via Ricasoli 60r. The most celebrated **Sicilian** ice cream in the city. ***Open*** *10am–midnight daily mid-May–Sep, 10am–8pm Tue–Sun Oct–Nov, mid-Feb–mid-May.*

Gelateria dei Neri ★★ Via dei Neri 20–22r. Vivoli gets more acclaim, but just as many locals think this is the best in town. Try the spicy Mexican chocolate, made with real chillies. ***Open*** *11am–midnight daily.*

Perché No! ★ Via dei Tavolini 19r. This shop has been knocking out great flavours since the 1930s: try the rum-laced tiramisù or *ciocolato bianco* (white chocolate). ***Open*** *11am–midnight Wed–Mon, closed Nov.*

Gelateria delle Carrozze Piazza del Pesce 3–5r. Great location on the north bank of the river just east of Ponte Vecchio: perfect for trips to Oltrarno. ***Open*** *11am–1am daily summer, 11am–8pm Thu–Tue winter.*

are long enough for families. The celebrated *Margherita* is €5.50, but there are another 20 mouth-watering options.

Open *12.30–3pm and 7.30pm–midnight Mon–Sat, closed Aug.* ***Main courses*** *€7.50–13.* ***Amenities*** *reservations essential for dinner.*

Trattoria da Rocco ★★ VALUE FLORENTINE LUNCH

Mercato di Sant'Ambrogio.

This tiny trattoria is one of the best bargains in the city. It's a trek from the centre, tucked away in the heart of Mercato di Sant'Ambrogio, an indoor food hall east of Santa Croce. It's a great place to introduce the children to a proper local, no-frills dining experience, with food they're bound to enjoy. Behind the take-away counter is an enclosed seating area, with tables big enough for four. Staff are friendly, but rushed off their feet so don't expect any special attention – you won't get much help in English either. Hearty dishes of lasagne, pasta and roast chicken rarely cost more than €5: it's €2–3 for a *primo* and €3–4 for *secondi*, €1.50 for drinks, 60¢ for bread and 80¢ for water. A bargain. Get here before 1pm if you want a table.

Open *midday–2.30pm Mon–Sat.* ***Main courses*** *€3–4.*

Oltrarno

I Tarocchi PIZZA

Via dei Renai 12–14r. ☎ 055 2343912.

This excellent pizzeria is popular with students, and makes a perfect lunch spot if you're wandering around Oltrarno. The long wooden tables and benches inside make better perches for families, though there are smaller tables on the narrow terrace facing the street. There's a huge range of pizzas (€5–6.50) and pasta, with tasty *calzoni* for €6.50. As usual, there's no children's menu, but the convivial staff are used to serving youngsters and will conjure up small portions and special dishes if asked and smiled at.

Open *12.30–2.30pm and 7–10pm Tue–Fri; 7–10pm Sat–Sun.* ***Main courses*** *€4–6.* ***Credit*** *AmEx, MC, V.* ***Amenities*** *reservations accepted.*

Il Cantinone ★ FLORENTINE LUNCH

Via Santo Spirito 6r. ☎ 055 218898.

This rowdy old cellar restaurant is popular with students and tourists, mainly for its *crostini*, thick slabs of bread smothered with ham, tomatoes, sausage and cheese. The long tables mean plenty of space for families. Food is simple, cheap and unbelievably tasty. Most *crostini* will set you back €5.50 and are more than enough for children – chop them in half for toddlers.

Open *12.30–2.30pm and 7.30–10.30pm Tue–Sun.* ***Main courses*** *€6–20.* ***Credit*** *AmEx, MC, V.*

4 Siena, Arezzo and the Central Hill-Towns

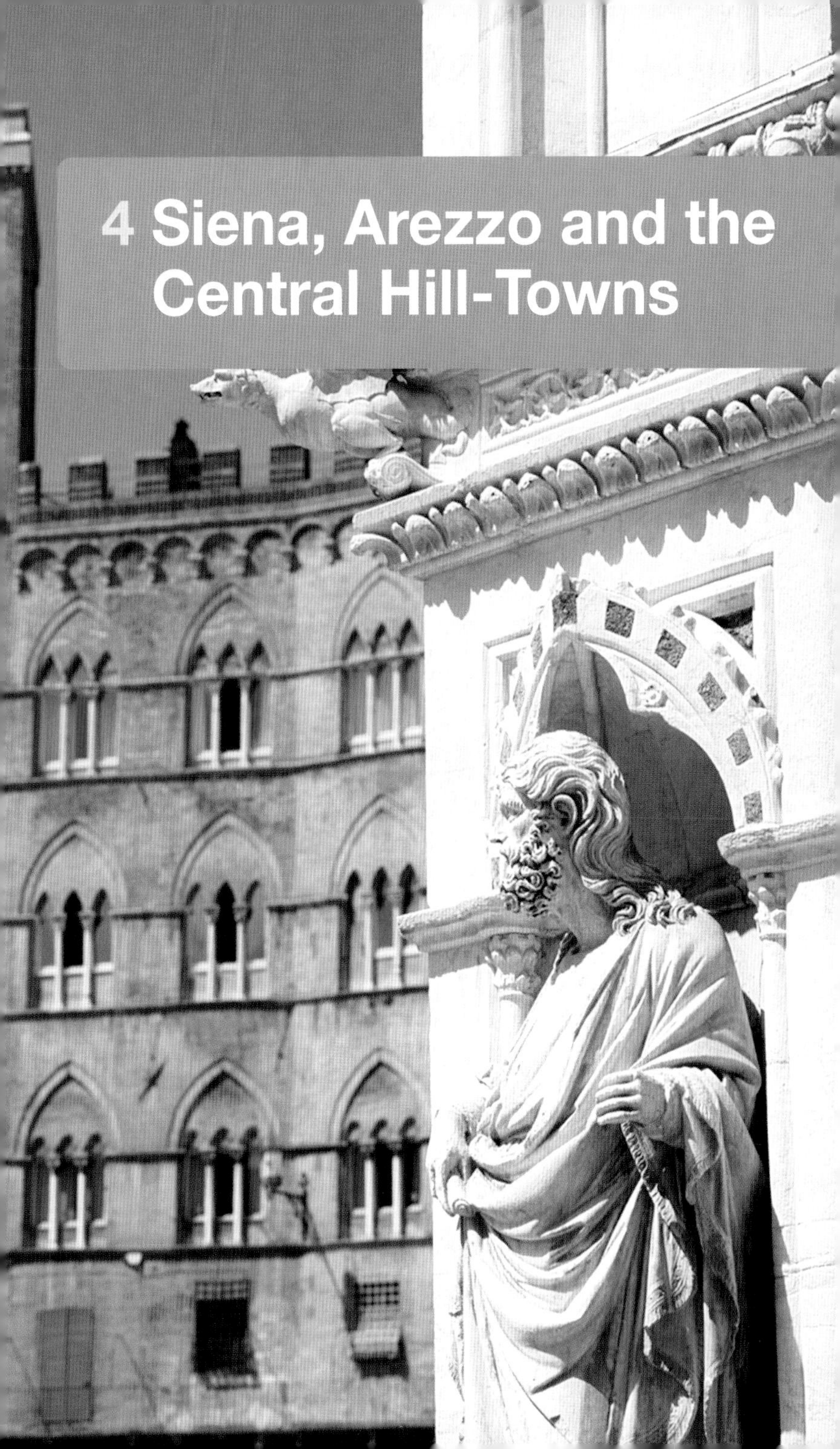

CENTRAL TUSCANY

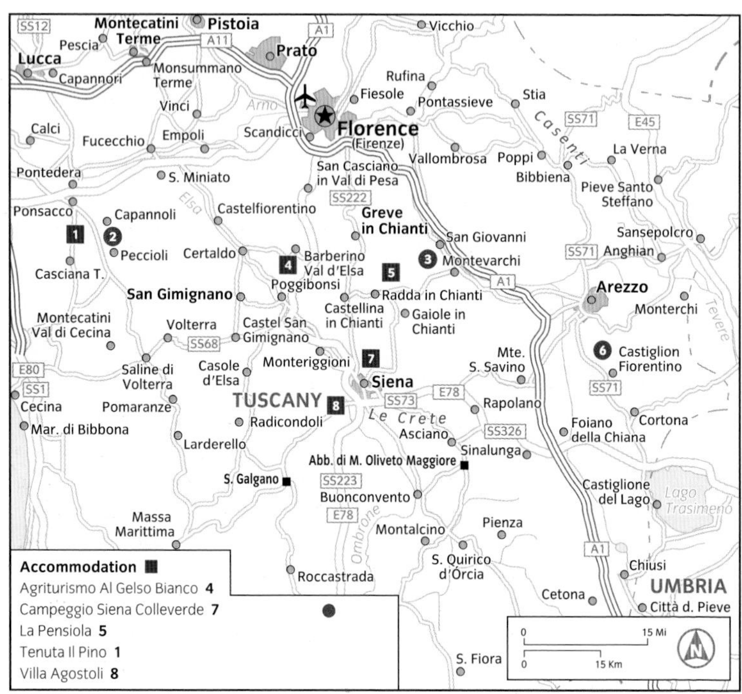

Central Tuscany is the bit that looks as it's meant to. Ridiculously corrugated hills roll and roll and roll their way to a misty horizon. To add to the savage beauty, up pops a medieval walled town whose foundations were laid before Christ, rearing up above orderly vine-clad fields.

Right at the core of the area is rose-coloured **Siena**. No Tuscan tour is complete without at least a day-trip or two into this ancient city. The astounding art is only one part of what makes a visit a special experience. Spiky **San Gimignano** and Etruscan **Volterra** complete the classic trio of atmospheric hill-towns. Throw in laid-back **Arezzo**, with one of the great treasures of Western art, and you have yourself a classic Tuscan itinerary. Villas dot the hillsides and there's plenty here for children if you know where to look: historic towns to explore, amazing works of art to discover and wild countryside to roam.

SIENA

One of Europe's finest medieval cities, **Siena** ★★★ occupies a series of steep ridges south of Florence. Like its former political rival, Siena has a rich artistic legacy dating to the

Children's Top Attractions of Central Tuscany

- Scaling Siena's **Torre del Mangia**, p. 81.
- Snapping classic Tuscan views in **Le Crete**, p. 88.
- Exploring **San Gimignano's historic centre** at dusk, p. 88.
- Eating ice cream with the **Gelato World Champions**, p. 90.
- Standing humbled before Piero della Francesca's **Legend of the True Cross**, p. 98.
- Kitting the children out medieval-style at **Volterra AD1398**, p. 93.
- Tucking into real **Tuscan food** at Antica Osteria dei Poeti, Volterra, p. 106.

pre-Renaissance period, and is a magical place for children to visit. It's easiest to see on foot because it's laid-back, elegant and less crowded than its neighbour to the north.

Founded by Roman Emperor Augustus as **Saena Julia** around 30AD, Siena became one of the richest Italian republics in the early Middle Ages, thanks primarily to successful banking families and a booming wool industry. The **Black Death** of 1348 dealt a massive blow, reducing the population by two-thirds and ushering in a period of decline. In 1555 Siena was finally seized by **Florence** and all development ceased, helping to explain why this city appears frozen in time.

Essentials

Getting There

By Car Driving to Siena is straightforward, especially from Florence, a one-hour cruise up the *SI-FI raccordo* (not actually a motorway). The problem is **parking**: it's virtually impossible to park your car in the *centro storico*. Try to get in before 10am (take the '**Siena Ovest**' exit) and aim for **Parking Fortezza** (follow the little football sign; it's by the *stadio*); it costs €1.60 per hour. **Don't** head for 'Parking piazza il Campo'. It isn't in the Campo at all; in fact, it's a 20-minute uphill walk away.

INSIDER TIP

If you know Siena already, there is a cheap option for parking. Against the north-western walls of the Fortezza there's a (for now) **free car park**. Funnily enough, it isn't signposted; you'll have to get in early and navigate by the sun. It worked for Columbus.

By Bus Forget the awkward train link: the easiest way to reach Siena on public transport is by **bus**. From Florence, **SITA** (*800 373760*. ***www.sitabus.it***) and **TRAIN** (*0577 204246*. ***www.trainspa.it***) use the terminal at Via Santa Caterina da Siena 17r, near Santa Maria Novella station. Take the **Rapido** rather

The *Palio* for Children

Every year, on 2nd July and again on 16th August, Siena's Piazza del Campo is host to Italy's most spectacular and exciting festival, the **Palio delle Contrade**. This chaotic and sometimes aggressive **bareback horserace** around the Campo involves 10 of Siena's 17 *contrade* (districts). Equally captivating is the pre-race flag-waving ceremony and parade. Frenzied celebrations greet the winning rider, and the day is rounded off with communal feasts in each district.

But taking small children to the *Palio* can be **difficult**. Crowds are overwhelming (50,000+), you'll end up standing for hours in the sun and it's a nightmare getting to a toilet. If you don't mind paying €150–300 each, reserve seats in the temporary stands; do this months, or preferably a year, in advance. Contact local travel agent **Il Palio Viaggi**, Piazza la Lizza 12 (*0577 280828*. ***www.palioviaggi.it***).

To experience the event for free, aim for the **trial races** ★, also held in the Campo (starting 29th June and 13th August, respectively). It's still busy, but bearable, at least during morning sessions. Trial races are not as fast and furious as the real thing, but are just as **photogenic** and fun to watch; there are usually six, held in the mornings (9am) and late evenings (7.45pm Jul, 7.15pm Aug).

than the *Diretto*: there are hourly services (fewer on Sundays) and it's faster, taking around 1¼ hours. Tickets are €6.50 in advance or €8 on the bus. In Siena, buses terminate at **Piazza Antonio Gramsci**, a short walk from the Campo.

Once there, Siena is best explored **on foot**: the *centro storico* is pedestrianised and compact – buses are mostly banned. Don't plan too much: there's **barely a flat street**, so little legs (and pushchair-pushers) will tire. The small orange buses known as **pollicini** can be useful for longer trips: tickets cost 90¢, are valid up to an hour, and can be purchased from the bus station or any *tabacchi*.

Visitor Information

The main **tourist office** is at Piazza del Campo 56 (*0577 280551*. ***www.terresiena.it***), open 9am–7pm Monday to Saturday. An indispensable **website** for family visits is ***www.terresienabambini.it***. You'll find **cashpoints** galore along Banchi di Sopra.

FAST FACTS: SIENA

Chemists **Antica Farmacia Parenti**, Banchi di Sopra 43 (*0577 283269*), has English-speaking staff.

Hospital The main one is **Le Scotte** (*0577 585111*), near the

FUN FACT Find the Fountain

Siena is divided into 17 contrade (districts), each with its own flag, council, church, insignia, patron saint and museum. They also each have a **fountain**, once crucial to their water supply (Fontebranda belongs to Oca; see p. 87). Try and find them. Getting all 17 would be quite an achievement.

train station on Viale Mario Bracci.

Internet Internet Train has several branches: Via di Pantaneto 54 (*0577 247460*) is open midday–7pm, Monday to Friday. At Via di Città 121 (*0577 247460*), hours are 10am–7pm Monday to Saturday; there are **Ethernet** cables for your laptop.

Toilets Public toilets are scarce, but there are some small facilities behind the Campo at Via di Beccheria 3 (just off Via di Città; 9am–6pm Mon–Sat and 9am–6.30pm Sun Oct–Mar; 9am–9pm Mon–Thu and 9am–11pm Fri–Sun, Apr–Sep), and on the other side of the square in Piazza del Mercato (similar times). You'll also find some on the northern side of San Domenico (8am–5.30pm daily Oct–Mar; 8am–7.30pm daily Apr–Sep). All cost 50¢.

SEEING SIENA

The ideal place to start a tour of Siena is **Piazza del Campo** ★, the fan-shaped heart of the city, ringed with cafés and shops, and home to a 19th-century reproduction of the **Fonte Gaia**, an ornate fountain sculpted in 1419 by Jacopo della Quercia.

Torre del Mangia ★★

AGES 7 AND UP

Palazzo Pubblico. 0577 292368.

Almost every child who sets eyes on the 102m **bell tower** of the medieval Palazzo Pubblico, dominating Piazza del Campo, wants to climb it. Make it your **first stop** of the day to get in before the tour groups arrive. The tower was built between 1325 and 1348 and is accessed by a separate entrance opposite the Museo Civico. The climb is an energetic yomp up 388 narrow steps to the top, rewarded by a marvellous panorama of the city rooftops and piazzas. With luck or planning you can be there when they

Fonte Gaia

SIENA

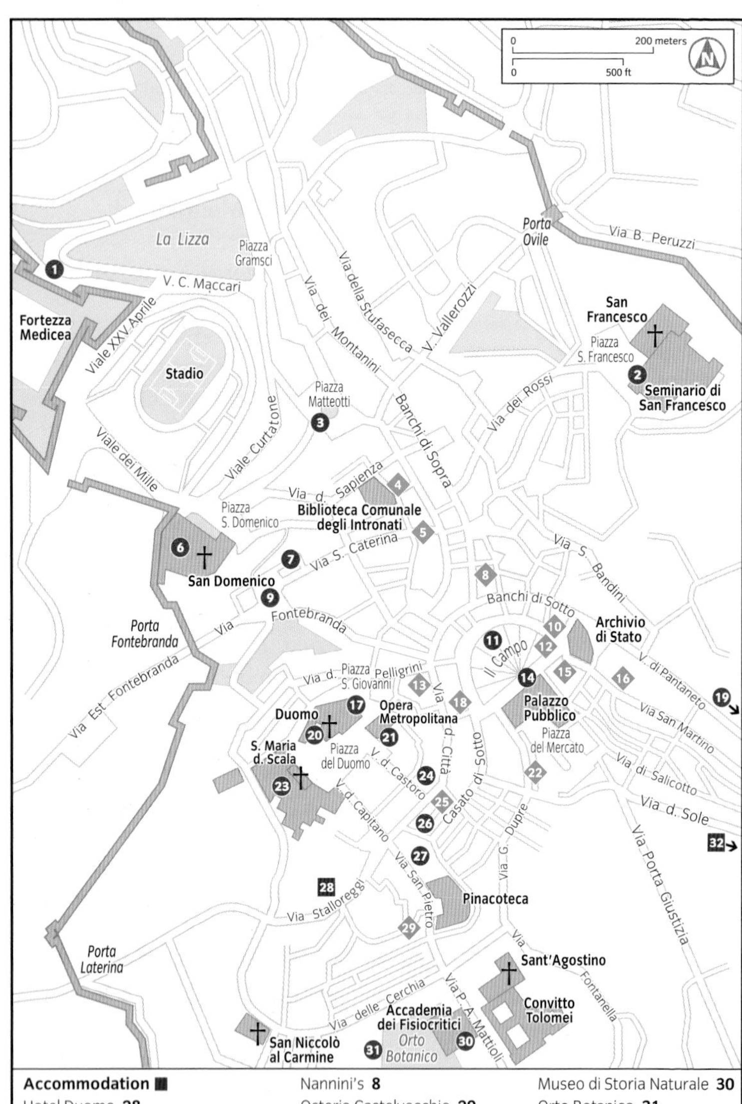

Accommodation ■
Hotel Duomo **28**
Hotel Santa Caterina **32**

Dining ◆
Antica Drogheria Mangianelli **18**
Antica Trattoria Papei **22**
Brivido **13**
Caribia **10**
Forno dei Galli **5**
Gallo Nero **16**
Key Largo Bar **12**
La Taverna di Nello **15**
Nannini's **8**
Osteria Castelvecchio **29**
Pizza al Taglio **4**
Pizzicheria di Miccoli **25**

Attractions ●
Bambimus **19**
Baptistery and Crypt **17**
Casa di Santa Caterina **7**
Duomo **20**
Fonte Gaia **11**
Fontebranda **9**
Museo dell'Opera **21**
Museo di Storia Naturale **30**
Orto Botanico **31**
Palazzo delle Papesse **24**
Palazzo Pubblico **14**
San Bernardino oratory **2**
San Domenico **6**
Santa Maria della Scala **23**

Shops/Services ●
Bookshop **27**
Conad City **3**
Enoteca Italiana **1**
Internet Train **26**

ring the bells, a temporarily deafening experience.

Open 10am–6.15pm daily, closes 3.15pm Nov–mid-Mar. ***Adm*** *€7, €12 with Museo Civico, free under-6s.*

Museo Civico ★★ AGES 7 AND UP

Palazzo Pubblico. ☎ 0577 292368.

The austere Gothic **Palazzo Pubblico** was home to Siena's city government for centuries, but most of it now houses the Civic Museum, principally a collection of fine medieval art. Two top-class rooms stand out for children: the **Sala del Mappamondo** ★★ showcases **Simone Martini**'s *Maestà*, a stunning 1315 depiction of Mary holding Jesus as a child. On the opposite wall is (though this is disputed) Martini's fresco of *Guidoriccio da Fogliano*, whose Sienese army is about to besiege a city. More sublime frescoes cover the **Sala della Pace** ★★★ next door: **Ambrogio Lorenzetti**'s astounding *Allegories of Good and Bad Government*, commissioned in 1338. One fresco depicts an idealised version of normal life in 14th-century Siena; a happy tableau of shops, builders, hawkers, dancers, school rooms and people working the fields beyond the city walls. There's plenty here to keep youngsters riveted – point out the 'dancing maidens', who were probably young men, as it would have been shocking to paint women frolicking in public at the time. Within a decade, bad government pretty much came to pass, as the Black Death killed 70,000 including Siena's leading artist. Tuscany's supreme work of civic art is a fitting memorial. As you leave through the **Anticamera del Concistoro**, children who've already seen San Gimignano's **Collegiata** (p. 91) should spot *St Sebastian* right away.

Open *10am–4.45pm daily 7 Jan–15 Feb and 26 Nov–22 Dec; until 5.45pm 16 Feb–15 Mar, 1–25 Nov and 23 Dec–6 Jan; until 6.15pm 16 Mar–31 Oct.* ***Adm*** *€7.50, €12 with Torre del Mangia, €4.50 students, free under-11s.* ***Amenities*** *disabled access, English, shop.*

Duomo AGES 5 AND UP

Piazza del Duomo. ☎ 0577 283048. ***www.operaduomo.siena.it****.*

Siena's opulent and stripey **cathedral** was built between 1136 and 1382 on the site of an earlier structure, and although you can't climb on the dome, there is a lot to see inside. Its most striking feature is the zebra-like exterior in black-and-white marble. The interior is equally ostentatious and fun to explore, with marble-inlaid **floor** ★, a star-painted ceiling and striped pillars. Its major-league artwork is the magnificent 13th-century stone **pulpit** ★ by Nicola Pisano, jammed with carved figures from the Bible: check out the lurid scenes of the *Last Judgement*, with sinners squirming in hell.

Pinturicchio's frescoed **Piccolomini Library**, showing scenes from the life of Pope Pius II in technicolour, will interest anyone who's already been to **Pienza**.

Siena's Duomo

Open *10.30am–7.30pm Mon–Sat, 1.30–7.30pm Sun Mar–late Aug; closed 6.30pm late Oct–Feb; 9.30am–7.30pm daily late Aug–late Oct.* ***Adm*** *€3 (inc. Biblioteca Piccolomini), free under-12s.* ***Amenities*** *disabled access, English, shop.*

Santa Maria della Scala ★★

AGES 3 AND UP

Piazza del Duomo 2. 0577 224811. ***http://santamaria.comune.siena.it****.*

There are several important galleries in Siena, but this **former hospital** is the best option with children. One of the earliest hospitals in Europe, it was founded in the 11th century and took care of the sick as well as helping the poor, pilgrims and *gettatelli* ('throw-away' orphans) abandoned by unmarried mothers.

The hospital closed in 1995, and today its halls and chapels are being transformed into exhibition spaces. Inexplicably, it's always much **quieter** than the more established galleries in town: the deserted basements have room for children to run around (literally).

Just beyond the main entrance, the **Pellegrinaio** ★★ (Pilgrim's Hall) is covered with cheery frescoes dating from 1440 by Vecchietta among others. They record **everyday hospital life** in the Middle Ages: compare the simple clothes of the poor with the robes of the rich, and spot carpenters, workers, bricklayers, doctors and those lucky orphans. But where's the anaesthetic?

Don't neglect the rest of the building; seek out the atmospheric **Oratorio di Santa Caterina** ★ and Matteo di Giovanni's brutal 1482 ***Massacre of the Innocents*** ★, hanging outside the **Cappella della Madonna**. The other highlight is in the hospital's bowels: the **Museo Archeologico** ★★ follows a labyrinth of tunnels,

TIP Pick Up a Pass

If you intend to visit more than one sight in Siena, pick up a *biglietto* *cumulativo*. Most useful is the **Opera della Metropolitana** pass, which covers the **Duomo**, **Baptistery**, **Museo dell'Opera** (for famous works by **Duccio di Buoninsegna** ★), **Crypt** and **San Bernardino** oratory for €10; it's valid for three days. It also allows you to scale the **Facciatone** ★, from inside the museum, with dizzying views down into the Campo. Most of these sights are free for under-11s, so the passes are only economical if you have older children. Buy the pass at the museum.

catacombs and creaking walkways, dimly lit and lined with display cases. The setting's the star, and makes the artefacts seem more interesting – mostly Etruscan ceramics and bits and pieces from the Bronze Age and local Roman ruins, including a collection of funerary urns and a tomb. Spoooooky.

***Open** 10.30am–6pm daily Mar–Nov, until 4pm Dec–Feb. **Adm** €6, €5.50 in advance, €3.50 students, €3 in advance, free under-11s. **Amenities** café, disabled access, English, shop.*

INSIDER TIP

Santa Maria della Scala's bookshop has an excellent selection of **children's reading**. To help make the city fun for young ones, get **Siena: Playing with Art** (€6), which takes youngsters on a voyage of discovery round the medieval city's art and history.

Museo di Storia Naturale (Accademia Fisiocritici) FIND

AGES 7 AND UP

*Piazzetta Silvio Gigli 2 (at Sant'Agostino). ☎ 0577 47002. **www.accademiafisiocritici.it**.*

This free **natural history museum** inside a 12th-century monastery is well off the tourist trail; you may have to ring the bell to get in and have the place to yourself. On the ground floor, hundreds of fossils are arranged in antiquated wooden cabinets around a courtyard, including a vast collection of seashells, bones and rocks. In the right-hand corner you'll find the off-beat Serini Collection of **terracotta mushrooms**, but the real highlight sits in the middle of the courtyard: the **skeleton of a Fin Whale** ★, the second-largest animal after the Blue Whale. Upstairs, corridors are lined with stuffed animals, birds, snakes, fish, insects and skeletons, including a small giraffe. The 'monstrosities' display case, with its twin-headed lambs and other freaks of nature, may be too much for toddlers.

***Open** 9am–1pm and 3–6pm Mon–Fri, closed Thu pm. **Adm** free. **Amenities** disabled access, English.*

Orto Botanico ALL AGES

Via Pier Andrea Mattioli 4. ☎ 0577 232874.

Downhill from the Museo di Storia Naturale, the **botanical garden** is a welcome patch of green, with plenty of space for children to join in playing with local youngsters, although opening times make picnics awkward. The gardens contain a well-stocked herbarium and special plants such as the 'living stones', with two wide leaves that look like rocks. The garden is also said to have a **ghost**: a local hero called Giomo, who died in battle in 1207. There are steep access steps and the garden itself is terraced: buggies beware.

Open *8am–12.30pm and 2.30–5.30pm Mon–Fri, 8am–midday Sat.* ***Adm*** *free.*

La Lizza and the Fortezza di Santa Barbara ALL AGES

Fortezza Medicea.

A short walk north-west of the Campo, **La Lizza** is another public garden, laid out in 1779 and home to the city's largest **market** – not to be missed for local delicacies – on Wednesdays. It's the best place for a picnic, with plenty to amuse the children: bronze horses, a fountain and pond packed with goldfish, ducks and even turtles. There's a slide and most days a carousel; in winter you can **ice-skate** ★ with your Tuscan neighbours. The gardens run up to the walls of the **Fortezza di Santa Barbara**, established by Charles V and rebuilt by Cosimo I in 1560. Today it's an exhibition and concert space, but little visitors can walk along the walls or let off steam in the gardens – a touch scruffy these days.

Inside the fort, however, you'll find the **Enoteca Italiana** (*0577 288497. E: info@enoteca-italiana.it*), which sells over 1,600 Italian wines. There are usually 10–15 bottles on their tasting table, costing €3–6.50 a glass. It's open midday–8pm Monday, until 1am Tuesday to Saturday.

Open *always.* ***Adm*** *free.* ***Amenities*** *disabled access, picnic area, shop.*

Museo d'Arte per Bambini (Bambimus) ★ AGES 3 TO 11

Via dei Pispini 164. 0577 46517. ***www.comune.siena.it/bambimus.*** *Bus: 50, 52, 53.*

Siena's informative **art museum for children** is tucked away on the third floor of a building near the Porta Pispini. Paintings and sculptures are set at child-friendly heights; there are objects to handle and actors dramatise the art at hands-on workshops, usually held on the first and last Saturdays of the month between 3pm and 6.30pm. You must make reservations in advance (phone or email). Someone can usually speak English, but the activities are enjoyable regardless of language and it's a chance to talk to the natives.

Open *10am–3pm Mon–Fri; closed 2 weeks in Aug.* ***Adm*** *free.* ***Amenities*** *disabled access, English, picnic area, shop.*

Trenonatura ALL AGES

Ferrovia Val d'Orcia, Piazza Rosselli 5. 0577 207413. ***www.ferrovieturistiche.it.***

This train runs on lines closed to scheduled services, an enjoyable

St Catherine (1347–80)

Not just **patron saint** of Siena, but also of Italy, Europe, nurses, firemen and sick people, St Catherine grew up in Siena. She had visions of God as a child and became a Dominican nun aged eight, but is best known today for **letters** she wrote to the Pope and other Italian leaders appealing for nationwide peace.

San Domenico in Piazza San Domenico (7am–12.55pm and 3–6.30pm daily Apr–Oct; 9am–12.55pm and 3–6pm daily Nov–Mar) is a spacious and rather plain church, enlivened by the **Capella di Santa Caterina**, which houses Catherine's venerated head, preserved in a glass case – her thumb is sealed in another cabinet by the chapel door. The **Casa di Santa Caterina** at Costa di Sant'Antonio (☎ *0577 44177*; 9am–12.30pm and 3–6pm daily) was once her home, preserved today as a religious sanctuary. Both are free.

Walk down the steps from the Casa di Santa Caterina to the **Fontebranda** and find the cross marking the spot where Catherine fell (the story goes she was pushed by the devil). The fountain dates from 1245 and is the best-preserved of Siena's medieval water sources.

jaunt through the undulating countryside to discover remote corners of Tuscany. It runs on Sundays, April to September, but not every week – it's vital to **check in advance**. The train, normally a 1950s diesel, makes a 140-km loop from Siena's main station in Piazza Stazione to **Asciano** (see p. 88), wine-producing country in Monte Antico and up the wild Val d'Orcia three times during the day. You can get off and explore if you catch the first train in the morning. It costs €15 from Siena or €10 from Asciano, and each paying adult can bring a child under 10 **free**. On the rare occasions when steam trains run, the charge is €25.

Shopping

Try **BookShop** at Via San Pietro 19 (☎ *0577 226594*. ***www.bookshopsiena.com***) for a wide selection of English-language children's books. The Siena branch of *bambini* specialist **Prénatal** is at Via del Moro 11 (☎ *0577 280340*. ***www.prenatal.it***), with a quality range of clothes for toddlers and early teens, baby supplies and crayons.

Siena is also packed with delicious delis and **food shops**, all great places to supply a lavish picnic in the hills. **Pizzicheria di Miccoli** ★ at Via di Città 95 is the best; the air inside is rich with the smell of expensive cured hams and sausage; it's also good for cheese. The **Antica Drogheria Manganelli** at Via di Città

Le Crete

The scarred clay hills east of Siena, known as **Le Crete Senesi**, are rightly famous for spectacular Tuscan **views** ★★★. For the best, drive the children and the camera along the **SS438** Asciano–Siena road; wind up at **Monte Oliveto Maggiore** (p. 173) or pass a couple of hours in Asciano. Its **Museo Corboli** (*0577 719524*), inside a 13th-century *palazzo* at Corso Matteotti 122, houses an impressive collection of Sienese art, Etruscan artefacts and restored civic frescoes, notably an allegory of the seasons on the ceiling of Sala 13. It's open 10am–1pm and 3–7pm Tuesday to Sunday between April and October, shorter hours Thursday to Sunday only otherwise (closed Mondays). Admission is €4, €2.50 for children 6–12. Pizza'n'pasta in the garden at **La Mencia** ★ (*0577 718227. **www.lamencia.it***), Corso Matteotti 85, is the cream on top.

71–73 comes a close second. Its aged wood cabinets are packed with everything from posh olive oils to truffle-scented polenta.

SAN GIMIGNANO

There ought to be a prize for the first guidebook writer not to mention 'medieval Manhattan' in the introduction to **San Gimignano** ★★. We've just blown it. But the similarities are remarkable, and not just the obvious towers. In high season San Gimignano is more like a **medieval theme park** than a real town, brimming with visitors crowding the piazzas and cobbled streets. But although there's a constant daytime din, there are quality shops and up-market restaurants, cracking paintings and a great tower to climb. And if you get here early or stay late, you will love the secretive ambience of the place. The **medieval centre at dusk** ★★★ is one of Tuscany's special places.

The town got its name from Gimignano, a Bishop of Modena, and in its heyday was a major stop on the pilgrim road to Rome, which gave the place great wealth. As in Siena, the **Black Death** of 1348 called time on the good times. The town slept for 600 years until mass tourism discovered its beauty and its **towers**. At one time, they numbered at least 72, symbols of medieval clan power, not to mention handy spots for pouring pitch out of when things got nasty. Now just one tower is accessible of the 14 that have survived.

While you're here, have a glass of Tuscany's only white DOCG wine (see p. 32), **Vernaccia di San Gimignano**.

San Gimignano

Essentials

San Gimignano is easiest reached by **car**. From Florence, get off the *raccordo* (main road) at '*Poggibonsi nord*' and follow the signs; from Siena you want the '*Colle Val d'Elsa sud*' exit. From the coast, take the SS68 just north of Cecina past Volterra and turn off at Castel San Gimignano.

Parking is an issue. The centre of town is pedestrianised. All park-and-ride car parks are well signed on the approaches. Car park **P1** is the farthest from the centre, but the cheapest (€1 per hour). There's a price cap for a 24-hour stay. At P1, it's €5; at **P3** (€2 per hour), closer but with a steep climb, it's €10. Go for P1: with children in tow, you'll be riding the bus (five

Panforte

Siena is famous for its panforte, a sweet, dense dessert sold in shops all over town, and especially along **Banchi di Sopra**, where you can buy it fresh by the *etto* (100g). It's made from candied fruit and nuts, glued together with honey, and resembles a gloopy fruit cake. Though popular across Italy, the first *panforte* was created in Siena in the Middle Ages: each shop has its own recipe and the most popular varieties are sweet **Panforte Margherita** or bitter **Panforte Nero**. Try a few slices from several shops to compare recipes. **Drogheria Manganelli** (see above) and **Antico Forno delle Campane**, Via Campane 11, are good places to start.

minutes) anyway. Stamp your car park ticket by the cashier's office to pay your return bus ticket too (€1). If you're only stopping for a couple of hours, **P2** (€3 per hour) is the closest.

INSIDER TIP

Keep your parking ticket handy. It's worth a €1 **discount** off the €7.50 *biglietto cumulativo* for all San Gimignano's civic museums.

The **tourist office** is at Piazza del Duomo 1 (*0577 940008. www.sangimignano.com*). They can recommend combined tickets for a multi-museum hop and rent **audioguides** to the town in English (€5), lasting three hours. Both main piazzas (della Cisterna and del Duomo) have **cashpoints**.

The third Saturday and Sunday in June sees the usual medieval shenanigans at the **Fiera delle Messi**, a *faux* knightly tournament. San Gimignano celebrates its **patron saint** on 31st January, when just about everything closes.

Inside the Walls

First orientate yourselves. **Piazza della Cisterna** ★ (named after the well) and adjacent **Piazza del Duomo** are the heart of town. The latter's vista is somewhat spoiled by a huge crane, which may not have gone by the time you read this. All streets lead to and from here.

You don't need a guidebook to tell you that the climb up the **Torre Grossa** (Piazza del Duomo. *0577 990312*), the highest of San Gimignano's towers, is going to end with a stunning **view** ★★ over the Val d'Elsa and beyond. Look hard enough and you might spot some poolside family accommodation or plot a family walk through the vines – the tourist office can suggest routes. Admission is €5, €4 for children 6–18. The same ticket is valid for some hardcore art at the **Pinacoteca** and **Palazzo Comunale**: all are open 9.30am–7pm daily March to October, 10am–5.30pm November to February.

If you're clever, you can get almost the same view for **free** by making the five-minute climb uphill from Piazza del Duomo to the ruined **Rocca**. Walk to your left towards the panorama when you get to the fort and look down. There's a view your little ones will appreciate: a small park with **swings and a slide**.

There are plenty of shops with local produce to be found along **Via San Giovanni**. You're being scalped, of course. Head for **Via San Matteo** ★, north of the main piazzas; it's slightly quieter and less touristy. Judging by the queues they don't need the plug, but the **Gelateria 'di Piazza'** ★★ at Piazza della Cisterna 4 (next to Protur; *0577 942244*) were Gelato World Champions in 2006. For a local flavour, try their **Crema di Santa Fina**, made with saffron.

Collegiata ★★ AGES 5 AND UP

*Piazza del Duomo. 0577 940316. **E: collegiata@cheapnet.it.***

Almost every bit of wall space inside this rather plain Duomo is covered in **fresco**.

It helps to know the **stories** behind religious art. On the far main wall from the entrance are scenes from the **Life of Christ**. No prizes for naming the only guy at the Last Supper without his halo. Looking right down the nave, the figure absorbing all the arrows is **St Sebastian**. Miraculously he survived, but was later bludgeoned to death on the orders of Roman emperor Diocletian. In a cruel twist, he's now the patron of archers. Above St Sebastian is a gruesome **Last Judgement** ★ by Taddeo di Bartolo. Androgynous human figures suffer all manner of ills at the hands of little devils.

The best frescoes in the church are Domenico Ghirlandaio's in the **Cappella di Santa Fina** ★★ opposite the entrance. They portray Santa Fina, a local girl who fell mortally ill aged 10 and lay on a plank of wood for five years to repent her sins. These appear to include accepting an orange from a boy. The scene on the right shows St Gregory foretelling Fina's death. On the left, mourners grieve, and you can see the towers of San Gimignano in the background.

***Open** 9.30am–7.10pm Mon–Fri, until 5.10pm Sat, 12.30–5.10pm Sun Apr–Oct; 9.30am–4.40pm Mon–Sat, opens 12.30pm Sun, Nov–Mar; closed second half Nov, second half Jan, 12 Mar, 1st Sun in Aug. **Adm** €3.50, €1.50 children 6–18. **Amenities** disabled access, English (audioguide €1).*

Museo della Tortura

AGES 12 AND UP

*Via del Castello 1–3. 0577 942243. **torture@ats.it**. On Piazza della Cisterna.*

Let's get this straight: there's some upsetting stuff in here. **Don't bring young or easily scared children.** That said, the **Torture Museum** showcases some astoundingly creative methods of inflicting pain, spanning the history of torture from the Spanish Inquisition to the Guillotine. Most pieces in the

TIP Have San Gimignano to Yourself

To get the full SG experience, it's best to stay here over night. Only at night and in the early morning does the town show its best. At **Hotel La Cisterna** (*0577 940328. **www.hotelcisterna.it***), you're within the medieval walls in a place with character, and assured a welcome. As an added bonus for youngsters, some rooms have a **bath**. Doubles are €85–130 with an extra bed €25–30, depending on room and season. Ask about bringing your car into town to unload.

Frescoes for Free

The door to the right of the tourist office in Piazza del Duomo leads into a courtyard of the Palazzo Comunale. As you emerge into the courtyard, turn to your right for some free 14th-century masterpieces: Taddeo di Bartolo's *Madonna and Child* is flanked by two works on the theme of justice by Sodoma, who painted the abbey at **Monte Oliveto Maggiore** (see p. 173). The best-preserved fresco is on the right, a monochrome **St Ivo**. All just painted on a wall.

nine rooms are originals. The 'Iron Maiden of Nuremberg', the 'Heretic's Fork' and 'Jock's Mare' are all far worse than they sound. Vivid descriptions in clinical English complete the grisly experience.

***Open** 10am–8pm daily Apr–Oct, until midnight Aug; 10am–5pm Mon–Fri, until 6pm weekends, Nov–Mar. **Adm** €8, €5.50 anyone in full-time education. **Amenities** English.*

VOLTERRA

You can't miss **Volterra** ★★. The ochre grimace it points at the world from way above the pastures of the Valdicecina is visible for miles in every direction. This **Etruscan** walled city grew wealthy from what's below your feet: alum for dyes and alabaster, a marble-like stone traditionally worked by Volterran craftsmen. Comparisons with San Gimignano are inevitable: Volterra is less pickled in its medieval state than its neighbour, with more locals and fewer tourists doing the rounds. Unfairly, but mercifully for visitors, it's permanently stuck at number two on the Tuscany day-trip chart.

Essentials

Volterra is only reachable with children by **car**. It's right on the **SS68**, 41km east of Cecina. If you see a space in the **Vallebuona** car park (follow *teatro romano*), grab it (not Saturdays 6am–3pm). Otherwise, drop the family at adjacent Porta Fiorentina and head for car park 3, **Docciola**: it's free and usually has spaces, even in peak season. The climb into town is long and steep. The '**Old Train**', a hop-on, hop-off hour-long circuit of the town and walls, doubles as car-park transport and tourist audio-guide. It runs 10am–7pm daily between June and September, shorter daily hours April, May and October, only occasionally at other times. Full fare is €5, with under 12s €3.

The **tourist office** (*☎ 0588 87257*. ***www.volterratur.it***) at Piazza dei Priori 19–20 can't do enough to help you. It's open 10am–1pm and 2–6pm daily. If you rent their **audioguide** (€5), they throw one in free for the youngsters to play with. There's a **cashpoint** opposite.

INSIDER TIP

You can download a street-map of Volterra at ***www.volterratur.it/immagini/Carta_Volterra.pdf***.

Volterra's famous *festa* is the **Astiludio**, 15th-century flag throwing on the first Sunday of September. Much better for children is **Volterra AD1398** ★★, on the third and fourth Sundays in August. The theme is self-explanatory; the added bonus being that youngsters get to don 14th-century dress (€10 max. charge), play-work as wool merchants or craftsmen and maybe speak a bit of Italian with the others.

The *biscotto* ice cream (€1.40) at **L'Incontro** ★ (Via Matteotti 18. *0588 80500*) is a wonder in itself.

Around Town

Very much the centre of town since the Middle Ages is **Piazza dei Priori** ★, whose **Palazzo** was the model for Florence's **Palazzo Vecchio** (see p. 51). If the tower in the eastern corner looks a bit squat after San Gimignano, take solace in the fact that Volterra's is festooned with a unique little pig (*porcellino*), hence the **Torre del Porcellino**. The modest-looking **Duomo** round the back of the piazza is notable for a painted wooden **Deposition** ★ carved in 1226, a magnificent Renaissance ceiling and some horrendous 19th century marble work. Finish your historical highlights tour at the **Porta all'Arco**, remains from the 7.5km of sandstone Etruscan wall.

The ideal family **picnic** spot is the **Parco Archeologico** (free admission). Despite being on the site of an Etruscan acropolis, it sports some not-so-ancient **swings and a slide**. It's open 8.30am–8pm all summer, closing 5pm in winter. Whichever way you approach the park, there's a short but steep climb up flagstones: you'll have to lug pushchair and passengers.

For offbeat toys and children's books that you don't see elsewhere, try **Lorien**, opposite the bakery at Vicolo delle Prigioni 5.

Museo Etrusco Guarnacci and Pinacoteca ★ AGES 8 AND UP

Museo*: Via Don Minzoni 15. 0588 86347.* ***Pinacoteca****: Via dei Sarti 1. 0588 87580.*

The three cultural must-sees of Volterra are linked on a single ticket: skip the **Museo di Arte Sacra**, but at the **Museo Etrusco Guarnacci**, you'll find one of Italy's important Etruscan collections. Downstairs are hundreds of haphazardly displayed funerary urns but the action starts upstairs: the intricate *Urna degli Sposi* (married couple's urn), the *Ombra della Sera*, a surprisingly touching elongated bronze of (maybe) a fertility god, and best of all (in Room 16), a series of carved reliefs showing scenes from the *Odyssey*. The vivid depiction of **Odysseus** ★

enticed by the Sirens is easy to spot.

Across town inside the Palazzo Minucci-Solaini, Volterra's **Pinacoteca** has several outstanding pieces of religious art. If time's tight, focus on the first floor: from Taddeo di Bartolo's **Enthroned Madonna** ★ polyptych to Rosso Fiorentino's Mannerist **Deposition** ★★★ took about a century. The comparison is stark: the first is a religious icon of exquisite beauty; the second a great work of modern art. That, in a nutshell, was the Renaissance.

***Open** 9am–7pm daily 16 Mar–Oct; 8.30am–1.45pm daily Nov–15 Mar. **Adm** €8, €5 children 6–18, €18 family. **Amenities** English (Museo audioguide €3), shop.*

alab'Arte AGES 7 AND UP

Via Orti S. Agostino 28. ✆ 0588 87968. www.alabarte.com.

Volterra's essential purchase is **alabaster**, ghostly-white calcium sulphate mined from local hills and worked by the town's artisans for millennia. Buy alabaster of varying quality and workmanship all over town, or take the children to the town's last **sculptural workshop**. You'll see alabaster in various stages of progress. If any statues catch your eye, you can buy finished pieces. Call ahead for your very own mini-tour.

If you go alabaster-crazy, there's a museum: the **Ecomuseo dell'Alabastro**, in Piazzetta Minucci. It's open 11am–5pm daily between 16 March and October, 9am–1.30pm weekends only otherwise; admission is €3, €2 6–18s.

***Open** 9.30am–12.30pm and 3–7pm Mon–Sat. **Credit** MC, V.*

Parco Preistorico FIND

AGES 2 AND UP

Via dei Cappuccini, Peccioli. ✆ 0587 636030. www.parcopreistorico.it. Badly signposted 1km north of Peccioli (22km north of Volterra).

Enjoy this family theme park on two levels. For you, there's the kitsch sight of an oversized plastic stegosaurus basking in a Tuscan wood. For the children, there's, well, all those **dinosaurs** – including a 12m hunk of brachiosaurus with his head above the pines. Of course, it's a lot of nonsense, but your children will love it. It's outside, shady and they can let off steam. The spectacle of

TIP Staying inside the Walls

Although nowhere near as crowded as San Gimignano, Volterra also shows its best without the day-trippers. Top family choice inside the walls is **L'Etrusca** ★ (✆ *0588 84073. www.volterraetrusca.com*), at Via Porta all'Arco 37–41, a romantic winding street that belongs in the Middle Ages. The apartments are spacious, well-equipped, bang in the centre of town and, unlike almost everywhere else in Tuscany, they can be booked per single night. Prices €210–665 per week. Stock up on local goodies and cook for yourselves. You'll feel like an Italian.

TIP The Best of Chianti

Though ideally sited for day trips into Florence, Siena and the hidden corners of the nearby Val d'Elsa, Chianti itself isn't much cop for children, especially young ones. A spin through the hills to admire the **vistas** might be enough. The **SS222**, the *Chiantigiana*, between Castellina in Chianti and Greve is the classic drive. Prettier still is the **SS429** meandering east through woodland and rolling vineyards from Castellina, that ends up close to **Cavriglia Nature Park** ★ (*055 967544. **www.parcocavriglia.com***). Here you'll find indigenous animals, a picnic area and a child-friendly restaurant. Note, the park is just west of Massa Sabbioni, *not* near Cavriglia; it's open daily 8am–dusk and free to get in. For the Chianti shire-town experience, poke round the shops and stop for a *caffè* in **Radda in Chianti**. Along the way, you're never far from a slurp of Tuscany's iconic wine. When you're buying, remember **Chianti 'Classico'** ★ denotes the original, and best, grape zone; pair it with a robust Tuscan meat dish and you're eating like a local.

Perhaps the very best time you can have together is hiding out in a villa or farmhouse, walking, relaxing and soaking up landscapes that have inspired writers and painters for centuries: Chianti boasts one of central Tuscany's **idyllic family retreats**, complete with cashmere goats (see p. 100). Tour operators (see p. 244) can offer plenty of alternatives.

a crimson **volcano** erupting plastic balls will stay with you for some time.

If you're touring in a **camper**, you can overnight at the park (with electricity and showers) for free.

Open *9am–dusk daily.* ***Adm*** *€4.* ***Amenities*** *bar/café, disabled access, English, parking, playground, shop.*

Parco Preistorico

AREZZO

The *città* of Piero Della Francesca, Vasari, a lopsided piazza, and of an unnatural number of dogs, **Arezzo** ★ is a little different from central Tuscany's other hill-towns. The town profits more from making exquisite gold jewellery and selling antiques than from the catering to the tourist euro. There may be some scruffy suburbs to overlook, but Arezzo's **medieval heart** is a gem and it's positively tranquil compared to San Gimignano and Siena. Even five minutes with *The Legend of the True Cross* would be plenty to justify jetting here from Honolulu.

Essentials

Driving to Arezzo is easy and quick. It's just 77km from Florence, 70km from Siena, 80km from Perugia and right by the **A1**. All **car parks** are signed as you approach the walls; the handiest is **Pietri** (free). Just to make things interesting, the sign for that park is **brown** while every other is white. There's a system of escalators (*scala mobile*) lifting you up hill to the **Duomo**.

Arezzo is on the main Florence–Rome line and served by a regular **train** (✆ *892021*. ***www.trenitalia.it***) service. A **Florence** train can take anything from a ½ hour to 1½ hours, and costs from €5.40. There's also a regular direct service from **Perugia** (1 hour, €4). From **Siena**, take the **TRAIN bus** (✆ *0577 204111*. ***www.trainspa.it***). Line 138 takes about 1½ hours and costs €5.

The **tourist office** (✆ *0575 377678*. ***www.apt.arezzo.it***) is at Piazza della Repubblica 82, outside the train station. It's open 10am–1pm and 3–6pm Monday to Saturday and when there's a

Arezzo's Famous *Festas*

Arezzo is home to one of Tuscany's iconic festivals: the **Giostra del Saracino** ★, a medieval jousting contest between the city's four *quartieri*. Expect extravagant fancy dress and Tuscan melodrama as they compete for the **Golden Lance**. The festival takes place twice a year: on the second-last Saturday in June and the first Sunday in September. Tickets are limited to about 900 for non-Aretines. Phone the office (✆ *0575 377462*) or email the society (***giostradelsaracino@comune.arezzo.it***) from mid-March onwards to get your ticket.

Less famous but just as likely to amuse little ones is the **Carnevale Aretino Orciolaia** ★ (✆ *0575 28353*. ***www.carnevalearetino.it***), with colourful floats, little trains and giant inflatable Teletubbies. It takes place on Sundays from late January to mid-February. The first Sunday of every month heralds a world-renowned **antiques fair** in Piazza Grande.

AREZZO

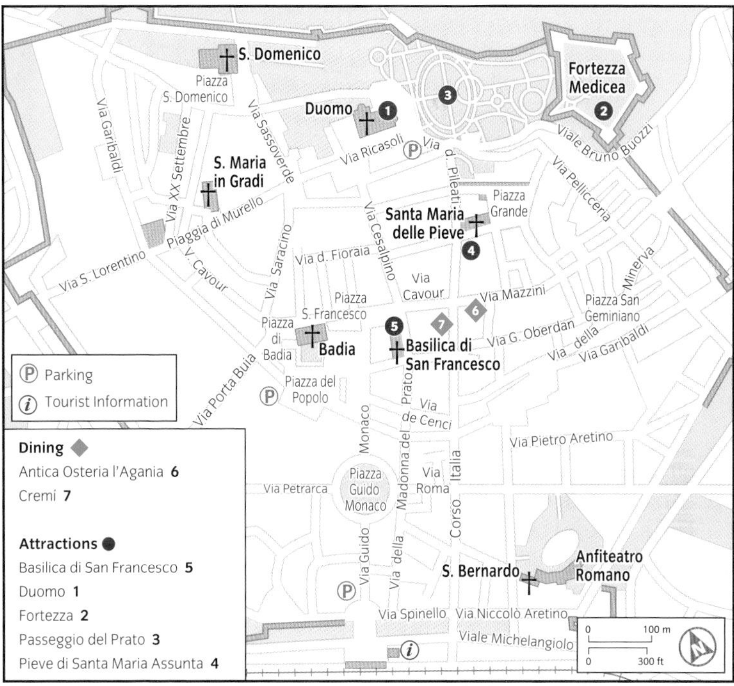

Sunday antiques fair from November to March; 9am–1pm only on regular Sundays. Between April and October it's open 9am–1pm and 3–7pm every day.

Around the Town

The half-ruined, 16th-century **Fortezza Medicea** is likely to be the children's highlight of a visit to Arrezo. The 360° **views** ★ from the ramparts stretch all the way to Florence and the arc of the Apennines. The fort is open 7am–8pm April to October, 7.30am–6pm November to March. The way in is through a tunnel from an adjacent park, the **Passeggio del Prato**, an ideal spot for a family picnic. Here you'll find **swings and a slide**. On your way downhill from the castle, don't miss crazy-sloping **Piazza Grande** ★. Its southern corner began sinking in about 1200 and has been unstoppable since.

Next you'll want to find **Corso Italia**: the home of Arezzo's *passeggiata*, all the best shops and **cashpoints** galore. At the top of the Corso, view the **Pieve di Santa Maria Assunta** (*0575 361319*) from the outside: every column decorating the **Romanesque** church has a

Piazza Grande, Arezzo

unique design. The bell tower has 40 windows.

The ice cream at **Cremí** (Corso Italia 100) is a treat.

The Legend of the True Cross ★★★ AGES 7 AND UP

*Piazza San Francesco. ☎ 0575 20630. **www.pierodellafrancesca.it**. Credit card bookings ☎ 0575 352727 or **https://ticketing.ribesinformatica.it/arezzo**.*

Inside the Cappella Bacci of the **Basilica di San Francesco** is the reason everyone comes to Arezzo: **Piero della Francesca**'s *Legend of the True Cross*. It's a giant of Western art: a piece of work whose size, grace and technical artistry is almost shocking. It took the artist 250 days between 1452 and 1466 to paint it, and latterly over 15 years to restore. Della Francesca's ability to suck all the movement from a moment, leaving frozen perfection, has never been bettered.

The ten slightly battered panels tell the story of the wood used to build Christ's cross, based on Jacopo da Voragine's '**Golden Legend**'. The wood is traced from the **Death of Adam** to the **Annunciation**. Although the battle scenes may look static to modern eyes, the **Meeting of Solomon and the Queen of Sheba** ★★ and the **Discovery and Proof of the True Cross** ★★ are majestic. The haunted gaze of the servant in **Constantine's Dream** ★★★,

FUN FACT Acqua Aretina?

Get your children drinking Arezzo's water; there's obviously something in it. For a small place, Arezzo's list of notable sons is long, including the philosopher **Petrarch**, art historian **Vasari** and **Guido d'Arezzo**, who invented the music score.

Art Matters

It goes without saying that Tuscany's rich cultural and artistic heritage is part of the region's *spirito* – part of what it means to be Tuscan, even in the 21st century. Tuscany's individual appeal is a concept as elusive as it is real when you feel it. But the importance of art and architecture goes even further: it has changed the course of modern warfare, saving lives in the process. In August 1944, the retreating Nazi army destroyed every bridge in Florence, except one: **Ponte Vecchio** (see p. 41). Partisans defending Volterra the same year risked their lives to brick up the hill-town's greatest Etruscan artefact, the **Porta all'Arco** (p. 93), in case it was targeted by a German assault. More remarkable still is the story of **Sansepolcro**. The British officer commanding the heights over the town in 1944 remembered he'd once read an essay by Aldous Huxley – entitled 'The Greatest Picture' – which accorded that status to Piero della Francesca's *Resurrection of Christ*, still in the town gallery. He ordered the shelling to cease lest a masterpiece be lost. Art, architecture, history, landscape and life: in Tuscany, these can never be separated.

on the lower-right of the stained-glass window, follows you around the chapel. You can see him (or is that the other way round?) from the entrance.

Booking in advance is **essential**. Each visit lasts a maximum of 30 minutes. Turn up at least 15 minutes before your booked slot to claim your ticket. If you develop a thing for Piero, you can follow his art trail to **Sansepolcro** and **Monterchi**.

Open *9am–6.30pm Mon–Fri, 9am–5.30pm Sat, 1–5.30pm Sun Apr–Oct; closes ½ hour earlier Nov–Mar.* ***Adm*** *€6, €4 18–25s, €2 under-18s.* ***Amenities*** *disabled access, English (audioguide), shop.*

INSIDER TIP

To get children warmed up for the visit, ***www.pierodellafrancesca.it*** has a couple of **educational games** (in English) inspired by Piero's masterpiece.

Parco Lignano ALL AGES

0575 979446. ***www.parcodilignano.it****. SS71 dir. Cortona; about 10 km out of Arezzo, turn off at Rigutino.*

Stop when you see the picnic tables in this **wooded park** on a spur of Monte Camurcina, south of Arezzo. It's a quaint spot above the Valdichiana with walking trails, a shaded **playground** and deer, geese and ducks to squawk at. In all honesty, it looks rather unremarkable to a 35-year-old, but your toddler will beg to differ. Continue uphill for top **views** ★, more walking but no services.

Open *always.* ***Adm*** *free.* ***Amenities*** *bar/café (3pm–midnight daily summer, 3–8pm Sundays winter), campsite (****info@parcodilignano.it****), parking, picnic area.*

TIP The Back Road

If you're heading to Florence, take the SS71 north from Arezzo into the little visited **Casentino**. Turn left onto the **SS70** just after Bibbiena and follow this road all the way to Pontassieve, just east of Florence. **Poppi** is the best spot to break your journey (avoid the 'zoo'). The whole detour, skirting the edge of the **Parco Naturale delle Foreste Casentinesi** (***www.parcoforestecasentinesi.it***), takes about two hours.

FAMILY-FRIENDLY ACCOMMODATION

For more ideas on finding accommodation, see p. 28.

Agriturismo Al Gelso Bianco ★★

*Via Sant'Appiano 47, Barberino Val d'Elsa. ☎ 055 8075658. **www.algelsobianco.it**. Signposted off road from Barberino to Sant'Appiano after 2km.*

This small complex centred around a converted 18th-century stone farmhouse is in the middle of nowhere in the heart of typical Tuscan countryside. Perched on a ridge above the vines and olive groves between Chianti and San Gimignano (25 minutes), the six newly renovated **apartments** are built for families. There are always potential new friends around. Apartments are terracotta-tiled, individually decorated and with proper kitchens (not 'kitchenettes'). For the best view on-site, ask for '**Ginestra**': its roof terrace looks right at San Gimignano's towers.

If you have tots, note that the pool area isn't fenced. Between June and September, it's **week-long bookings** only.

***Apartments** 6. **Rates** 1-bed €650–940 per week, 2-bed €920–1580 per week. Cots free. Closed mid-Jan–Feb. **Credit** MC, V. **Amenities** babysitting, highchairs, parking, pool (outdoor), restaurant, sauna, WiFi. **In apartment** A/C, kitchen, safe, sat TV, shower only.*

Hotel La Cisterna, San Gimignano, see p. 91.

La Penisola Goat Farm GREEN

*Loc. La Pensiola, Radda in Chianti. ☎ 0577 738080. **www.chianticashmeregoatfarm.com**. 3km north-east of Radda.*

Meet the goats: this converted stone farmhouse doesn't just stare right at **classic Chianti views**, it's also the only place in Italy currently making goat cashmere. Tot entertainment is on tap, with the ethically reared herd and a litter of Bolognese dogs running about the place. (The goats kid in May.) The house itself is a loving conversion, with a vine-shaded outdoor dining area and plenty of space in the bedrooms.

The English manager can help arrange vaguely 'child-friendly' **wine tastings** in nearby Volpaia and Álbola.

***Apartment** 1. **Rates** 3-bed (sleeps 6) 650–2000 per week. **Credit** MC, V.*

Amenities *English, garden (goat-free), parking, pool (outdoor).* ***In room*** *kitchen, sat TV, shower only.*

Villa Agostoli ★

Strada degli Agostoli 99, Siena. 0577 44392. ***www.villaagostoli.it****. 5km west of Siena.*

This complex of villas and apartments is situated on a lush hillside of olive groves and vineyards just a 10-minute drive from the centre of Siena, offering space and **freedom** for families (especially large ones) with a car. Each villa is fully equipped with kitchen, spacious bathrooms and plenty of amenities, with enough room for four or five people, while the gardens are perfect for picnics and playing. The pool is a real winner with children, and each house has a terrace equipped for eating al fresco.

Small villas *10.* ***Rates*** *2-bed €490–1370 per week, 3-bed €860–1650 per week.* ***Credit*** *AmEx, MC, V deposit only.* ***Amenities*** *disabled access, parking, pool (outdoor).* ***In room*** *A/C, fridge, TV.*

Garden Hotel

Via Custoza 2, Siena. 0577 47056. ***www.gardenhotel.it****. 1.5km north of Siena; bus: 6, 10.*

A smart hotel in a converted 17th-century villa among tranquil gardens also incorporates three modern properties nearby – ask to stay at '**the Villa**' for atmospheric rooms. The obvious appeal for families is the bucolic setting, still close to all the attractions, and the large triple or quad rooms for up to five, depending on the ages of your children. The small pool is the perfect place to end the day, and there's also a tennis court on site. The city is a short bus ride or 20-minute walk.

Rooms *24 (in villa).* ***Rates*** *Double €103–157, triple €143–197, quad €168–222. Cots €15. Breakfast included.* ***Credit*** *AmEx, MC, V.* ***Amenities*** *babysitting, bar, disabled access, parking, pool (outdoor), restaurant.* ***In room*** *A/C, fridge, safe, shower only.*

Hotel Santa Caterina

Via Enea Silvio Piccolomini 7, Siena. 0577 221105. ***www.hscsiena.it****. Bus: A, N, 2.*

Set in a charming 18th-century villa just outside Porta Romana in Siena, this friendly hotel offers cosy triple rooms for families. In low season, children under 18 go free – you pay double rates for a

TIP Siena on a Budget

Hotels in Siena book up fast, especially in summer, and choice is limited in the *centro storico* if you're looking for large rooms, good prices and facilities for children. Many families opt to visit the city as a day trip; if you have a car, accommodation options widen considerably. See ***www.agrituristsiena.com*** for a list of local *agriturismi*. The best campsite is **Campeggio Siena Colleverde** (Strada di Scacciapensieri 47. *0577 280044*), 2km north of the city, which has a shop, bar and outdoor pool. It's open mid-March to mid-November; pitches start at €8.

triple. The rooms themselves are all tastefully decked out with antique wooden furniture and tiled floors, but the best extras for families include the terraced garden (where you can breakfast in the summer) and bike rentals, which the owners can arrange on arrival.

***Rooms** 22. **Rates** Double €144–155, triple €155–210. Cots €15 in high season, free low season. **Credit** AmEx, MC, V. **Amenities** babysitting, bar, disabled access, parking (€15). **In room** A/C, fridge, sat TV.*

Hotel Duomo ★

*Via Stalloreggi 38, Siena. 0577 289088. **www.hotelduomo.it**.*

Stay in a converted 12th-century *palazzo* with one of the best locations in town, a short walk from Siena's Duomo. The choice of reasonably priced triples and quads makes it perfect for families: ask for one of the 13 rooms with a **view** of the cathedral (the best are 61 and 62 with panoramic terraces). All are modern and functional, despite the archaic exterior, though bathrooms are a little cramped.

***Rooms** 23. **Rates** Double €80–150, triple €110–200, quad €150–250. **Credit** AmEx, MC, V. **Amenities** babysitting, parking (€25 double, €20 triple, free quads). **In room** A/C, shower only, sat TV.*

Residence L'Etrusca, Volterra, see p. 94.

Tenuta Il Pino ★★ FIND

*Santo Pietro Belvedere, Capannoli. 0587 607273. **www.tenutailpino.com**. On SP26 2km west of Capannoli.*

Hiding behind an olive grove mid-way between Volterra and Pisa is the Valdera's first *agriturismo*, now nearly two decades old. Accommodation is in the original *agriturist* spirit: rough around the edges, but spacious, clean and built for **adventurous families**. The four apartments are crafted from the original farmhouse: conversion is minimal, with terracotta floors, original (small) windows and worn Tuscan antique furniture left *in situ*. The real attraction for families is the farm. It's a *fattoria didattica*, where you can spend the afternoon learning to **cook a Tuscan feast** (€40 inc. meal) or baking bread, while the children are off working the farm's Etruscan dig or **making ceramics** on-site (€20 approx.). Or you could all just sit by the pool and watch the grapes grow – whatever suits. It's **weekly bookings only** in high season.

***Apartments** 4. **Rates** 3-bed €410–900 per week, 2-bed €315–685 per week, 1-bed €270–420 per week. Cots free. **Amenities** parking, pool (outdoor), restaurant. **In room** kitchen, sat TV, shower only.*

FAMILY-FRIENDLY DINING

On the Go in Siena

Historic bakery **Forno dei Galli** (Via dei Termini 45. *0577 289073*) sells *schiacciata* (flatbread) and slices of pizza to take away. It's open 9am–7pm daily, and often runs specials (like

TIP Parents' Tuscany, Too

If you're lucky enough to have friends, grandparents or a nanny in tow, Tuscany has countless magical corners awaiting your **escape**. Without the children. For romance, dreamy landscapes and a weekend by yourselves under the Tuscan sun, try some of these:

- Pamper yourselves silly at the award-winning **Terme di Saturnia Spa and Golf Resort** (p. 182).
- Book two nights at the luxury **Westin Excelsior** (p. 69) to tour the paintings and sculptures in Florence's unparalleled museums.
- Dine by candlelight on gourmet Tuscan food at Chiusi's **Zaira** (p. 185) or Volterra's **Antica Osteria dei Poeti** (p. 106).
- Contact Montepulciano's **Consorzio** (p. 169) to arrange a wine-tasting itinerary in the surrounding countryside's finest Vino Nobile cantinas.
- Book a table at Montalcino's **Re di Macchia** (p. 185), a night at the **Porta Castellana** B&B (p. 182) and wake up to breakfast on the terrace as the mists rise from the Val d'Orcia below.
- Escape to Asciano for wonderful walks and bike rides in the clay hills of **Le Crete** (p. 88) and fine Renaissance frescoes at the abbey of **Monte Oliveto Maggiore** (p. 173).

'*panino* kids' for €1). Not far away at Via delle Terme 94–96, **Pizza al Taglio** sells fat slices of mushroom, sausage and Margherita pizzas for €3. Upmarket **Nannini** at Via Banchi di Sopra 22–24 (*0577 41591*) is the most lauded café in town, worth popping in to check out the range of cakes (including *ricciarelli* – almond cookies) and hot chocolate (€2.30). **Key Largo Bar**, just off the Piazza del Campo on Via Rinaldini, is great fun if you can squeeze onto the narrow **balcony** upstairs – perch on small benches overlooking the Campo and munch on cakes, pizza (€1.50) or *panini* (€2.50).

Caribia ★, next to Key Largo, has the best *gelato* in Siena, with a range of flavours including cherry, apple and rice pudding. It's open 10.30am–11pm daily. Almost as good is **Brivido** ★, at Via dei Pellegrini 1.

INSIDER TIP

While the touristy cafés on Siena's Piazza del Campo are overpriced, you can't beat the location **at night** ★: eat a large lunch and grab an evening table for snacks and drinks.

Restaurants

Antica Osteria l'Agania

TUSCAN/ARETINE

Via Mazzini 10, Arezzo. 0575 295381.

This informal little *cantina* up a side street near Arrezo's Piazza Grande specialises in Aretine cooking. Since 1905 they've been serving up *ribollita* (vegetable soup-cum-stew), *fegatelli* (liver) *all'Aretino* and *bistecca alla Fiorentina* to a mixed local and tourist crowd. Judging by the stickers on the door, they've been in every restaurant guide going since about 1906. Children will enjoy creating their own **pasta'n'sauce combo** from a choice of six of each, including plain tomato and buttery sage sauces.

Open *midday–2pm and 7–10pm Tue–Sun.* ***Main courses*** *€6–14.* ***Credit*** *AmEx, MC, V.* ***Amenities*** *A/C, highchairs.*

La Mencia, Asciano, see p. 88.

Trattoria Chiribiri ★ VALUE
CLASSIC ITALIAN/TUSCAN

Piazzetta della Madonna 1, San Gimignano. ☎ 0577 941948.

These eight tables at the southern tip of walled San Gimignano have virtually none of the attributes required for family dining: it's cramped, there's no children's menu or highchairs, they don't take credit cards and the food is Italian *trattoria* classics. But the welcome mat is out whatever your age, and the food is **brilliantly executed** considering the tight squeeze. Beef in Chianti, wild boar stew, *ossobuco*, ravioli with pumpkin, plus straight lasagne and spaghetti with meat sauce: all are here. It's an oasis of value in the heart of rip-off city.

Open *11am–11pm daily.* ***Main courses*** *€6–14.*

Gallo Nero ★ MEDIEVAL THEMED

Via del Porrione 65–67, Siena. ☎ 0577 284356. www.gallonero.it.

This is the most entertaining restaurant in Siena, at least if any of your children are into **knights**, castles and anything medieval. It's not just the décor, but the food too: ordering from the *Medioevale* menu is all part

Glorious gelato

of the fun. You'll find faithfully recreated dishes from the Middle Ages, mostly elaborate concoctions taken from cookbooks of the time. Try the *salsiccie* (sausages), peasant favourite *pici penne* (made with a simple sauce of flour and eggs), or *fagioli del purgatorio con cotiche* (white beans with pork rind).

Open *midday–3pm and 7–11pm daily.* ***Main courses*** *€9–12.* ***Credit*** *AmEx, MC, V.* ***Amenities*** *reservations accepted.*

La Taverna di Nello

TUSCAN/ITALIAN

Via del Porrione 28, Siena. ☎ 0577 289043.

The chief appeal of this traditional Tuscan restaurant in Siena is the open kitchen – children can watch chefs chopping, stirring and frying beneath archaic pots and pans. The décor has a rustic feel, and includes plenty of interesting touches: lanterns, racks of wine, and sheaves of corn hanging from the ceiling. Being close to the Campo it's a handy place for lunch, and the food is good, too, with a solid range of Italian favourites.

Open *midday–3pm and 7–10.30pm Mon–Sat, closed Jan.* ***Main courses*** *€9–18.* ***Credit*** *AmEx, MC, V.* ***Amenities*** *reservations accepted.*

Osteria Castelvecchio ★

VEGETARIAN ITALIAN

Via di Castelvecchio 65, Siena. ☎ 0577 49586.

Families with enthusiastic vegetarians should make for this **hip restaurant**, set in a historic building close to Siena's Duomo. Although it does serve meat, the focus is overwhelmingly vegetables and modern vegetarian cuisine. Menus change daily, and feature at least two kinds of *risotto*, home-made soups and excellent spaghetti. The dining rooms are small, so not so great for very young ones or pushchairs, but the bright, orange-pastel coloured walls and brick vaults create a cheerful vibe amidst the grey medieval stone.

Open *12.30–2.30pm and 7.30–9.30pm Mon–Sat.* ***Main courses*** *€7–10.* ***Credit*** *AmEx, MC, V.* ***Amenities*** *reservations accepted.*

Antica Trattoria Papei ★

SIENESE

Piazza del Mercato 6, Siena. ☎ 0577 280894. Behind Palazzo Pubblico.

This popular restaurant is becoming a favourite with day-trippers, but is still the best place to introduce the children to quality Sienese cuisine. It's good value, and there are plenty of large tables inside – ask to sit in the upstairs room with timbered ceiling for more ambience. The tables outside are smaller, but it's hardly a picturesque location anyway (the piazza comes with added car park).

The menu caters to all tastes: youngsters can have the pasta basics, but the kitchen also knocks out superb *gnocchi*; as usual, a plain veal cutlet is no problem For the more adventurous, specialities are *pappardelle*

TIP A Sienese Picnic

Dining in Siena can be enjoyable, but isn't particularly cheap or child friendly. Picnics are a viable alternative, the best spot being **La Lizza** (see p. 86). The biggest **supermarket** in the centre is **Conad City** in the Galleria Metropolitana off Piazza Matteotti, open 8.30am–8.30pm Monday to Saturday, 9am–1pm and 6–8pm Sunday. Alternatively, stock up on fancy deli food along **Banchi di Sopra**.

(large *fettucine*) in wild boar *ragù* or duck stewed with tomatoes. Round it off with *cantuccini* biscuits and the *vin santo* is plonked down on the table.

Open *midday–3pm and 7–10.30pm Tue–Sun.* ***Main courses*** *€7–10.* ***Credit*** *AmEx, MC, V.* ***Amenities*** *reservations accepted.*

Il Porcellino VALUE TUSCAN

Vicolo delle Prigioni 16, Volterra. 0588 86392.

Despite the obvious tourist orientation, the cooking at Volterra's Il Porcellino is just about good enough to attract **locals** and their families, too. Dishes are simple and regional: *pappardelle* with wild boar, rabbit stew, *bistecca alla Fiorentina*. Children are welcome as usual – and though there are no pizzas, the menu has just about everything else simple and Italian you can think of, as well as plain-as-you-like **roast chicken** for €4.

There's a small **terrace** outside on the quiet lane.

Open *midday–3pm and 6.30–10pm Wed–Mon.* ***Main courses*** *€4–14.* ***Credit*** *AmEx, MC, V.* ***Amenities*** *reservations accepted.*

Antica Osteria dei Poeti ★★ TUSCAN

Via Matteotti 54, Volterra. 0588 86029.

Don't be fooled by the location right on Volterra's tourist drag: this is a **seriously good** traditional Tuscan eatery. The small, characterful dining room serves up the staples you'd expect, including *pappardelle* with hare, *gnocchi* with truffles and local peasant soup, *zuppa Volterrana* (mixed seasonal vegetables and beans poured over bread). For something with a flourish, try the rabbit with aromatic herbs or sliced Chianina beef with pecorino cheese and toasted walnuts. There's the usual simple pasta options or roast pork for the children. The lengthy Tuscan wine list has plenty to tempt, from €7 to €120 a bottle.

It's Volterra's best food experience, at an affordable price; it's also open early at lunch and dinner.

Open *11.30am–3pm and 6.30–10pm Fri–Wed.* ***Main courses*** *€7–16.* ***Credit*** *AmEx, MC, V.* ***Amenities*** *reservations accepted.*

5 Pisa, Lucca & Northern Tuscany

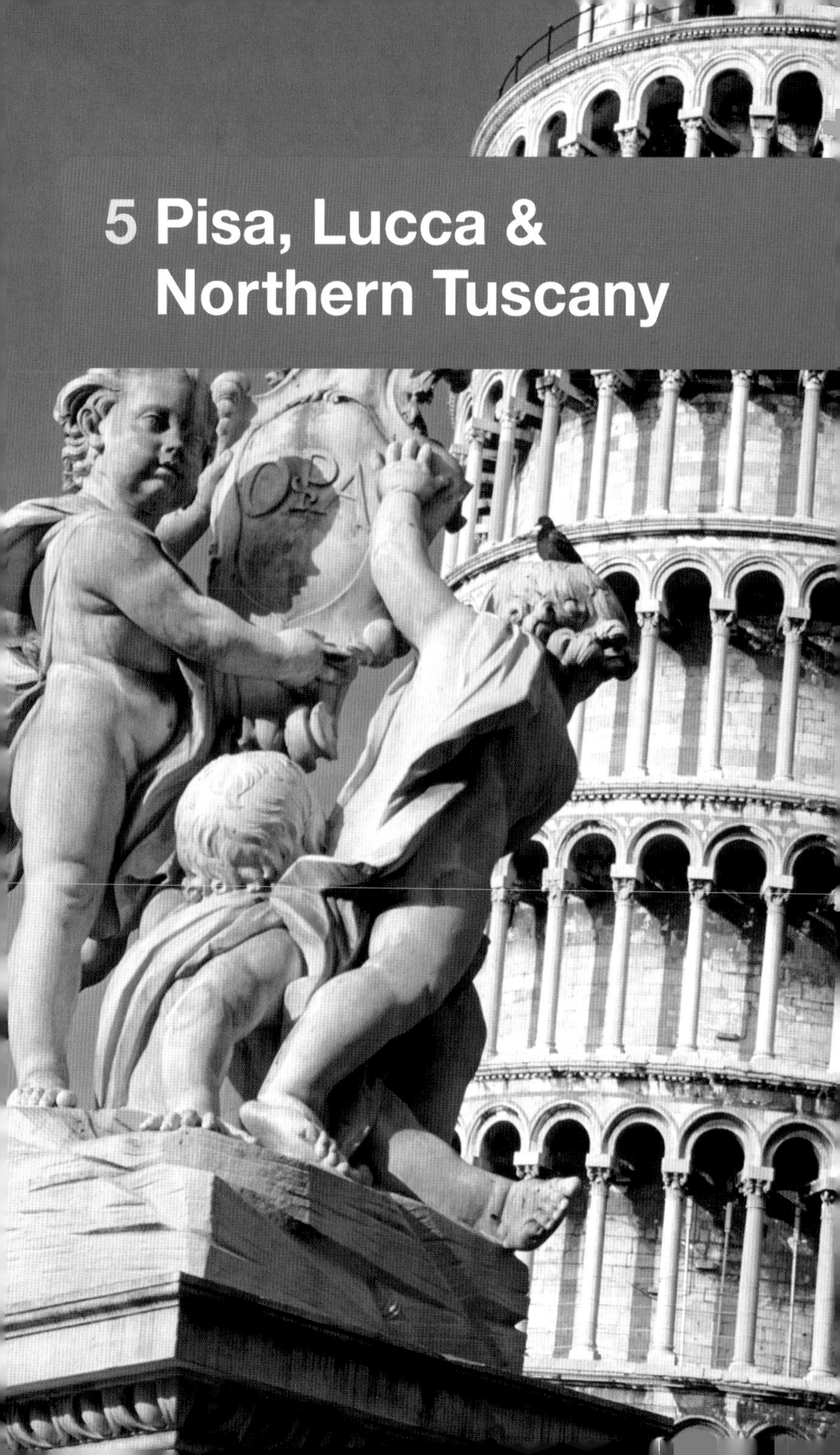

NORTHERN TUSCANY

Despite the presence of an iconic tower looming over it, a visit to the Tuscan north doesn't stop there; Pisa's **Campo dei Miracoli** is Italy's most dramatic piazza and Roman galleys have been unearthed from the silt of the river Arno. Lucca's elevation from hidden gem for those in the know to major tourist stopover has been rapid: the medieval ramparts are some of the best-preserved in Tuscany and the cathedral needs to be seen to be believed. Under-visited **Pistoia** has a quiet charm, but there are still peaceful corners and truly great art everywhere.

The great outdoors also pulls visitors northwards. The chic beaches of the **Versilian coast** are wide, shallow and perfect for families; wealthy Florentines flock here in August to see and be seen. The mountainous **Garfagnana** and the **Alpi Apuane** are paradises for walkers and cavers, dotted with charming villages and small towns in which to hide away. And you can still find a part of Tuscany that most won't even have heard of, let alone visited: rugged, forested and castle-dotted **Lunigiana**, ripe for exploring by car, and ideal for a real villa holiday away from the crowds. For the children, the north of Tuscany means great sandy stretches of beach to run around on, miles of virgin countryside to hike and astounding architecture and art.

Children's Top Attractions of Northern Tuscany

- Scaling Pisa's **wonky tower**, p. 113.
- Chilling out on **Campo dei Miracoli**. p. 113.
- Discovering **Roman ships** buried in the mud, p. 115.
- Circling **Lucca's walls** on bikes or rollerblades, p. 121.
- Hanging from zip-slides and Tibetan bridges in the **Lunigiana**, p. 131.
- Tucking into Tuscany's tastiest **pesto**, p. 136.
- Enjoying family fun at Viareggio's **Carnevale**, p. 127.
- Tracking wolves and lynx at Pistoia's **Moonlight Zoo**, p. 124.

PISA

Tuscany was the epicentre of the **Renaissance**, and is home to the world's most inspiring art collections, but the one sight certain to drive children wild with excitement has its roots way before all that: the **Leaning Tower of Pisa**. It's a mesmerising piece of botched engineering, and one that the children will want to climb right away.

Pisa was a busy trading port during the Roman era (when the sea came farther inland) and by the early Middle Ages was one of Italy's most powerful **maritime republics**, controlling an empire that included Corsica, Sardinia and the Balearics. After its mighty navy was destroyed in battle with Genoa in 1284 and when the river Arno began to silt up, the city never recovered its fortunes. Today it's a sophisticated and bustling city with a cobbled *centro storico* scattered with trendy bars and cafés and a respected university founded in 1343, one of Europe's oldest.

Essentials

Getting There

By Air For UK and Irish flights to Galileo Galilei airport, see p. 38. To get into the city take the **LAM Rossa** (red) bus, which connects the airport, train station and Campo dei Miracoli in around 30 minutes (90¢). **Trains** connect the airport to Pisa Centrale every 30 minutes (6 minutes; €1.10). **Taxis** cost €6–8 into the centre and take 10–15 minutes. There is ample **parking** at the airport (€2 per 30 minutes; €3 per hour; €12 per day).

By Car Pisa is easy to get to by car, with the **A11** connecting it to Florence (1 hour) and the **A12** passing just to the west. Take the **Pisa Centro-Aeroporto** exit (rather than Pisa Nord). It's difficult to **park** inside the old centre. Either use free 'park and rides' on the edge of town or drive farther in and pay. The best free spots are **Park Brennero** at Via Paparelli (closed Wednesday and Saturday morning for the market) and

Souvenirs, Pisa

Park Pietrasantina, both north of the centre and connected to the main sights by LAM Verde (green, for the centre) and LAM Rossa buses (red, for the Leaning Tower). The closest to the Tower is **Parcheggio Piazza dei Miracoli** (*050 8312152*. €1.50 per hour 6.30am–11.30pm; 75¢ per hour 11.30pm–6.30am) at Via Cammeo 51 near Porta Nuova, just west of Campo dei Miracoli. Note that a new car park is being built under **Piazza Vittorio Emanuele II**, which should be open by the time you

TIP

Getting Around Pisa

Pisa's smart centre is small enough to explore on foot, but there is a comprehensive local bus network run by **CPT** (*050 505511*. ***www.cpt.pisa.it***) if anyone gets tired. Fares are 90¢ for a single journey within an hour; you can buy 4 tickets for €3.15 and 10 for €7.50 from the bus station or *tabacchi* stores, otherwise the single fare is €1.50 on the bus. Children under a metre in height travel free with an adult.

As in Florence, an enjoyable and hassle-free alternative is the tourist bus service operated by UK-based **City Sightseeing** (UK *01708 866000*. ***www.city-sightseeing.com***). **Line A** (City Tour; 10am–6pm every hour) starts just east of the Leaning Tower at Piazza Arcivescovado and makes a loop around the city. **Line B** starts in the same place and makes three runs a day (9am, 2pm, 6pm) to Parco San Rossore outside Pisa. Tickets (€15, €7 for children 5–15) are valid for 24 hours and can be used on both lines – start anywhere. Buses run daily between 17th March and 31st October.

PISA

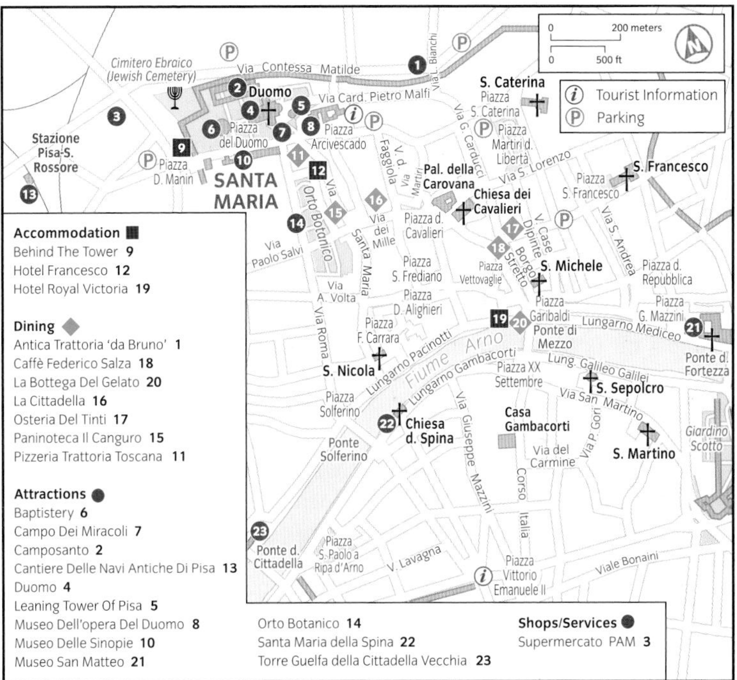

read this. Out of peak season, it will be quiet enough to head for the Leaning Tower (you can see it for miles) and find something in the surrounding streets (€1 per hour).

By Train **Pisa Centrale** is the main train station, connected by fast services with Rome, Genoa, Milan, Turin, Naples and Livorno. Local trains shuttle from **Lucca** (25 minutes; €2.30) and **Florence** (1¼ hours; €5.40) throughout the day. From Lucca, get off at **San Rossore** if you're heading to the Leaning Tower. Forget the bus.

Visitor Information

The most convenient **tourist office** for the Leaning Tower is in Piazza del Duomo (*050 560464*), inside the Museo dell'Opera del Duomo. It's open 9am–6pm Monday to Saturday and 10.30am–4.30pm Sunday, although all ticket offices in Campo dei Miracoli double as information centres. You'll find fewer tourists and more enthusiasm at the office near the **station**, Piazza Vittorio Emanuele II 16 (*050 42291*), open 9am–7pm Mon–Fri and 9.30am–1.30pm Saturday. The **airport** also has a tourist desk (10.30am–4.30pm and 6–10pm daily).

The official city **websites** are fairly informative: ***www.pisa.turismo.toscana.it*** (in Italian) and ***www.comune.pisa.it/english***; ***www.pisaonline.it*** is more comprehensive.

Family-friendly Festivals

Pisa's best festivals both happen in June. The **Festa di San Ranieri** ★★ (16–17th June) honours the patron saint of Pisa, a local boy who died in 1160 and was buried inside the Duomo. The celebrations begin with the *luminara*, when 70,000 candles on white wooden frames (*biancheria*) light up the Arno. The following afternoon four teams compete in a regatta, dressed in medieval garb representing the ancient quarters of the city.

The **Gioco del Ponte** ★ (last Sunday in June) is great fun to watch, kicking off with a procession along the river Arno, followed by a sort of tug-of-war across Ponte di Mezzo. Two teams compete to see who can push a cart to the opposite end of the bridge first.

Fast Facts: Pisa

Chemist **Farmacia Comunale No. 5** is open 24 hours and a short walk west of Campo dei Miracoli at Via Cammeo 6a.

Hospital **Ospedale Santa Chiara** at Via Roma 67 (✆ *050 992111*) has English-speaking doctors.

Internet **Koine Internet** at Via dei Mille 3 is open 10am–midnight Mon–Fri, 1pm–midnight Sat–Sun (50¢ for 5 minutes, €2.50 for 30 minutes, €3.50 for an hour).

Pisa's Duomo and Campanile

TIP Campo dei Miracoli: Joint Admissions

Admission charges to the sights around Campo dei Miracoli (except the Leaning Tower) are tied together, although you can visit the medieval **Duomo** on a single ticket (€2). For the full art-and-architecture package, the **Baptistery**, **Campo Santo**, **Museo dell' Opera del Duomo**, **Museo delle Sinopie** (fresco sketches) and Duomo costs €10; to visit 3 of these is €8, and 2 costs €6. Seeing any individually (apart from the cathedral) is €5.

Toilets Public toilets can be found on Campo dei Miracoli, towards the **Campo Santo** entrance (50¢).

What to See & Do

Pisa's celebrated cluster of dramatic religious sites squat around the lawns of the **Campo dei Miracoli** ★★★ ('Field of Miracles'), 1km north-west of the centre and the river Arno, and a long walk from the train station – take the LAM Rossa (red) bus. Here you'll find the medieval Duomo, the long loggias of the Campo Santo, the richly inlaid Baptistery and yes, the Leaning Tower itself. The Campo, or Piazza del Duomo as it's known locally, is crawling with tourists in high season (although apart from the area behind the Duomo and Leaning Tower, parking yourself on the grass is frowned upon). Everything is free for children under 10, except the tower – and you must be 8 or older to climb it. For disappointed youngsters, a worthy alternative is the **Torre Guelfa**, see p. 116.

Leaning Tower of Pisa ★★★

AGE 8 AND UP

Piazza del Duomo 17. ☎ 050 560547. Advance tickets ***www.opapisa.it/box office/index.jsp****.*

If there's one sight guaranteed to impress the children, it's the curiously lopsided **bell tower** of the Duomo: the *Torre Pendente*. Started in 1173, construction continued (with two long interruptions) for about 200 years and was completed in 1360. The lean wasn't intentional; it started during the early phases of construction, and has been thrilling visitors ever since (see 'Why Doesn't It Fall Down?', below).

The only way to climb the arcaded tower is to book a **guided visit** in the office on the north side of the piazza – in peak season book online well in advance. You should be punctual and children 8–18 need to be accompanied by an adult (8–12s must hold your hand at all times). Leave bags at the cloakroom next to the ticket office, behind the Duomo opposite the Tower. The climb is surprisingly steep, with 293 steps to the top, around 55m up, but it's great fun as you really notice the lean and you are rewarded with fantastic views over Pisa. Watch out for slippery steps...

Open 10am–5pm daily Nov–Feb (9am–6pm 25th Dec–6th Jan), 9am–6pm daily Mar; 8am–8pm daily Apr–Sep, 9am–7pm daily Oct. ***Adm*** *€15 (€17 online).* ***Amenities*** *English, shop.*

INSIDER TIP

Don't buy so much as a *caffè* around the Campo dei Miracoli without checking the price first. It's not unusual to be charged **triple** what you're expecting.

Duomo AGE 5 AND UP

Piazza del Duomo 17. 050 560547. ***www.opapisa.it****.*

Pisa's magnificent **cathedral**, banded in red and white marble and decorated with tiers of arches and columns, is an exuberant example of Romanesque architecture, built between 1063 and the end of the 12th century. It's stunning from the outside and inside the snowy marble interior Giovanni Pisano's magnificent carved **pulpit** ★ (1302–10) in the nave is covered in relief panels illustrating scenes from the New Testament. It is supported by figures of the Archangel Michael and Jesus. Try to identify the Annunciation, the Nativity, the Adoration of the Magi and the Last Judgement. Nearby is a copy of the '**Lamp of Galileo**' (see 'The First Scientist', below).

Open *10am–1pm and 2–5pm daily Nov–Feb (9am–6pm 25th Dec–7th Jan), 10am–6pm daily 1st–13th Mar, until 7pm 14th–20th Mar and Oct, until 8pm 21st Mar–30th Sep.* ***Adm*** *€2 (free 1st Nov–1st Mar and Sun am), free under-10s.* ***Amenities*** *disabled access, English.*

Orto Botanico ALL AGES

Via Luca Ghini 5. 050 560045.

Lose the crowds and take a breather after the chaos of the Leaning Tower; this quiet slice of green, just south of Campo dei Miracoli, does the job perfectly. Established in 1544 and moved to here in 1595, it's the **oldest botanical garden** in Europe. It contains a school, ponds, shady palm trees, greenhouses and separate herb gardens – and there is plenty of space to run around. The eccentric original botanical institute is a sight to be seen, with its shell-embellished façade.

The First Scientist

Galileo Galilei (1564–1642) was born in Pisa, and is regarded as the founder of modern physics. In 1590 he's reputed to have climbed the Leaning Tower and dropped two wooden balls, of differing sizes, from the top. When they hit the ground at the same time, he had proof that **gravity** exerts the same force on objects no matter what they weigh. It makes a good story, but experts now think it's bunk.

The **Duomo** has its own Galileo legend: he supposedly discovered the laws of **pendulum** motion (a pendulum's swings always take the same amount of time) by watching the bronze chandelier now known as the 'Lamp of Galileo'.

Why Doesn't It Fall Down?

So, why doesn't it?

Until recently the Leaning Tower *was* falling down, just very, very **slowly**. If construction had been faster, it would have collapsed years ago. By 1990 the tower was leaning at a rate of 1.2mm per year and was closed to the public. An ambitious project to stabilise it involved removing soil from the base and adding lead counterweights; now it leans about 4.1m off-centre and is much safer. The lean is caused by a combination of gravity pulling towards the ground and subsidence under the foundations, but at the current angle the tower appears to be in equilibrium. The weight and foundation at its base balance the forces pulling it earthwards – for now.

How did it get like that?

The primary theory is that the ground underneath is too unstable and sandy to hold the weight of all that marble. Check out the magnificent **Baptistery** opposite: it's got a distinct lurch of its own.

Who built it?

This is a bit of a mystery. Giorgio Vasari, who wrote *Lives of the Artists* in 1550, claimed the original architect was local boy **Bonanno Pisano**, though recent studies have revealed an obscure architect, **Biduino**, as a more likely candidate. Giovanni di Simone worked on it in the 13th century, and Tommaso Pisano finished it off in 1360. The actual work was done by hundreds of builders, masons and craftsmen.

What's it for?

It's the bell tower (*campanile*) of the Duomo, housing seven **giant bells**.

How big is it?

The tower is 58.36m high from its foundations and 55.86m from the ground on the lowest side, 56.70m on the highest side. It weighs 14,453 tonnes.

Open *8.30am–1pm Mon–Sat.* ***Adm*** *free.* ***Amenities*** *disabled access, picnic area.*

Cantiere delle Navi Antiche di Pisa ★★★ FIND AGE 7 AND UP

Via Bianchi Bandinelli. 320 7599707. www.cantierenavipisa.it. Opposite San Rossore station.

Pisa's best-kept secret is a series of ancient Roman galleys discovered on the edge of reclaimed marshland that once served as **the city's harbour**, where the Auser and Arno rivers emptied into the sea. The museum is closed until at least 2010, but here you get to see the boats being painstakingly excavated, which is far more interesting for children. Join a **tour** (1¼ hour) and guides usually speak English.

Sometime between the 3rd century BC and 5th century AD, a series of catastrophic floods sunk at least 33 boats and preserved them in the mud. Since 1998, when a construction team stumbled on the first wreck, 11 have been recovered. The first part of the tour gives a bird's-eye view of the main dig site (sadly, you can't go down) where the shapes of wrecks are clearly visible. Beyond here lie laboratories where the restoration process is under-way: wooden hulls are encased in fibre glass 'cages' and treated with chemicals for several years before going on display. There's also an exhibition of items retrieved from the wrecks, coins and amphorae in pristine condition, with Roman fish paste still in them. Yeugh.

Tours *9am, 10.30am, midday, 2pm, 3.30pm Fri–Sun; by advance booking Tue–Thu.* ***Adm*** *€10 (English guide), €8 (Italian), free under-10s.* ***Amenities*** *English, shop.*

Torre Guelfa della Cittadella Vecchia ★★ AGE 5 AND UP

Lungarno Simonelli, Piazza Terzanaia. 055 3215446.

This is the best alternative to the Leaning Tower for crestfallen youngsters under 8 who were looking forward to climbing *something*. The solid-looking **red-brick tower** forms part of a ruined fortress built in the 15th century, right by the river. Destroyed in the Second World War, the tower was faithfully rebuilt in 1956. Inside there's an exhibition of Pisan coats of arms, but the real highlight is the clamber to the top and the **view ★★** back to Campo dei Miracoli. You can picnic on the lawn outside, or by the river Arno.

Open *3–7pm Tue–Sun Mar–Oct; 2–5pm Sat–Sun Nov–Feb.* ***Adm*** *€2, free under-10s.* ***Amenities*** *parking, picnic area.*

Museo Piaggio FIND

AGE 10 AND UP

Viale Rinaldo Piaggio 7, Pontedera. 0587 27171. ***www.museopiaggio.it****. Signposted 14km south-east of Pisa off SS67.*

Though Piaggio have made trains, planes and automobiles, they are known worldwide for one thing: the cute little **Vespa**. No surprise then that their **company museum** is largely given over to celebrating 60 plus years

TIP A Pisan Picnic

The cheapest place to stock up on picnic items near the centre of Pisa is **PAM**. The branch at Viale delle Cascine 1 (8am–8.30pm daily) is a short walk from Campo dei Miracoli, while Via Pascoli 8 (7.30am–8.30pm Mon–Sat, 9am–1pm Sun) is closer to the station. Alternatively, for cheap burgers (€3.90), sandwiches (€4) and slices of pizza (€4), try **Paninoteca Il Canguro** at Via Santa Maria 151, with stand-up tables only. It's open 10am–midnight daily during April and May but closed Sundays otherwise. For a treat, pop into **Caffè Federico Salza ★** at Borgo Stretto 57, a 19th-century café with pastries and sumptuous hot chocolate (8am–8.30pm Tue–Sun).

Messing About on the Arno

Between April and October take an open-top boat ride along the river Arno to admire Pisa from a new angle and give your feet a break. **Il Navicello** (☎ *050 530101. **www.ilnavicello.it***) runs trips into the **Parco Naturale Migliarino San Rossore Massaciuccoli** and back. Tickets (buy on board) are €8, €7 for children 3–10. You can catch the boat at San Paolo, not far from Santa Maria della Spina church, or at Roncioni on the north bank near San Matteo museum.

To properly explore the **Parco Naturale Migliarino San Rossore Massaciuccoli**, which has some super wildlife and **birdwatching** trails, the only way is by pre-booking guided tours on foot, bike or **horseback** ★. They depart from the visitor centre in Cascine Vecchie, 4½km west of Campo dei Miracoli. Guided visits on bikes of 2½ hours cost €9.80 and €8 for children 12 and under; on horseback a 1½ hour guided outing is €19.50. Email ***visitesr@tin.it*** or call ☎ *050 530101* (☎ *338 3662431* for riding tours). There is also a limited area around the visitor centre open to free public wandering on weekends and national holidays: bike hire costs €6 per hour or €16 all day (€4/or €13 for children's bikes). There's a **little train** that often runs after Sunday lunch. The park closes at 7.30pm.

of Italy's iconic scooter. This is the only place in the world where fashion-conscious mums, dads and teens get to see models from the 1940s and 50s all together – including the 1943 'Paperino' ('Donald Duck'), a prototype for the original 1946 Vespa. As well as the bikes, there are old adverts, early designs and photos, plus a multimedia presentation on the development process from idea to production line for budding designers. There are '**do not touch**' signs everywhere: this isn't a place to bring agile young sprites.

***Open** 10am–6pm Wed–Sat. **Adm** free. **Amenities** disabled access, English, shop.*

Museo di Storia Naturale at Certosa di Pisa ★ AGE 7 AND UP

*Via Roma 79, Calci. ☎ 050 2212970. **http://storianaturale.museo.unipi.it**. 6km east of Pisa; follow signs for 'certosa di Calci'.*

Tucked away inside the largest Carthusian monastery in Italy, the University of Pisa's **natural history museum** diverts children for an hour or two. There's a huge collection of stuffed carnivores and reptiles – and the giant whale skeletons in the glass-walled gallery have a lovely view over olive groves and the rolling terrain of the Monte Pisano. The highlights are the multimedia re-creations of landscapes from the age of dinosaur, all reconstructed from local fossil records. A realistic **giant mako shark** will scare

Glorious *Gelato*

La Cittadella at Via dei Mille 18 (7am–7.30pm daily) is an excellent place to grab a *gelato* between Campo dei Miracoli and the city centre. At the bottom of Pisa's main shopping street, Borgo Stretto, near the river at Piazza Garibaldi 11, **La Bottega del Gelato** ★ (*050 575467*) serves the best in town: try a cone (€1.30–2.50) of exotic fruit flavours, chocolate fondant, Nutella, pine nuts or trifle (*zuppa Inglese*). It's open 9am–midnight daily.

little ones. For children with sight problems, there's an animal-themed **tactile room** ★. Signage inside the museum is largely in Italian, but if you call ahead they will try to organise a guided tour in English.

Visits to the lavishly Baroque **monastery** itself are by guided tour (1 hour; usually Italian only). Most interesting are the cells where the monks passed their years in silence. Tours leave hourly on the half-hour 8.30am–6.30pm Tue–Sat; the last visit on Sunday goes at 12.30pm. It costs €4, €2 18–25s and under-18s are free.

Open *10am–7pm Tue–Fri, until 8pm Sat–Sun Jul–mid-Sep; 9am–6pm Tue–Sat and 10am–7pm Sun otherwise.* ***Adm*** *€7, €3.50 children 6–18.* ***Amenities*** *parking.*

Shopping

The **touristy stalls** around the Campo dei Miracoli may seem a bit tacky, but children will love the Leaning Tower T-shirts, mugs and pens all for under €15. You should at least buy a model of the tower: a small one will set you back €1.

Old-fashioned toy store **Città del Sole** has a branch at Via San Lorenzo 65 (*050 970930*) while **Hobby Centro** at Borgo Stretto 57 (*050 580888*) has a large selection of traditional games. It's open 4–8pm Monday, 9am–1pm and 4–8pm Tue–Sat. Baby chain **Prénatal** has a branch at Borgo Stretto 14 (*050 579618*).

LUCCA

Lucca ★ has just about ditched its 'undiscovered' label. This cobbled provincial capital, wrapped in a perfect set of walls, is now firmly on the Tuscan town trail. But it's still one of Italy's most delightful towns, with a flamboyant cathedral, lovely squares, and numerous charming Liberty-style shop fronts advertising the occasional quirky bargain; there's plenty to keep you occupied for a day or two.

Essentials

Lucca is easiest to reach by **train** (*892021. **www.trenitalia.it***). There are regular links with **Florence** (1½ hour €4.90), **Pisa**

LUCCA

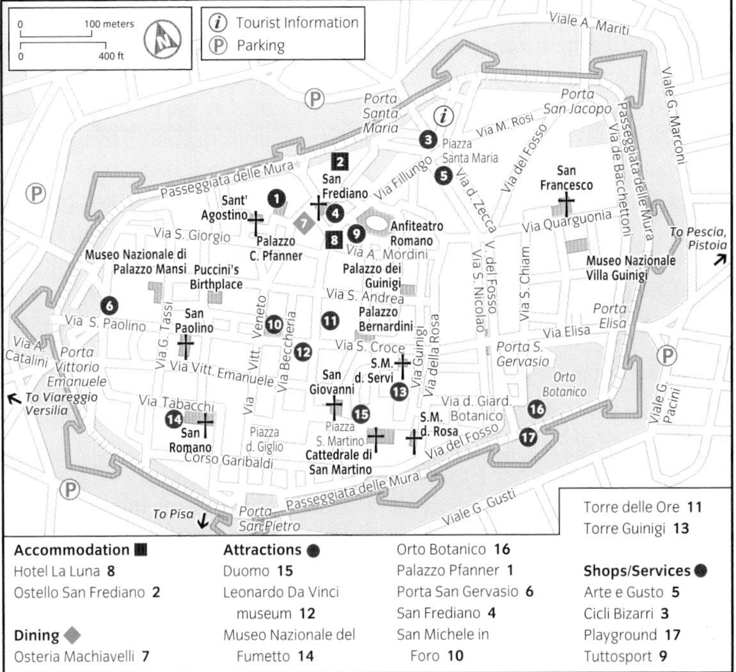

(25 minutes €2.30) and **Pistoia** (50 minutes €3.40). The station is in Piazza Ricasoli, just south of the walls.

Getting there by **car** is simple enough: Lucca is bang on the **A11**, 72km west of Florence. The town is busy and **parking** can be tricky. Your only options for free are outside the walls: north of town there's the vaguely signposted **Palasport**. Just inside the eastern walls, it's €1 per hour to park underground at **Piazza Mazzini**; turn right as you come through Porta Elisa. It's a 10-minute walk to the action.

The main **tourist office** (☎ *0583 919931*. ***www.luccaturismo.it***) is at Piazza Santa Maria 35. It's open 9am–8pm daily between April and October, 9am–12.30pm and 3–6.30pm Mon–Sat otherwise; don't expect too much enthusiasm. Events are advertised in English-language monthly **Grapevine** (€2).

Children might enjoy some of the modern acts at Lucca's **Summer Festival**: the programme is regularly updated at ***www.summer-festival.com***. Recent headliners have included Joss Stone, George Michael and Norah Jones.

Around the Town

In theory, Lucca is a **pedestrian** *città*, but that's 'pedestrian' in the

Italian sense of allowing cars and buses to drive everywhere. It's a town of secret alleys, misshapen piazzas and hidden courtyards, tricky to get oriented in. Find **Via Fillungo** ★, the medieval mall, and take it from there. You'll eventually come across **Piazza Anfiteatro**, where the outline of a Roman amphitheatre has been preserved. The gates into the piazza are the very ones that gladiators walked through. And the phenomenal façade you'll bump into in Piazza San Michele is **San Michele in Foro** ★. The inside's a let-down, but the exterior is a masterpiece of elaborate **Pisan-Romanesque styling**.

Cattedrale di San Martino

AGE 10 AND UP

Piazza San Martino. 📞 0583 490530.

Lucca's gloriously asymmetrical Pisan-Romanesque **Cathedral of San Martino** is a forbidding space. The towering ceiling and constant twilight conceal some rather grim Baroque art. Inside a chapel that looks like Brighton Pavillion, the ***Volto Santo*** is a poignant image of Jesus on the cross, reputedly carved by Nicodemus at the time of the Crucifixion. Carbon dating nevertheless places the cross firmly in the 13th century, but it's processed through the town by candlelight every 13th September in the **Luminara di Santa Croce** ★. Far more interesting is the **Tomb of Ilaria del Carretto** ★ in the Sacristy (€2). Jacopo della Quercia's masterpiece depicts Ilaria, wife of Paolo Guinigi, 15th-century ruler of Lucca. She died in childbirth and the dog at her feet symbolises fidelity. The stray lock of hair on her forehead and the folds in her dress make you forget that what you're seeing was hewn from local Carrara marble. A vast antique market is held in the piazza outside on the third Sunday of each month; it spreads into the streets around the cathedral.

Cathedral of San Martino, Lucca

TIP Montecarlo or Bust?

For a local tipple, including Montecarlo DOC and a special red from Valgiano, **Arte e Gusto** (☎ *0583 953611*) at Via Fillungo 220 sells wines only from the Lucchese area.

***Open** 9.30am–5.45pm Mon–Fri, until 6.45pm Sat; 9.30–10.45am and 12–6pm Sun. **Adm** free. **Amenities** English, shop.*

Museo Nazionale del Fumetto (Comic Museum) ★ FIND

AGE 7 AND UP

Piazza San Romano. ☎ 0583 56326. ***www.museonazionaledelfumetto.it.***

The giant plastic **Spiderman** above the door gives it away: this isn't *just* the pretty, medieval convent of San Romano. In 2004 part of the building and courtyard were converted into a multimedia shrine to the **comic**.

The adult collection features Italian cult classics mixed with familiar international names, including original 1940s *Topolino* (Mickey Mouse) comics, 1960s *Batmans* and 1980s *Supermans*. Best of all is the **Viaggio nel '900**, where you can wander among lifesize models of Clark Kent's phone box and Mickey's kitchen. Children of all ages are free to scrawl in themed creative spaces like Disney's *Art Attack* room and a *Casa di Pooh*.

Under-12s must be accompanied at all times. There is English signage and leaflets, but unless you read Italian, a handful of the exhibits will be a little remote.

***Open** 10am–7pm (5.30pm winter) Tue–Sun. **Adm** €6, €4 children 4–10. **Amenities** disabled access, English, shop.*

Biking the Walls ★★

AGE 3 AND UP

Blame Marie-Louise Bourbon, for it was she who turned Lucca's defensive ramparts into shady boulevards of plane, chestnut and ilex. Built between 1500 and 1645, the 11 bastions, six gates and 4km of flat wall are ideal for **cycling and sightseeing**. Start in Piazza Santa Maria: hire your bikes next to the tourist office at **Cicli Bizzarri** (☎ *0583 496031*). It's open 8.30am–1pm and 2.30–7.30pm Mon– Sat, and Sundays March–September. Bikes are €2.50 for an hour (plenty for one circuit); tandems or *Cammellini* (tot bikes hooked to the back of yours) are €5.50.

On summer afternoons and weekends, the ramparts are crowded with families, joggers, cyclists and people having picnics or lazing on the grass. Head clockwise, with the town on your right. You'll soon see a couple of oak trees growing from the roof of the **Torre Guinigi**. They're best viewed from right above Porta Elisa, where there are **swings and a slide**. About a minute farther along, there's the same again and with shade. On the right is the **Orto Botanico**,

Lucca

complete with Tuscan plants and lily-pads. The elevated ramparts provide an alternative view of the cathedral (see above), and square **campanile**; the red-brick tower visible just after is the **Torre delle Ore**, Lucca's clock tower. Still farther, the gate standing in a field next to another playground is the medieval **Porta San Gervasio**. Just before you get back to Piazza Santa Maria, look down into the manicured Baroque gardens of the **Palazzo Pfanner**. The church of **San Frediano** stands behind with a fine 13th-century **mosaic** ★ shimmering on its façade.

A couple of warnings: there's plenty of room on the ramparts but **no fence** on the inner edge of the walls. Cycle that side of young ones if they're pedalling themselves; there were two fatal accidents in 2006. And those little taps you keep seeing: they're **drinking water**, so use them. It gets very hot and sunny up there in summer.

INSIDER TIP

A cool way for older children to 'do' the walls is on **rollerblades**. Alas, no one in Lucca rents them out yet. Bring your own or buy them in child sizes at **TuttoSport** (☏ *0583 91600*) at Via Mordini 25.

PISTOIA & ITS PROVINCE

Many visitors to Tuscany neglect Pistoia ★ in favour of its more famous neighbours, but if you take the trouble to spend some time in this vibrant little town, you won't regret it.

Situated at the base of the Apennines, the city has long shed its medieval reputation for mindless violence to become northern Tuscany's **market garden**. It is famous for its plant nurseries; the

Leo in Lucca

If you can't get to Vinci (see p. 126), there's a small Leonardo da Vinci museum (***www.matart.it***) at Via Roma 20. It's along similar lines, with the added bonus that you can touch and operate most of the 40 wooden models from Leonardo's countless books, known as *Codices*. It's open daily 9.30am–7.30pm; entry is steep at €5, €4 for anyone in full-time education, under-6s free.

surrounding plains are lined with orderly rows of trees and shrubs in back-to-back *vivaii*. Its medieval, walled *centro storico* is almost intact and incorporates some wonderful buildings and great art. It repays an extended stroll.

If you're ensconced in Florence, three **trains** (*892021. **www.trenitalia.it***) an hour leave Santa Maria Novella for Pistoia. The journey takes 40 minutes and costs €2.80.

Start at the **tourist office** (*0573 21622. **www.pistoia.turismo.toscana.it***) at Piazza del Duomo 4: Pistoia's a maze, so you'll need a map. Head for the tallest tower you can see to find it; the office is open daily 9am–1pm (open 10am Sundays) and 3–6pm. **Piazza del Duomo** ★ itself is a fine civic square, superior to anything in Lucca, dominated by the zebra-hooped **Baptistery** and Romanesque **Cattedrale di San Zeno** (*0573 25095*). The cathedral's interior is less overbearing than Lucca's, rich in monuments and the half-ruined **crypt** is fun to explore. Admission is free; it's open 8am–12.30pm and 3.30–7pm, and between May and September it only closes at lunchtime on Sundays and holidays.

Ospedale del Ceppo, Pistoia

If you've got time, walk five minutes north of the piazza to see the **Ospedale del Ceppo**, or rather the glazed terracotta **frieze** on its façade. Carved by Giovanni della Robbia in the early 1500s, it features a motley collection of Pistoiese pilgrims and sick people. The building is still a hospital.

INSIDER TIP
On Saturday mornings you'll find stalls selling great value **children's shoes** in Piazza dello Spirito Santo.

Sant'Antonio Abate (Cappella del Tau) ★ AGE 5 AND UP

Corso Silvano Fredi 70. 0573 24212.

This plain stone cube right on a main road, houses Pistoia's little-known **art treasure**. The interior surface of the chapel was frescoed by **Niccolò di Tommaso** and **Antonio Vite** in (probably) the 1370s. Parts of the walls are badly mutilated, but the ceiling is almost complete. The frescoes relate Biblical stories, starting from the back-right corner as you walk in (facing you is **Paradise**).

The ceiling and top level illustrate stories from the **Old Testament**: the *Creation* and *Noah's Ark* are easily spotted. The middle level narrates the **New Testament**: look for the *Nativity*, the *Annunciation* and the *Slaughter of the Innocents*. If you ask, there's a photocopied sheet (Italian only) to help you out. It's an intimate place, which you'll likely have to yourself – worth the trip here alone, never mind 15 minutes of your time.

Right across the road, **Magico Chiosco** knocks up cheap, tasty *panini* (from €1.70).

Open *8.15am–1.30pm Mon–Sat.* ***Adm*** *free.*

Pistoia Zoo AGE 2 AND UP

Via di Pieve a Celle 160. 0573 911219. ***www.zoodipistoia.it****. 2km west of 'Pistoia Ovest' exit from ring road.*

It's no wonder the **Giardino Zoologico di Pistoia** is packed with Italian families at weekends: it's by far the best in Tuscany. The 600 animals, including big cats and lots of snakes, keep little ones transfixed. Every weekend there's a free, all-day 'Incontri Bestiali' programme: children (and parents) can touch and learn about tortoises, harmless snakes, goats and the like. Structured children's programmes ('*per piccoli visitatori*') highlight the zoo's commitment to conservation. Activities (ages 3–12; Italian only) are held in the **Biodiversity Lab** and in the zoo every weekday morning in summer plus the second Saturday of every month. Best of all is the **Moonlight Zoo** ★ (10pm June to September only): your one-hour guided visit takes in animals that don't do much during daylight. See wolves, owls and lynx at their most active.

INSIDER TIP
A **taxi** to the zoo from Pistoia station (*0573 534444*) costs a fixed €10 and your receipt is worth 10% off zoo entry.

Public Scribbles

Young Italians, especially south of the Apennines, are unfathomably attached to their indelible markers. The **graffiti** is rarely original. An amorous 'so-and-so *ti amo*'; *forza!* the local team; occasionally, the mayor is a *fascista* or *comunista*. Saying something rude about the neighbours is delivered with untranslatable relish – one reason not to teach the children *too much* Italian vocabulary, perhaps. The Sienese have centuries of issues with the Florentines; *Lucchese* look down their noses at the Pisans. But they're all agreed, Romans are... we're too polite to write exactly what. *Campanilismo* – literally, loyalty to one's bell tower – is alive and well in teenage Tuscany.

Email the zoo in advance (***E:*** ***info@zoodipistoia.it***) to book. One of the Moonlight guides speaks English – ask when he's guiding.

Open *9am–7pm daily Apr–Sep, until 5pm Oct–Mar.* ***Adm*** *€10.50, €8.50 children 3–9.* ***Children's programmes*** *€15 inc. entry.* ***Moonlight Zoo*** *€10/8 (€29 family) inc. entry.* ***Amenities*** *parking (€2), picnic area, playground, restaurant.*

Parco di Pinocchio ★ AGE 2–7

Collodi. ☎ 0572 429342. ***www.pinocchio.it/park.htm****. Signposted off SS435 15km east of Lucca; BluBus 109 from Pescia station.*

More 'themed park' than theme park, this little world of Carlo Lorenzini's creation, Pinocchio, lies midway between Lucca and Pistoia. Negotiate some tricky first impressions (**overpriced**, needs a lick of paint) and you will start to enjoy yourself. The main 'Paese dei Balocchi' lies beyond the giant mosaic, a fantastical maze of steps, ramps and bronze statues of characters from Lorenzini's tale, skilfully designed to keep tots wondering what's round the next corner. The giant whale at the story's climax is revealed gradually through a bamboo forest.

INSIDER TIP

If the children don't know **Carlo Lorenzini**'s surreal story, make your first stop the **mechanical theatre**, where an English handout and original 1920s marionettes bring them up to speed.

As well as the maze, there's **Painting Corner** (10am–12.30pm and 3–5.30pm), three live **shows** a day (Italian only), carousels (€1) and Pinocchio-themed face-painting (weekends only). The whole park could use a clean up, but the old-fashioned style is perfect for imaginative youngsters.

Open *8.30am–dusk daily.* ***Adm*** *€10, €7 children 3–14.* ***Combined ticket*** *€18/14 with Villa Garzoni Gardens and Butterfly House (☎ 0572 429590).* ***Amenities*** *bar/café, disabled access, entertainment (Mar–Sep), English, parking, picnic area, restaurant (children's menu €10), shop.*

Eating Local

After a visit to the Parco di Pinocchio, head for Cecco ★ (*☎ 0572 477955. **www.ristorantececco.com***), at Viale Forti 84 in Pescia. The menu features seasonal choices from local market gardens: the freshest artichoke, asparagus or Sorano beans to accompany *ossobuco* or *bistecca alla Fiorentina*. In addition to its gourmet reputation, service is impeccably **friendly**. Main courses are in the range €9–16, and there's a fine local wine list. They also rent basic, air-conditioned rooms (€45 double, €15 extra bed).

Museo Leonardiano ★

OVERRATED **AGE 12 AND UP**

*Vinci. ☎ 0571 933251. **www.museoleonardiano.it**. 24km south of Pistoia.*

Yes, *that* Vinci (actually, it's just outside Pistoia's province, but let's not quibble). Such has been the success of Tuscany's original Leonardo da Vinci museum that it has spread: the **Castello dei Conti Guidi**'s two floors of marvellous machines were joined in 2004 by another at **Palazzina Uzielli**. Though the new building has some multimedia additions, like PC terminals showing the machines in 3D, the drill's the same: models of the weird, wonderful and downright genius from the Renaissance master's *Codex Atlanticus*. Highlights include the massive crane, the famous flying (actually, flapping) machine and some cool stuff on **optics**.

That's the good news. Alas, the presentation is too dry for young ones. In fact, the physics is so complex that it's really not for children at all. English descriptions disappear when you need them most, in the optics room (there are photocopied sheets if you ask). Worst of all, the museum is **way too small** when big groups turn up, which is all the time. I blame Dan Brown.

That said, it's just about worth the drive for mechanically minded older children and adults – the trip south from Pistoia through the olive terraces is a corker, and there's a super **campsite** nearby (p. 133). **Avoid** the rest of Vinci, though: it's a well-oiled rip-off machine whose efficiency would have made Leo proud. There are similar Leonardo museums in Florence (p. 59) and Lucca (p. 123); for more on Leo see p. 54.

***Open** 9.30am–6.15pm daily Mar–Oct, until 5.15pm Nov–Feb. **Adm** €5, €3.50 children 14–18 or adult accompanying under-18s, €2 children 6–14. **Amenities** English, shop.*

VIAREGGIO

A smart, popular seaside resort since the 19th century, Viareggio is the principal town of **Versilia**, Tuscany's Riviera. It has retained an air of faded gentility with grandiose belle-époque buildings lining its long seafront: think

Brighton with better sand. In summer, it is heaving with holidaymakers (mostly from Florence) and in many ways is the quintessential Italian beach destination. It'll be bucket-and-spade heaven for your children.

Essentials

Viareggio is at the junction of the **A12** and **A11**, 22km from both Pisa and Lucca. If you drive, there are plenty of central spaces and **car parks**; but arrive late on a summer weekend and you may have trouble getting on the seafront. Parking generally costs about 75¢ for the first hour and 75¢ each half-hour thereafter.

By **train** (*892021*. ***www.trenitalia.it***), there are easy, regular connections to/from **Lucca** (20 minutes €2.30), **Pisa** (20 minutes €2.30) and **Florence** (1½ hour €6.30). If you're based in any of those, don't come by car in summer.

The main **tourist office** (*0584 962223*. ***www.aptversilia.it***) is tucked away in a courtyard at Viale Carducci 10. It's open 9am–2pm and 3–7pm Mon–Sat (7.30pm in summer) and 9am–1pm Sunday (also 4–7pm July and August). There's a **cashpoint** next door. The train station also has a small tourist office (Piazza Dante. *0584 46382*. ***stazione.vg@aptversilia.it***).

INSIDER TIP

Hotels in Viareggio are often overpriced. Do as Florentines do and make it a **day trip** destination.

Carnival

Since 1873, Viareggio has hosted Italy's second-biggest **Carnevale** ★, after Venice. The seaside comes alive with floats, masked dances, noise and party atmosphere with a child-friendly flavour. Events take place throughout **February**, with the main parades on Sundays and Shrove Tuesday. Tickets for these cost €13, €9 for 11–12-year-olds; under-10s go free. Call *0584 47077* or email ***biglietteria@ilcarnevale.com*** to book. It's advisable to book accommodation well in advance. See ***www.viareggio.ilcarnevale.com*** for more.

Around the Town & Down the Beach

The town's famous 'sight' on the promenade, the Art Nouveau **Gran Caffè Margherita**, is a puffed-up architectural oddity,

Viareggio Carnival statue

but the interior is worth a peek. The all-things-marine displays at the new **Museo della Marineria** (0584 391004. ***www.museomarineria.info***) across the canal at Via Peschiera 9 kills half an hour. It's open Friday to Sunday 6–11pm in summer, 4–7pm in winter, and costs €2.50, free for under-14s. While you're over there, see the **day's catch** traded at what is still a working **fishing port**.

The real draw is Viareggio's **beach** ★: wide and flat, it has a shallow shelf so little ones can paddle safely. Various private '**bathing companies**' (*stabilimenti balneari*) guard their own stretches. In return for a fee, you get a patch of groomed sand, facilities to change and shower, and a parasol and sunlounger; some (bizarrely) even have swimming pools. Prices fluctuate by day and season, and you'll get a deal if you're here for a week and book with one company for the duration. The friendly **Tre Stelle** at Viale Margherita 64/1 (*0584 44370*) has just enough *aloha* to keep it interesting; it's €7 per day (€5 low season).

There's also a public beach, **Le Dune** ★, 1½km south of town along Viale Europa. If you're out this way, there's a playground with **swings and slides** at the corner of Viale Kennedy and Viale dei Tigli, and plenty of shady strolling or **cycling** under the *pineta*.

Parco Pitagora FIND AGE 1 TO 11

Via Aurelia, Lido di Camaiore. 0584 611008. ***www.parcopitagora.com****. Off SS1 1½ km north of Viareggio, junction Via Pitágora.*

Ask the tourist office to show you this park on the map: it's dastardly to find, but worth it for the children. There are carousels, a mini-train, **bouncy castles**, trampolines, bumper hovercraft, tyre swings, slides... you get the idea. Older children can play basketball or video games and

Puccini's Lake

Separated from Viareggio by a glorious avenue of lime trees, Torre del Lago is forever bound to the composer of *Tosca*, *Madam Butterfly* and *La Bohème*: Giacomo Puccini (1858–1924). Book a guided tour of his **villa** (*0584 341445.* ***www.giacomopuccini.it***); plus, a few companies run one-hour boat trips on reed-fringed **Lago di Massaciuccoli**. It's a WWF reserve, part of the **Parco Naturale di Migliarino San Rossore Massaciuccoli** (see 'Messing About on the Arno', p. 117), where you can spot rare marsh birds and enjoy the silence. Buy tickets on board: €6, children €3. The lake also provides the backdrop for the opera-fest that is the summer **Puccini Festival** (*0584 359322.* ***www.puccinifestival.it***). There's a seasonal **ticket office** at Viale Puccini 257/a; expect to pay €35–125.

Lago Massaciuccoli

there is plenty of shade for everyone. Entry is free, you pay for rides with **tokens** on sale 10am–12.30pm, 3.30–7.30pm and 9pm–midnight: they're 80¢ each or €10 for 20.

***Open** 9.30–midnight daily Jun–Sep, 9.30am–7pm daily Oct–May. **Adm** free. **Amenities** baby change, café/bar, disabled access, parking.*

Oasi LIPU di Massaciuccoli

ALL AGES

*Via del Porto 6, Massaciuccoli. ☎ 0584 975567. **www.oasilipumassaciuccoli.org**. 6km south of Massarosa, dir Pisa.*

If you can't make it down to the nature reserves of the Maremma, this is the best spot in northern Tuscany for a young **ornithologist**. A series of raised walkways above the silent reed-beds link birdwatching hides on the fringes of Lago di Massaciuccoli opposite Torre del Lago. Residents include the marsh harrier and several species of wader. Check the website or call ahead for events. **Guided boat tours** of the lake and its inhabitants (€9) leave from the jetty on summer Sundays after lunch.

***Open** daily, except Tue Nov–Feb. **Adm** free. **Amenities** canoe hire, disabled access, parking.*

TO THE HILLS! TUSCANY'S FAR NORTH

Tuscany's north-east corner is defined by the impassable Apennines, which shadow the **Garfagnana** and the **Lunigiana** ★. Just north of the Alpi Apuane, the Garfagnana is a treasure box of wild crags, endless chestnut forest and miles of rock formations above and below ground. Its trough was cut by the river Serchio, which threads along the core; the only busy bit of the valley follows the SS445 along its banks. Escape from there, and you're in an emerald green heaven for walkers, climbers and potholers. If that sounds like you,

FUN FACT **Ghostly Sightings**

When the Garfagnana's main dam enclosing Lago di Vagli empties every 10 years for cleaning, a former iron-working village reappears. **Fabbriche di Careggine**'s rebirth from 70m of water is expected again in 2014.

you'll need expert guidance: contact the **tourist office** in Barga (*0584 724743*). Also look out for Vittorio Verole-Bozzello's *Discover Garfagnana* (€15), with 38 itineraries.

The Lunigiana, named after its port, is west of Garfagnana and even **emptier**. Aside from the **marble quarries** at Carrara on its edge, its insular, Ligurian terrain is rarely visited by anyone, Italian or British. You'll have isolated villages, rugged vistas, twisting mountain roads and terraced olive groves all to yourself.

Grotta del Vento ★ AGE 4 AND UP

Vergemoli. 0583 722024. ***www.grottadelvento.com****. Gallicano turn-off from SS445, 16km south-west of Barga.*

Dip your toes into the Garfagnana at the **Wind Cave**, a massive complex of formations, waterfalls and bottomless pits cut from the karst, an ideal place to bring physical geography alive for GCSE students. Trips through the cave are guided only (knowledgeable guides speak English) and there are three itineraries: the obvious choice with young children is the first and even that has **300 steps**. The white and gold tongues of **calcite** inside the living cave are things of surreal beauty: they are hard as marble, look like sponge and forever change with stalactites, stalagmites 'cave pearls' and spaghetti rock formations shifting and growing. Come when it's raining and you're accompanied by the constant din of rushing water.

Take **warm clothing**: it's always 11°C inside the cave. Get here early during peak season or at weekends. Baby backpacks and pushchairs are not allowed; front-loading baby slings are fine. Drive up the ramp when you see the '*Grotta del Vento*' sign: you don't need to pay €3 to park outside.

Open *10am–6pm daily (****itinerary 1*** *leaves on the hour except 1pm;* ***itinerary 2*** *11am, 3pm, 4pm, 5pm;* ***itinerary 3*** *10am, 2pm); itinerary 1 only Mon–Sat Nov–Mar.* ***Adm*** *itinerary 1 €7.50, €5 children under 11; itinerary 2 €12/8.50; itinerary 3 €17/11.50.* ***Amenities*** *bar/café, English, parking, shop.*

Carrara's Marble Quarries

ALL AGES

0585 844136. ***infocarrara@aptmassacarrara.it****. Colonnata, Fantiscritti and Torano are north of Carrara; follow signs from town.*

David woz here: the piece of rock that became Michelangelo's **David** (see p. 57), started life in the marble quarries just outside Carrara. Tour the three major quarries by car, on a well-signed and trodden trail.

The world-famous mines at **Colonnata**, **Fantiscritti** and Torano are all still operational. Carrara's tourist office advise that you don't attempt the drive up to Torano, but you can get close enough to appreciate the scale and smell the dust. Allow 1½ hours for the circuit by road.

To visit a working *galleria*, email ***infocarrara@apt massacarrara.it*** for '*visita una cava di marmo*' guided tours.

Open *always.* **Adm** *free.* **Amenities** *shops (marble souvenirs).*

INSIDER TIP

The most spectacular way into the Lunigiana by car is the **SS446** from Carrara to Fosdinovo. The road follows a ridge with unbelievable **views** ★★ of the Apennines and back to the Versilia coast. From Carrara follow signs for **Castelpoggio** or **Campocecina**.

Parco Avventura Fosdinovo ★★ FIND ALL AGES

320 9060749. ***www.parco avventurafosdinovo.com****. 500m north of Fosdinovo dir. Fivizzano.*

Get harnessed up for **extreme** fun at this new adventure park on the edge of the Alpi Apuane. Hidden in a pine wood off the road are a quad-bike circuit, mountain bike tracks (rent or bring your own) and a whole bunch of **treetop fun**: zip-slides, Tibetan bridges, cargo nets and the like. There are six different levels of difficulty, starting with a *percorso* for 4-year-olds, but the focus is on **teens** and young adults. Despite the madcap atmosphere, safety is taken very seriously. Recommended for all but the most confirmed vertigo-sufferer – bored teens most of all. Sundays are busy and prices are a little steep.

Open *10am–7pm daily May–15th Sep; 11am–5pm Sat–Sun Mar–Apr and 15th Sep–Nov.* **Adm** *€20, €15 under-18s, €6 baby courses only; 3 hour maximum stay.* **MTB hire** *€3.50 per hour, €5.50 half-day.* **Mini-quads** *€8 for 15 minutes* **Amenities** *café, English, parking, picnic area.*

Museo delle Statue-Stele Lunigianesi ★ AGE 7 AND UP

Castello del Piagnaro, Pontrémoli.
0187 831439. ***www.lunigiana.net****.*

This little museum, in a 16th-century castle above **Pontremoli** ★, hosts one of Tuscany's **weirdest** collections. Iron Age stone figures (known as *stele*) have been found in Europe from Galicia to the Crimea, but rarely so precisely carved or in such concentration as around the Lunigiana. That so many have been decapitated is a sure sign the Catholic Church got here before the archaeologists.

For more itineraries around Pontrémoli, Tuscany's northernmost town, the old pilgrim road, the **Via Francigena**, or the Lunigiana, contact the provincial tourist office: **APT Massa-Carrara** (*0585 240063.* ***www.apt massacarrara.it***).

Open *9am–midday and 3–6pm daily Apr–Sep; 9am–midday and 2–5pm Tue–Sun Oct–Mar.* **Adm** *€4, €2 children 6–16.* **Amenities** *English (audio-guide), shop.*

TIP

Ski Toscana

Skiing 1400m up in the Apennines at Abetone (**☎** *0573 60231*. ***www.pistoia.turismo.toscana.it***) is none too shabby between December and March. A day-pass costs €28–33 for adults and €23.50–27.50 for under-10s, depending on the season. Take the SS12 65km north from Lucca. The resort (with slopes for all abilities) is right by the main road.

FAMILY-FRIENDLY ACCOMMODATION

Hotel La Luna

Corte Compagni 12, Lucca. ☎ *0583 493634.* ***www.hotellaluna.com***.

Good family hotels inside Lucca's walls are rare, but if you skip the **overpriced** breakfast buffet (€11), this place offers decent value just off Via Fillungo. Rooms are plain, bathrooms could do with an update but are plenty big enough for a family, and downstairs there's a TV room and **free Internet** to keep the children in touch with the outside world. Note, only room 122 has a bath.

You can drive right up to the hotel to unload. They have a covered car park, for which you'll need to book ahead.

Rooms *29.* ***Rates*** *Double €112, triple €140, quad €150. Breakfast €11. Cot €16 per night.* ***Credit*** *MC, V.* ***Amenities*** *bar, parking (€12).* ***In room*** *A/C, safe, sat TV.*

Behind the Tower ★★ VALUE

Porta Nuova, Pisa. ***www.behindthetower.com***.

This simple **rental apartment** is ideal for families of up to five, providing the freedom of having a fully equipped kitchen and a lot more space than a hotel room – it's also a **major deal**, so book early. The rooms are bright and modern: there's one bedroom with a double or twin, and a living room with a sofa-bed big enough for two. Alternatively a third bed is available (free) for the bedroom or kitchen. The spotless bathroom is compact but big enough. Owners Marcel and Gloria will pick you up from the airport (free) and provide all the local information you need, though the central location is only five minutes' walk to Campo dei Miracoli. For now there is **no air conditioning**, only fans in summer, and no TV.

Note that you must contact the owners via email to book; it's pointless turning up at the door.

Apartment *1.* ***Rates*** *3–6 nights at €80 per night for 4, or €500 per week.* ***Credit*** *AmEx, MC, V online deposit only.* ***Amenities*** *disabled access.* ***In apartment*** *fridge, shower only.*

Hotel Francesco

Via Santa Maria 129, Pisa. ☎ *050 554109.* ***www.hotelfrancesco.com***.

This no-frills hotel 100m south of Campo dei Miracoli has triple rooms that make a reasonably cheap central option for families.

Note that these can fit four comfortably if someone is small enough to sleep in the double bed, or if you **book a cot** in advance (free). Alternatively, try and secure rooms 201 and 202, which can be connected and share an elegant terrace overlooking the botanical garden. Rooms are bright and modern but fairly plain.

***Rooms** 13. **Rates** Double €70–100, triple €100–135. Cots free. Breakfast €5. **Credit** AmEx, MC, V. **Amenities** babysitting, bike rental (€10 per day), disabled access, Internet (free), parking (€8), restaurant. **In room** A/C, fridge, safe, sat TV.*

Hotel Royal Victoria ★

*Lungarno Pacinotti 12, Pisa. ☎ 050 940111. **www.royalvictoria.it**.*

Pisa's first hotel (opened in 1839 and still owned by the Piegaja family) is also the most welcoming for families, set in a romantic series of medieval houses and towers by the river. Children under 12 stay free, meaning that a family of three can stay in a double rather than a triple (in practice this doesn't save much). The hotel has a choice of configurations for triples (3 single beds or 1 double and 1 single) and quads (4 singles or 1 double and 2 singles), while the family suite sleeps 4 (1 double, 2 singles). None of the rooms are non-smoking, but guests are asked voluntarily to observe a ban, and none of the staff smoke. All rooms are fairly spacious, but get one that faces the river for the best views.

***Rooms** 48. **Rates** Double €138, triple €147, quad €152, suite €244. Cots free. **Credit** AmEx, MC, V. **Amenities** babysitting, bar, disabled access, parking (€18), restaurant. **In room** A/C, fridge, safe, TV.*

Borgo Antico Fattoria di Casalbosco, Pistoia, see p. 113.

Camping Barco Reale ★

*Via Nardini 11, San Baronto. ☎ 0573 88332. **www.barcoreale.com**. On SP9 between Pistoia and Empoli.*

This campsite might just have the best **views** in northern Tuscany: from its ridge on Monte Albano you look down on Pistoia and Prato to the north and all the way to Livorno and the Ligurian Sea to the west.

The **mobile homes** are plain, adequately sized and well-equipped (bring your own towels) – and the site's a

TIP

Budget Lucca

The best value inside Lucca's walls is to be found at the Ostello San Frediano ★ (☎ *0583 469957. **www.ostellolucca.it***), at Via della Cavallerizza 12. Public areas are cool and quiet, even quite grand; split-level family rooms have private bathrooms and reasonable amounts of space. You'll need to book well ahead: at €92 for a room sleeping four just off Via Fillungo, it's a **serious deal**. Breakfast is €1.60 extra; they don't provide cots.

child-friendly bonanza, with activities all summer, and plenty of shade and the *montagna*'s breeze when the day heats up. Between late June and mid-August, it's always full: booking ahead (Sat–Sat only) is **essential**. Eurocamp (see p. 245) come here.

Pitches *230 (+ 26 mobile homes) (closed Oct–Mar).* ***Rates*** *Adults €6.70–9.50, children €2.60–5.80, pitch €9.50–14, discounts for 5+ nights.* ***Mobile homes*** *family of 4 €40–117 per night. Cots free.* ***Credit*** *MC. V.* ***Amenities*** *children's club (May–Sep), disabled access, entertainment, Internet (€3 per ½ hour), playground, pools (outdoor), restaurant, shop.* ***In mobile homes*** *kitchenette, safe, sat TV.*

Hotel Villa Rinascimento ★★

Santa Maria del Giudice. ☎ 0583 378292. ***www.villarinascimento.it****. Off SS12 8km south of Lucca.*

You'd be hard pushed to find a better **base** for exploring northern Tuscany than this 15th century villa set among the olive groves of Monte Pisano, just 15–20 minutes from Lucca or Pisa. Large grounds, the architectural flourish of a first-floor *loggia* and **scrambled eggs** for breakfast complete a near-perfect package.

Individually decorated family rooms have plenty of space, terracotta floors and exposed beams. Bathrooms are large, but just starting to need an update; some have baths. Of the 14 value (but smaller and less characterful) rooms in the annex, odd numbers have a better view and a sun terrace.

The same owners also offer **apartments** (***www.villacheli.it***) nearby for rental by the night or week.

Rooms *31 (closed mid-Jan–Mar).* ***Rates*** *Double €132–150, double in annex €95–103. Cots free. Extra bed €16–33. Breakfast included.* ***Credit*** *MC, V.* ***Amenities*** *bar, Internet (free), parking, playground, pool (outdoor), restaurant, tennis.* ***In room*** *A/C, sat TV.*

FAMILY-FRIENDLY DINING

Osteria Machiavelli ★ VALUE TUSCAN

Via Cesare Battisti 28, Lucca. ☎ 0583 476219.

This small, local bar-cum-osteria in a quiet street north of Piazza San Michele is the best place in town to introduce the family to a **workers' lunch**, Tuscan-style. The menu always has plain pasta, or even roast beef and chips, for fussy little eaters, but the **set lunch** at €11 is the star. If you're lucky, it might feature *minestra con farro* (vegetable broth with local pulses) and pork chop with a mushroom *ragù*, accompanied by a ¼ of house wine (the red's a **Montepulciano DOC**), water and a *caffè* to finish. The place itself is a bit haphazard – the restaurant doubles as a wine store, somewhere for the cooks to eat after service and an office for the proprietor's paperwork – but great fun.

***Open** 9.30am–3pm and 6.30pm–midnight, closed Sun lunch. **Main courses** €5–10. **Credit** AmEx, MC, V. **Amenities** highchairs, reservations accepted.*

Antica Trattoria 'da Bruno' ★

PISAN

*Via Luigi Bianchi 12, Pisa. 050 560818. **www.pisaonline.it/trattoriaDaBruno**.*

Pisan specialities abound at this rustic trattoria, with a definite slant towards seafood, a reminder of Pisa's maritime history. It's one of the best places in town to introduce your children to **authentic Pisan food**, and the communal tables are perfect for large groups. For a more genuine experience, aim for dinner rather than lunch – evenings are mellower, local affairs and as a family you'll get special attention. Favourites include Tuscan beans with olive oil, sea bass ravioli, grilled swordfish and Pisan stockfish – and there's also roast meats like beef and lamb or *zuppa Pisana* (a soaked-bread and veggie broth). If your children can recognise any of the photos of 'famous' customers on the walls, buy them an ice cream.

***Open** 7–10.30pm Mon, 1–3.30pm and 7–10.30pm Wed–Sun. **Main courses** €12–20. **Credit** AmEx, MC, V. **Amenities** reservations accepted.*

Osteria del Tinti **TUSCAN/ITALIAN**

Vicolo del Tinti 26, Pisa. 050 580240.

This cosy local restaurant knocks out high quality food down a tiny side street off Borgo Stretto. The cellar-like rooms have plenty of atmosphere and hold lots of appeal for curious youngsters, though there aren't many tables that seat more than four. Pasta is excellent: the *testaroli* with olive oil and cheese and *gnocchi al Roquefort* are worth the visit alone. Relatively simple dishes like grilled tuna and *zuppa Toscana* should satisfy most, while the adventurous can opt for wild boar (*cinghiale*) with polenta.

***Open** 12.30–3.30pm and 7.30–11pm Tue–Sun. **Main courses** €11–15. **Credit** MC, V. **Amenities** reservations accepted.*

Pizzeria Trattoria Toscana

PIZZA & PASTA

Via Santa Maria 163, Pisa. 050 561876.

Although this cheerful restaurant is aimed squarely at **tourists** piling into Campo dei Miracoli, it's a convenient option and easy with tired children in tow. The English-speaking staff can conjure up basic pasta dishes for finicky eaters – and fall over themselves to accommodate baby requests; it's also **open all day**. There's plenty of space inside, though the covered terrace might be a little tight depending on how many are eating (four is fine).

Food is adequate rather than exceptional, but you can't go wrong with the pizzas, good value (€3.60–6.50) with a large choice of toppings. Note, their house red wine is perhaps the worst in Tuscany, and they stick a 15% service charge on your bill.

***Open** 8am–11pm Thu–Tue. **Main courses** €5–10. **Credit** AmEx, MC, V. **Amenities** reservations accepted.*

Trattoria Da Bussè ★★★
VALUE **LUNIGIANESE**

Piazza del Duomo 31, Pontrémoli. ☎ 0187 831371.

Hidden in Pontrémoli's warren of ancient streets, Da Bussè is *the* place in the north to pay homage to fantastically cheap **home cooking**. It's not just the food either: you really do feel as if you're lunching in someone's country kitchen. Specials are traditional and local, obviously, with a whiff of Liguria about them: *testaroli* (a pancake-like pasta), rabbit stew, salami and veal. If the **pesto**'s on, which at lunchtime it usually is, you'll be treated to the best in Tuscany. There's a *gelateria* on the piazza to round off a perfect lunch.

***Open** 12.30–2.30pm Sat–Thu, also 7.45–9.30pm Sat–Sun. **Main courses** €6–9.*

Trattoria La Darsena **SEAFOOD**

*Via Virgilio 150, Viareggio. ☎ 0584 398249. **www.trattorialadarsena.it**. At junction of Via Euro Menini.*

There are plenty of places to eat decent **seafood** in Viareggio, but few that you don't leave feeling a bit scalped. The much recommended La Darsena's location away from the seafront ensures a more discerning clientele, better cooking and (slightly) better prices. The atmosphere's informal without being scruffy – and of course, families are welcome. Classics like *spaghetti alle vongole* (with clams), lobster and mixed fried fish are joined by the catch of the day, cooked however you fancy. The cover charge (€3) is a bit steep; there's a *gelateria* next door.

If it's full, or Sunday, a good local alternative is **Osteria Barcobestia** (☎ *0584 384416*) at Via Coppino 201, though service can be slow if it's full. If the children won't eat fish, don't bother with either.

***Open** midday–2.30pm and 7.45–10.30pm Mon–Sat. **Main courses** €11–22. **Credit** AmEx, MC, V. **Amenities** reservations accepted.*

Villa Rinascimento

6 The Tuscan Coast: Livorno to Lazio

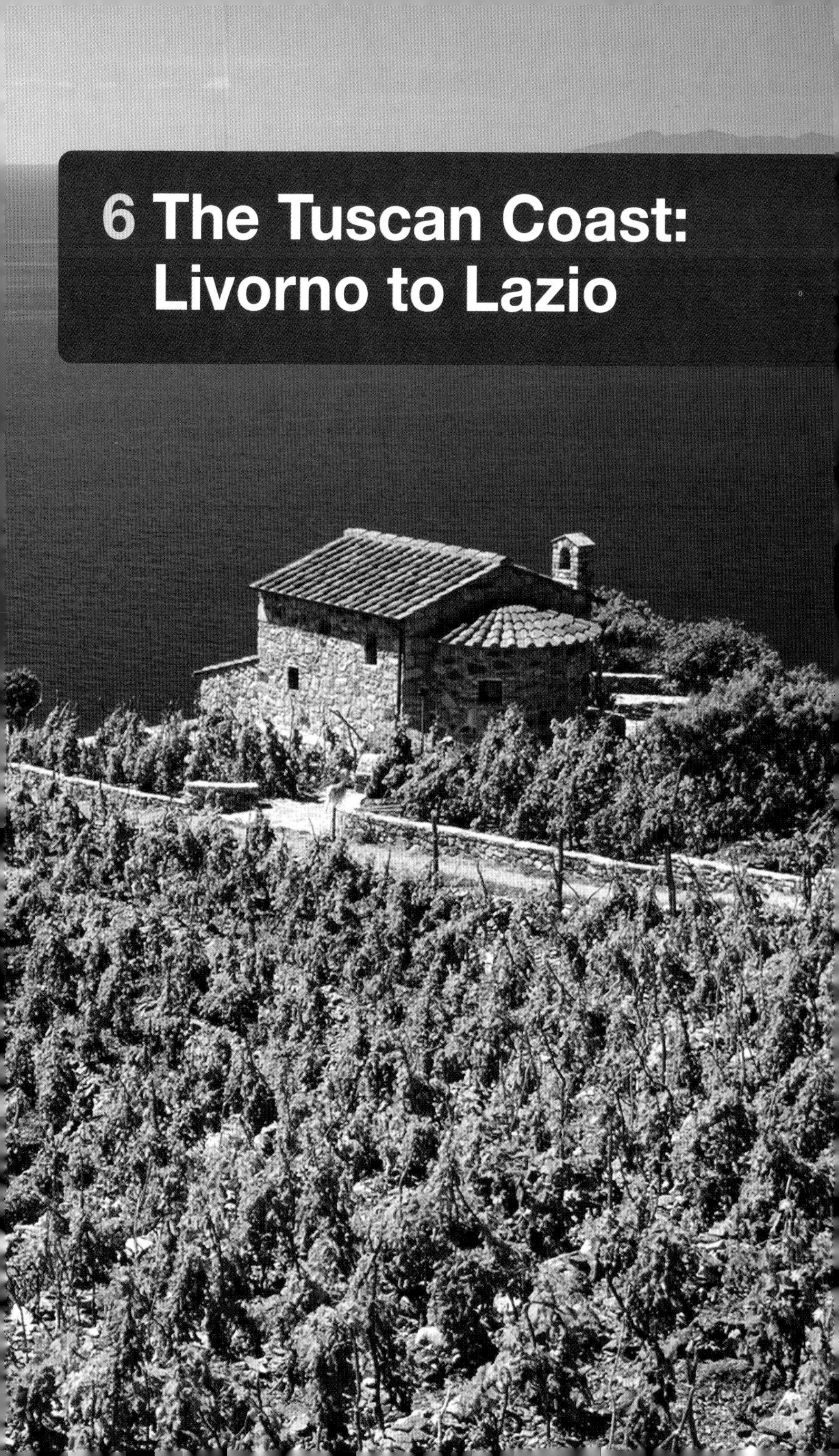

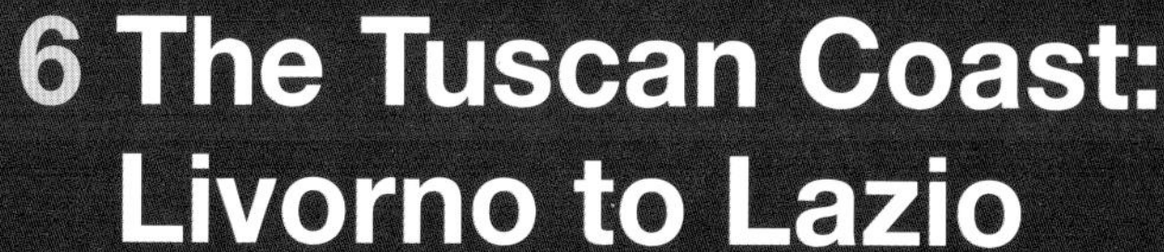

THE **TUSCAN COAST**

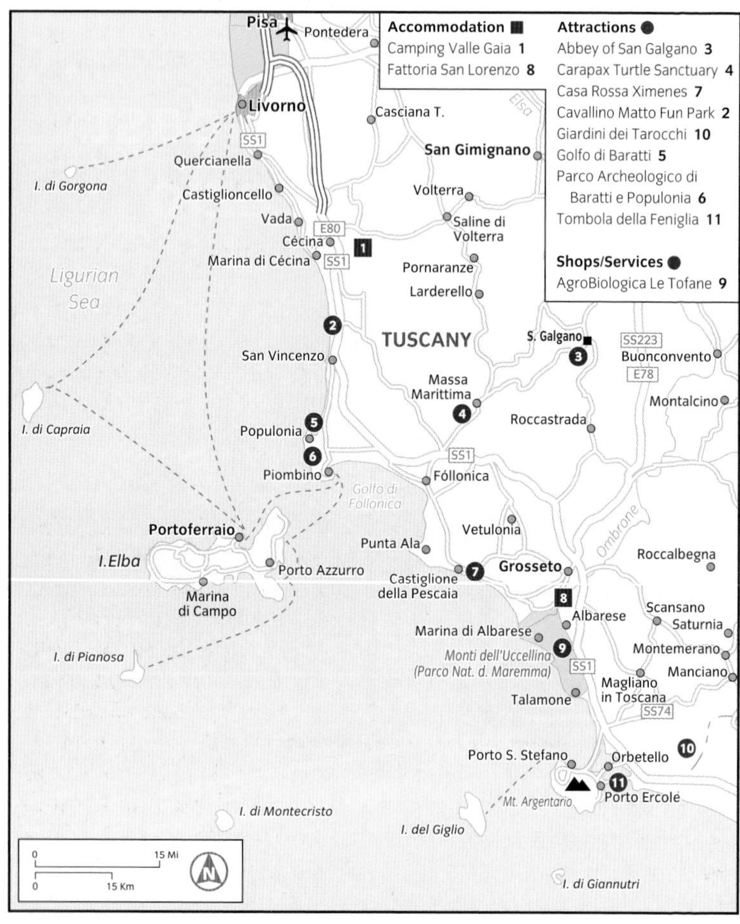

For a region with a shore that spans three seas, Tuscany is not well known in the UK for its beaches. But it sure is to the Italians, who populate whole sandy stretches of Mediterranean, Tyrrhenian and Ligurian coastlines every summer. Many beaches are packed to the gunnels and not all are idyllic, but there are occasional gems if you know where to look. And you will benefit from the smart bars, cafés and restaurants that follow whenever Italians appear in force.

The beaches of the holiday island of **Elba** are among Europe's best, and although packed in the height of summer, in May or September you could be in the Seychelles. Tuscany's coast is also the best stretch to grab some nature. The **birdlife** in the marshes and foothills of the Maremma, as well as Orbetello's salty seawater lagoon, make binoculars an essential luggage item. The culture-deprived can bail inland to

Massa Marittima, where fine art and architecture sit happily alongside a couple of crackers for the children – they'll love going underground in a mine and seeing giant tortoises. And we haven't even got started on the coast's hiking, museums or sublime seafood restaurants. You'll just have to read on.

The best news of all is that most of this area isn't much visited by English-speaking holidaymakers. If you're after an authentic Italian holiday experience, which the youngsters will love as well, this is the place to be in Tuscany.

LIVORNO

Of the hundreds of people who disembark from cruise ships in **Livorno** harbour every day, only a handful make it into the city. It was badly damaged during World War II bombing raids and many of its graceful 18th- and 19th-century buildings have been replaced with some fairly hideous architecture.

But fear not: Livorno isn't entirely without alternative merits – there are plenty of things to do together as a family. Livorno's **seafood cuisine** is famed throughout Italy, chiefly *cacciucco*, a fish soup-stew. The canals around Venezia Nuova are yours to explore and there's no need to worry whether you're paying tourist prices, because you're the only ones in town.

Essentials

Easy to find, Livorno is 20 minutes south of Pisa along the **A12** or **SS1**. Driving in the centre is a *casino* (roughly, 'mad-house'); **park** for free at the station (well signposted) and take a **bus** (10 minutes) from **Piazza Dante**. If you insist on driving in, there's covered **parking** in town (€1.30 per hour) in Piazza Menin; all-day at Via Roma 19 costs €10. Good luck. For **trains** (☎ *892021. **www.trenitalia.it***) linking the city with

Children's Top Attractions of Tuscany's Coast

- Hiking in the **Parco Regionale della Maremma**, p. 154.
- Poking around in **rock pools** at Sant'Andrea, p. 148.
- Finding your own patch of sand at **Fetovaia**, p. 149, or the **Tombola della Feniglia**, p. 158.
- Gawping at the **Mediterranean panoramas** from Monte Capanne, p. 150.
- Discovering the world underneath **Massa Marittima**, p. 150.
- Catching some **calcio** at family-friendly football club, AS Livorno, p. 142.
- **Birdwatching** through a webcam at Diaccia Botrona, p. 153.

the **Costa degli Etruschi**, see p. 143. There's also a regular, quick link with **Pisa** (15 minutes €1.70), and **Florence** (1½ hours €6.30).

The most useful of Livorno's three **tourist offices** is the booth in the middle of Piazza del Municipio (☎ *0586 204611*. ***apt7 livorno@costadeglietruschi.it***). It's open Monday to Saturday 9am–5pm and Sunday 9am–1pm. There are **cashpoints** galore in town, especially along Via Cairoli.

Livorno's best event for children is the **Effeto Venezia** in early August, when the city's canal quarter springs to life, sort-of.

Around the City

A tour of Livorno's sights won't take long – it isn't that kind of place. The best part for an aimless but charming mooch and a coffee is the ambitiously named **Venezia Nuova** (New Venice), between the **Fortezza Nuova** and **Fortezza Vecchia**. The forts are a bit shabby, but the colonial streets and canals, especially along **Via Borra**, have some atmosphere and an untainted local flavour. For a closer look at the waterways, **boat trips** (€10, €5 children 6–12) run irregularly from the tourist office in Piazza del Municipio.

Livorno's major work of public art, the statue of Ferdinand I in Piazza Micheli, is far better known for the Mannerist **Quattro Mori** (Four Moors) at his feet. They were cast by **Pietro Tacca** in 1626. South of the centre, the best seafront promenading and panoramas are to be found at the **Terrazza Mascagni**.

If you're packing a picnic, be sure to call in at Livorno's stacked **food market** on Via Buontalenti.

Livorno's New Venice

FUN FACT Brits Were Here

Livorno has a long British history. While we named Venezia 'Venice' and Firenze 'Florence', poor old Livorno got '**Leghorn**', since immortalised as a breed of chicken. They seem to have forgiven us. The poet **Shelley** sailed to his death from Livorno. The port itself was designed by an Englishman: 'Roberto' Dudley's plaque is on the wall behind the Quattro Mori in Piazza Micheli.

Museo di Storia Naturale del Mediterraneo ★ FIND

AGES 8 AND UP

Via Roma 234. 0586 266711. ***musmed@iol.it****. Bus: 5, 8n/r to Piazza Matteotti.*

The complexity of entrance options to the **Museum of Mediterranean Natural History** is Byzantine: the areas most suited to non-Italian-speakers are the **Orto Botanico** and **Sala del Mare**. The second of these is the highlight, especially the **giant skeleton of a fin whale** ★ washed up on Livorno's beach in 1990. Children can touch the jaw and ribs and try to work out just *how* far it is to the tip of the tail. At the far end of the small **Orto Botanico**, in the Zona Umida, there's a pond with turtles and a kitchen garden with medicinal plants.

There's plenty more in the museum – geology, palaeontology, even a Planetarium – but you or the children need to speak Italian to get much out of it. Plans are afoot to make displays bilingual. If you email ahead, the museum can often arrange a guided visit in **English**.

Open *9am–1pm Tue–Sat, also 3–7pm Tue, Thu and Sat; 3–7pm only Sun.* ***Adm*** *€4, €2 children 7–12 Mare or Orto; €6, children €3 Mare/Orto/Sala Invertebrati; €10, children €5 everything; €20 family everything.* ***Amenities*** *disabled access, shop.*

Museo Civico Giovanni Fattori AGES 12 AND UP

Via San Jacopo in Aquaviva 65. 0586 808001. ***Emuseofattori@comune.livorno.it****. Bus 1,8.*

Livorno's arty highlight is inside the extraordinary Rococo-meets-colonial **Villa Mimbelli**, south of the centre. The Museo Civico Fattori exhibits the work of the local **Macchiaioli School**: kind-of impressionists without the water lilies. Alas, Cézanne it ain't: among three levels of average work, the highlights are jammed on the top floor. If you've been to the Maremma, Giovanni Fattori's 1893 painting of bearded *butteri* (cowboys, see p. 155) will be of interest. Fattori aside, the only other painting of note is Lodovico Tommasi's rather lovely, autumnal **La caduta delle foglie**. Still, it marks a change of gear from wall-to-wall religious art.

Another bonus is the setting: inside there's a lush civic park, with **swings and a slide** for the children. If you're here weekdays between 4pm (5pm Fridays) and 7pm, there's a **Ludoteca** ★ that

Serie A on the Cheap

They might not be a household name, but AS Livorno ★ (*gli amaranto,* 'the purples') are on the up. In 2004 the team returned to Italy's elite Serie A after a 55-year wait, and then promptly qualified for the UEFA Cup in 2006. They're a friendly little football club, happy to see English-speaking visitors of all ages. Tickets go on sale about 7–10 days before games: it's around €15 to sit in the Curva Nord with the crazies, €25–28 for the quieter Gradinata (no roof), and €35–40 for the Tribuna Coperta. Children under eight only pay €1, and under-14s get €7–8 off the full-price. Although the Curva Nord has no reputation for trouble, it is **loud**, and occasionally angry: young children probably shouldn't be there.

Their Stadio Armando Picchi is in Piazzale Montello, not far from the Museo Fattori. You can usually **park** outside, or take **bus 1** from the station, **bus 5** from Piazza Grande. Buy match tickets from the **Punta Amaranto** at the main stadium entrance (including on matchdays), or at Piazza Mazzini 81, next to **Bar Terzo**. You need to show photo ID. See the club website (***www.livornocalcio.it***) for a fixture list.

they're welcome to join (from age three up), including games, creative play, skateboards, books and of course a swarm of little Tuscans to make friends with. The annual membership fee is €11, so it only makes sense if you're around Livorno for more than a day or two.

Open *10am–1pm and 4–7pm Tue–Sun.* ***Adm*** *€4, €2.50 children 7–18.* ***Amenities*** *disabled access.*

Isola Capraia AGES 10 AND UP

Ferry from Livorno.

When you get that I-want-to-be-alone-on-a-Tuscan-island feeling, **Capraia**'s the one you want. This scrub-covered slab of desolate beauty has just one road. It's the quietest accessible island in the Tuscan archipelago, with empty hiking trails, hidden coves and azure views galore, although no decent beach. If your luck's in, you might spot the rare **Audouin's gull**.

Getting there is a journey you'll only want to make with older children: it takes 2½ hours and costs €12.50 each way to cross, and there's usually just one ferry a day. Occasionally in high season you can get the 8.30am from Livorno and return on the 6pm (make sure you book). Check timetables with **Toremar** (*081 0171998.* ***www.toremar.it***). **Agenzia Viaggi e Turismo Parco** (*0586 905071.* ***agparco@tin.it***) can arrange family packages, including **diving** ★.

For expert advice, contact the island's **tourist office** (*0586 905138.* ***www.prolococapraiaisola.it***).

THE ETRUSCAN COAST

Just south of Livorno, the **Maremma Pisana** begins. Or, at least, it did until someone decided to rebrand it the **Costa degli Etruschi**. Once a sparsely inhabited malarial swamp, it now hosts most of the Tuscan mainland's summer seaside action. Guidebooks are often snotty about it, with good reason. Stretches exhibit the dark side of the Italian seaside experience: concrete, campsites and crowds. If you know how to navigate your family around the place, however, you can avoid the worst excesses; but if you like a beach all to yourself, you've come to the wrong place.

The coast is easiest by **car**: it follows the **SS1** south from Livorno to Piombino. It's also straightforward by **train** (*892021. **www.trenitalia.it***). Every hour or so a *Regionale* service connects Livorno with **Cecina** (25 minutes €2.80) and **San Vincenzo** (40 minutes €4). A regular-ish stopper also calls at **Castiglioncello** (18 minutes €2.30) and **Bolgheri** (37 minutes €3.40).

There are a couple of **websites** worth consulting before you go: the superb official portal ***www.costadeglietruschi.it*** and unofficial ***www.costaetrusca.com***.

Beaches

You need to pick your spots here. The **Bay of Quercetano** has the views, but its beaches are small and rocky. There's a decent, though busy, stretch of white sand around **Vada**: just south or 1½ km north of the main piazza park on either side of the road and cut through the scrub. You might get more space at the sandy southern extreme of **Marina di Bibbona**. Park (free except July and August) and walk 10 minutes through the *pineta* and dunes.

San Vincenzo was the scene of the Florentine army's rout of Pisa in 1505, remembered by Vasari's frescoes in the **Palazzo Vecchio** (p. 51). Its beach is broad, flat and fluffy, but the concrete wall rather spoils the view. Further south, the beach at **La Torraccia** is a popular sea-fishing spot with

Tourist Offices

HQ for Costa degli Etruschi tourism is in Livorno (*0586 204611. **www.costadeglietruschi.it***), upstairs at Piazza Cavour 6. Most resorts have well-signposted seasonal offices, occasionally more than one, but only three are open all year: in **Castiglioncello**, at Via Aurelia 632 (*0586 754890. **apt7castiglioncello@costadeglietruschi.it***); in **Marina di Cecina**, at Piazza S. Andrea 6 (*0586 620678. **apt7cecina@costadeglietruschi.it***); and in **San Vincenzo**, down by the marina at Via della Torre (*0565 701533. **apt7sanvincenzo@costadeglietruschi.it***).

enough coarse sand to park a family. Leave your car by the brick tower. Your best bet along this coast, however, is the **Golfo di Baratti** ★. Park on the left of the road (€5 for 5 hours in summer); if you reach the archaeological park (see below), you've gone too far. Views of the promontory of **Populonia** are super; the sand improves the further east you walk.

Out & About

Besides the sea, there are one or two things to amuse. Marina di Cecina has a small **Museo Archeologico** (*0586 680145. **www.comune.cecina.li.it/museo.archeologico/index.html***), in the colonial Villa Guerrazzi north of town. It's well signposted and open 6–10pm Tuesday to Sunday between June and August, 3.30–7pm weekends only February to May and September to November. Entry is €4 adults, €2.50 for 6–18s. A family ticket costs €8; another €4 gets you all into Cecina's 'archaeological park' for a roam, too.

Farther inland, Suvereto's **Museo Artistico della Bambola** (Via Magenta 14. ***www.comune.suvereto.li.it/museums.asp***) documents the history of **dolls** and doll making. The collection includes wooden dolls, porcelain dolls and rag dolls. Open 5–7pm Saturdays and Sundays, and also 9–11pm between July and September, it's **free** to get in.

Wine buffs might want to pass through medieval **Bolgheri**, home of legendary reds **Sassicaia** and **Ornellaia**.

Cavallino Matto Fun Park

AGES 3–8

*Via Pò 1, Marina di Castagneto. 0565 745720. **www.cavallinomatto.it**. 1km from SS1 Donoratico exit.*

Tuscany's **almost-a-theme-park** does exactly what it says on the tin: highlights include mini-roller coasters, log rides, mazes, inflatables, a pirate ship and a show where people jump off high things. It's not Disney, but your under-10s will love it. You, on the other hand, may end up grumbling about the price and appreciating the shade under the pines.

***Open** 10am–7pm daily mid-May–mid-Sep, until 8pm Aug; weekends only mid-Sep–Oct and Apr–mid-May; closed Nov–Mar. **Adm** €16, €14 children 3–10, free under 90cm height. **Amenities** disabled access, parking, picnic area, restaurant, shop.*

Acqua Village OVERRATED

AGES 6 AND UP

*Via Tevere 25, Cecina Mare. 0586 622539. **www.acquavillage.it**.*

This **tatty** water park in a car park outside Marina di Cecina only warrants a mention because it's advertised everywhere – and your children could conceivably have a good time. It's a seaside staple, after all. If it buys you a couple of days of touring in central Tuscany, go for it. Otherwise, beg or bribe your way out.

There's another branch in **Follonica**.

The Oil Trail

The hillside village of Castagneto Carducci, inland from San Vincenzo, is said to produce Italy's best olive oil. There isn't much to do bar wandering the steep cobbled streets and slurping ice cream. Reserve a terrace table at La Gramola on Via Marconi 18 (*0565 763646. **www.lagramola.it***) for proper pizza from a wood oven, erratic service and fine views of the Etruscan Coast below.

***Open** 10am–6pm daily Jun–mid-Sep. **Adm** €15, €12 children 4–11. **Amenities** bar/restaurant, parking, shop.*

Parco Archeologico di Baratti e Populonia ★ AGES 5 AND UP

*0565 226445. **www.parchivaldicornia.it**. Signposted from SS1.*

The Etruscan Coast's major Etruscan site got a major revamp in 2007. The original two areas covered 80 hectares and have been joined by an Etruscan-Roman Acropolis and Roman road at the top of Populonia's promontory. The finds confirm that Populonia's status as a major iron and metal-working centre didn't end with the Etruscans.

Scientifically the most interesting site remains San Cerbone, the only Etruscan necropolis ever found by the sea. It's the easiest to explore with youngsters: relatively intact circular tombs litter a field right by the visitor centre. With older children, a two-hour round trip on foot to Le Grotte, where a series of tombs are hewn from solid rock, is well worth it – not just for the views. English signage everywhere makes it all easy to follow and understand.

A complex ticketing structure can't hide the fact that it's overpriced. Two- and three-site tickets are valid for up to a week; combining it with lunch at La Barcaccina (p. 162) one day and a trip to Baratti's beach across the road the next, can just about extract your value.

***Open** 10am–7pm daily Jul–Aug, closed Mon Jun and Sep; 10am–6pm Mar–May and Oct; 10am–4pm Sat–Sun Nov–Feb. **Adm** one site €9, €6 children 6–14; 2 sites €12, €9 children; 3 sites €15, €12 children; family (5 people) 2 sites €32, 3 sites €39. **Amenities** bar/pizzeria, English, parking (free/€1), picnic area, playground, shop.*

INSIDER TIP

There's nothing left of the medieval hamlet of Populonia Alta bar *turismo* and *tipico* shops. but its Castello (***www.castellodipopulonia.it***. €2, €1 for children 6–14) has the best panorama ★ up the Etruscan Coast. It's open 10am–12.30pm and 2–6pm daily, right by the Acropolis area.

ELBA

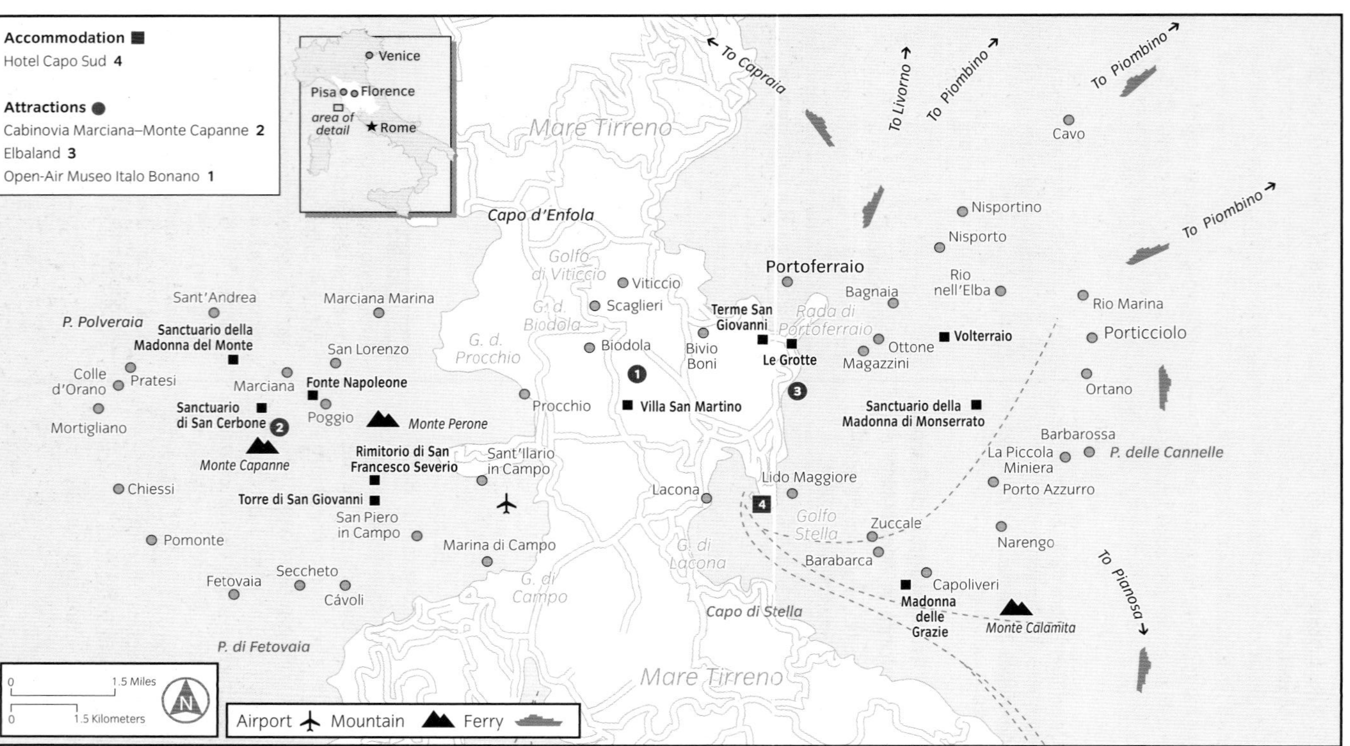
Accommodation
Hotel Capo Sud 4
Attractions
Cabinovia Marciana–Monte Capanne 2
Elbaland 3
Open-Air Museo Italo Bonano 1
Venice
Pisa
Florence
area of detail
Rome
Mare Tirreno
To Capraia
To Livorno
To Piombino
To Piombino
To Piombino
To Pianosa
Cavo
Capo d'Enfola
Nisportino
Nisporto
Portoferraio
Rio nell'Elba
Rio Marina
Porticciolo
Golfo di Viticcio
Viticcio
Scaglieri
G. d. Biodola
Biodola
Terme San Giovanni
Rada di Portoferraio
Bagnaia
Ottone
Magazzini
Volterraio
Bivio Boni
Le Grotte
Ortano
G. d. Procchio
Procchio
Villa San Martino
Sanctuario della Madonna di Monserrato
Barbarossa
La Piccola Miniera
P. delle Cannelle
Porto Azzurro
Sant'Andrea
Marciana Marina
P. Polveraia
Sanctuario della Madonna del Monte
San Lorenzo
Colle d'Orano
Pratesi
Marciana
Fonte Napoleone
Poggio
Monte Perone
Mortigliano
Sanctuario di San Cerbone
Monte Capanne
Rimitorio di San Francesco Severio
Sant'Ilario in Campo
Lido Maggiore
Lacona
Chiessi
Torre di San Giovanni
San Piero in Campo
Golfo Stella
Zuccale
Narengo
Pomonte
Marina di Campo
G. di Lacona
Barabarca
Capoliveri
Seccheto
Fetovaia
Cávoli
G. di Campo
Capo di Stella
Madonna delle Grazie
Monte Calamita
P. di Fetovaia
0 1.5 Miles
0 1.5 Kilometers
N
Airport
Mountain
Ferry

ELBA

As places to be exiled go, Napoleon struck lucky with **Elba ★★**. If the mainland's beaches are a touch underwhelming, you can't say the same about Italy's third-largest island. Every bend in the road reveals an expanse of rock, sea or sand more picturesque than the last. It's a little busier these days than it was in the 19th century: almost **2 million visitors** come every year to have their fill of azure water.

Family travellers should follow some simple rules. Most importantly, **don't come between late July and the end of August**. Everything's full, prices are astronomical, resorts are noisy and roads are clogged. May is a great time to come, when the greens and browns of the island's scrubby interior are interlaced with yellow, red and violet blooms. In September, the water is warmer and the island quieter than in peak season. If you're budgeting, factor in the price of the **ferry**: cars are expensive to bring and Marina di Campo is easy on the bus. Yes, prices are steep, but you're in a pretty special place.

Island Essentials

Two ferry companies link Piombino and **Portoferraio** on Elba: **Toremar** (✆ *081 0171998. www.toremar.it*) and **Moby** (✆ *199 303040. www.moby.it*). Frequencies (at least half-hourly in summer) and prices vary by season, becoming hideously expensive on August weekends. The crossing takes an hour. Toremar also runs a **hovercraft** (*aliscafo*) service (€9.40) for passengers only, four times a day (40 minutes). Except from late July through August, you should be able to roll up and sail, but you'll get a better price with Moby if you **book in advance**. Compare prices and schedules at *www.traghetti.com*.

If you want to leave your car at Piombino, there's a **long-stay car park** signposted by the docks (€8–12 per day). There's also a

Portoferraio Harbour

cashpoint, a pizzeria and an Autogrill inside the port building.

Unless you have a car, Elba's remote areas and beaches are hard to reach. However, **Procchio** (20 minutes) and **Marina di Campo** (½ hour) are served hourly-ish until dusk by **ATL buses** (*0565 914392. www.atl.livorno.it*). You want route 116 from opposite the Toremar dock in Portoferraio; there's a ticket office adjacent, at Viale Elba 22. Some buses continue to **Fetovaia** (45 minutes). The service on route 117 to **Capoliveri** (½ hour) runs infrequently.

The only **tourist office** open all year is in Portoferraio (*0565 914671. www.aptelba.it*), at the far left end of the quay as you sail in, at Calata Italia 43. It's open 10am–1pm and 2–5pm Monday to Saturday between October and May; 9am–7pm Monday to Saturday, 9.30am–12.30pm and 3.30–6.30pm Sunday, all summer. They are the best people to ask for advice about **diving** ★ around the island. Another useful trip-planning resource is *www.elbatuttanatura.com*.

The Beaches

Despite 147km of coastline, you're not going to 'discover' any beaches on Elba. Every tiny patch of sand is **busy** in summer. Unless you come way out of season, you're unlikely to find a deserted spot. There's a very good reason for this: Elba's beaches are great.

Most often recommended to families are the mile of sand at

'Cavoli Beach, Elba'

Marina di Campo ★ and its northern counterpart at **Procchio**. Both are wide with shallow shelves and easy to park near for free. You're never far from a pizza or *gelato* on either beach, and can rely on them being packed all summer. The *Spiaggia Grande* at **Lacona** is also wide and flat, with soft sand. West of Procchio, there's pay parking around the stunning cove at **Sant'Andrea** ★★. The small beach is white and sandy, with shallow rock-pools at the eastern end.

Well signposted south of Capoliveri, the small sand-and-pebble coves at **Innamorata** ★ and **Morcone** are oriented perfectly for sunset. You will find a parking spot at either if you hunt around. Further north, follow the signs from the main road for **Zuccale** ★ and **Barabarca** ★. Park at the end of the road (Zuccale to the right,

TIP A Glass of Elba

Uncharacteristically for Tuscany, the island's best wine is white: Elba Bianco DOC. Follow it down with anything pulled out of the sea and you're more than halfway to the perfect lunch.

Barabarca the left). It's €2.50 for the day. You walk down a path to both, so **no pushchairs**.

The **natural beauty** quotient jumps a notch higher on the island's south-west. The coves at **Fetovaia** ★★ and **Cavoli** ★★ are idyllic: white sand, transparent, turquoise sea and summer crowds. Fetovaia has more shade and the sand is less grainy, but Cavoli's crescent just edges the beauty contest. There's pay parking around both.

There are **disabled facilities** at Marina di Campo (*0565 976966*), Procchio (*0565 907366*), Lacona (*0565 964364*), Fetovaia (*0565 988037*) and Cavoli (*0565 987288*).

For an extended stay, with lashings of beach, 153 are described in the book ***Elba: all its Beaches*** (aka '*Tutte le Spiagge*'; €10), available at Piombino port and bookshops on Elba (try **Il Libraio** at Via Veneto 10, on Portoferraio's quay).

Elsewhere on Elba

If you're not coming here for the beaches, there's no point in coming at all. Still, the rest isn't without interest. The main harbour and capital of **Portoferraio** was a major iron-ore centre for centuries, hence the name and the forts you'll spot from the ferry – defence always follows the money, after all. The **Fortezza Medicea** (*0565 944024*) has a great view over the harbour. It's open 10am–1pm and 3.30–7.10pm Thursday to Tuesday. Admission is €3 (children €2); enter on Via Guerrazzi.

If you're on the way to Procchio or farther west, plan half an hour at the **Open-Air Museo Italo Bolano** (*0565 914570*). It's signposted by the side of the road in San Martino. Eerie ceramic sculpture adorns a shady garden. It's free to get in, open Monday to Saturday 10.30am–1pm and 4–7.30pm from May to September.

The tourist office in Portoferraio has a list of **play parks** (*parco giochi*) on the island. The best is **Elbaland** (*335 8194680*. ***www.elbaland.com***), on the Portoferraio-Porto Azzurro road. As well as **bouncy castles** and trampolines, there are wild boar, butterflies and goats to check out. Your ticket (€7, children €9) allows you to come in and out as often as you like for two days. It's open from 11am until sunset, mid-March to mid-September.

Once you've done all that, there's always a **boat trip**. Advertised, erm, everywhere.

Cabinovia Marciana–Monte Capanne ★★ AGES 3 AND UP

☎ 0565 901020. Signposted between Poggio and Marciana.

There's no doubt where you'll catch the best **views** ★★★ of Elba: 1,019m up Monte Capanne. The 20-minute ride in open cages to the highest point on the island is your only other **essential stop** bar the beach. The 360° views take in the arc of the Tuscan coast from Livorno to Monte Argentario. Seawards, the Mediterranean panorama spans the Tuscan archipelago and out to Corsica. Look for Populonia Alta above Piombino, and try to pick up your favourite Elban beach: you can see *that much* detail.

Some logistics: there's no room for **pushchairs**, so babies need to go up in pouches (back or front). It is possible to **hike** down (1½ hours); wear proper boots and don't take anyone under eight. And remember to hold on to your hats: ours are still up there somewhere.

***Open** 10am–12.15pm and 2.30–5pm daily. **Adm** €10 single, €15 return, €7 children 4–10. **Amenities** bar/restaurant, parking, picnic area.*

MASSA MARITTIMA

Gripping the side of a hill 350m up in the Colline Metallifere (the Metaliferrous Hills) back on the mainland is the misnamed 'maritime' capital of the Alta Maremma, **Massa Marittima** ★. This mining town was hit hard by plague of 1348 and took 600 years to bounce back. It's now an **overlooked gem**: an empty hill-town of shuttered buildings, steep, narrow lanes and a fine cobbled piazza, well off the usual trail. The only sounds you'll hear during lunchtime *riposo* out of season are the occasional marital dispute from a first floor window. Bliss.

Piazza Garibaldi, Massa Marittima

Essentials

Getting to Massa Marittima by **car** is a doddle: the town is on the **SS439**, 13km inland from the main coastal highway (SS1). There's a large **car park** (€1 per hour) on Piazza Mazzini, just before Massa's pedestrian zone if you're approaching from the coast, though parking is cheaper (but less convenient) in the tangle of back-streets.

The only feasible public transport option is the **RAMA bus** (*0564 475111. www.grifo rama.it*) from Follonica (€2).

The mega-helpful **tourist office** (*0566 902756. www.amatur.it*) is at Via Todini 3–5, down the side of the Museo Archeologico. There are **swings and a slide** on Via Valle Aspra by Piazza XXIV Maggio. The handiest **cashpoint** is the Banca Toscana in Piazza Garibaldi.

Massa's main event is the **Toscana Foto Festival** ★ (*0566 901526. www.toscanafotofestival.com*) during the first half of July, with exhibitions around town and workshops to join if you're an enthusiast. The town's *terzieri* battle it out in the **Balestro del Girofalco**, on the Sunday after 20th May and the second Sunday in August. Expect crossbows and flag juggling.

In & Around Town

The lower town, the **Città Vecchia**, is dominated by **Piazza Garibaldi**. Here you'll find Massa's **Duomo** ★, dedicated to San Cerbone Vescovo (8am–midday and 3–6pm daily), a fine Romanesque-Gothic pile dedicated to Massa's patron, the Bishop of Populonia between 570 and 575, who made his name taking a flock of geese to see the Pope. The **bell tower** is especially photogenic.

For the top views in town, climb the hill to the **Città Nuova**. The direct route up Via Monconi is the quickest, but beware: it's short, sharp and nigh on impossible with a pushchair. At the top you'll bump into the 40m **Torre del Candeliere** (*0566 902289. www.coopcollinemetallifere.it/musei/torre.html*). The castle keep and fine views over the chequerboard plains below are available Tuesday to Sunday 10am–1pm and 3–6pm between April and October, 11am–1pm and 2.30–4.30pm November to March. Admission is €2.50, €1.50 for children 6–14. The artistic highlight of Massa's upper tier is the **Museo di Arte Sacra** (*0566 901954. www.coopcollinemetallifere.it/musei/artesacra.html*). Hours are 10am–1pm and 3–6pm April to October, open an hour later and closed an hour earlier otherwise; closed Mondays. Entry is €5, children €3. Sienese Ambrogio Lorenzetti's **Maestà** ★ moved here recently from the modest **Museo Archeologico** in Piazza Garibaldi's Palazzo Podestà.

Museo della Miniera ★

AGES 6 AND UP

Via Corridoni. 0566 902289. ***www.massamarittimamusei.it/anticaminiera****. Follow yellow signs 700m uphill from Piazza Garibaldi.*

The Other Sword in the Stone

Halfway between Siena and Massa Marittima is a roofless Gothic ruin: the 13th-century Cistercian **Abbey of San Galgano** (8am–11pm daily; free). It's a mighty structure sitting alone in its windy field in the middle of nowhere, and as long as you don't catch a tour bus, quite atmospheric. The vaulted ceiling in the chapterhouse is also impressive.

There are several legends regarding Saint Galgano himself. One has noble young **Galgano Guidotti**, dedicated to worldly pleasures, out riding when the Archangel Michael appeared with flaming sword. Galgano fell to the earth, took his own sword from his belt and threw it against a nearby rock. It was swallowed, remaining stuck like a cross. You can see 'the sword' driven into its rock up the hill at the circular **Cappella di Montesiepi**. The adjacent chapel has faded frescoes by Ambrogio Lorenzetti.

Parking is €1.50 per hour; there's a **bar-deli-giftshop** that sells loaded *panini* (€3).

Did you know that **mules** were more economical mine workers than machines until the 1950s? Or that Massa's miners kept their lunch in metal tins so foot-long rats couldn't chew through them? Don your hard hats for this look at a miner's life in the Colline Metallifere and you'll soon know it all. The 700m-long authentic **replica** of a working 1940s mine, complete with echoes and eccentric machinery, is a sure winner for children. It's all on the flat, so little walkers should be fine as long as you wrap them up warm – the mine is 12°C all year.

The only catch is the superb guide's **patchy English**: to get the most out of a tour (30–40 minutes), at least one of you should understand Italian passably.

***Guided tours** approx. hourly 10am–4.30pm Tue–Sun, until 5.45pm Apr–Oct. **Adm** €5, €3 children 6–15.*

Carapax Turtle Sanctuary ★

GREEN **AGES 2 AND UP**

*0566 940083. **www.carapax.org**. 5km south-west of Massa; follow 'centro tartarughe' signs from SS439.*

This wildlife sanctuary rescues, studies, breeds and releases hundreds of **turtles**, tortoises and terrapins every year, with an especial interest in rare species. That's *tartarughe* big and small, local and exotic, from Calabria to Kazakhstan, including a giant Sahel tortoise. On top of that, they've got the whole thing set up for child-friendly tours, with a **playground** and picnic area, and water stops at regular intervals along the one-hour trail. There's signage in English for each pen, although the **biodiversity** displays are in Italian only. Paths are steep and stony: positively **no pushchairs**. There's also a breeding colony of **White Storks** (chicks appear in May).

In summer, **visit early or late** or all you'll see are several sleepy shells.

Open *9am–6pm daily Apr–Sep, until 7pm Jul–Aug; 9am–5pm daily Oct; 9am–5pm Sat–Sun Mar.* ***Adm*** *€7, €6 children, €17 family.* ***Amenities*** *bar, English, parking, picnic area, playground.*

CASTIGLIONE DELLA PESCAIA

Just south of Follonica is the bucket-and-spade town of **Castiglione della Pescaia**, stuck on the side of a rocky outcrop of Monte Petriccio. Despite its nightmare one-way system and parking hell, it's well worth the detour, for the super seafood restaurants (see p. 153) and wetlands.

The town overlooks the marshy mouth of the Bruna river, 23km west of provincial capital, **Grosseto**. From Follonica going north-west, it's 23km down the SS322.

The **tourist office** (*0564 933678.* ***infocastiglione@lamaremma.info***) is at Piazza Garibaldi 6, opposite the marina and right next to a **car park**.

Around the Town

The major draw here is the seaside: there's a south-facing **beach** right by the coast road serviced by several bathing companies. If you have time, though, there's better sand farther south at **Marina di Alberese** (p. 156). Castiglione's **Borgo Medioevale** (old town) makes a pleasant if tortuously steep walk, but it's mostly deserted. The action migrated downhill to the sea long ago.

Nearby **Punta Ala** has a mature par-72 golf course on aptly named Via del Golf (*0564 922121.* ***www.puntaala.net/golf***). A day-pass costs €65–75 adults, €39–45 juniors. Less adventurous clubbers might prefer the **crazy golf** (€5, children €4) 2km west of Castiglione on the SS322, next to the Esso garage.

Museo Multimediale Casa Rossa Ximenes & Nature Reserve ★ GREEN AGES 6 AND UP

0564 484580. ***www.diacciabotrona.it****. 500m east of centre; turn after Ponte Giorgini.*

This museum and marsh is one of Europe's most important **wetlands** preserves – a perfect place to take a young bird watcher. The 'multimedia' museum is housed inside the 18th-century Casa Rossa. It's equipped with feeds from three **webcams** scattered about the marsh that you can pan and zoom to get close to the birdlife without disturbing them. There's also an interactive guide to the marsh's inhabitants (in Italian only) and their calls (in Bird only). Depending on the season, residents include the marsh harrier, flamingo, and bittern.

Out on the marsh itself, a haphazard network of rough paths (unsuited to pushchairs) meanders through the stillness of 2,300 hectares of empty Diaccia Botrona. It's ideal for birdwatching. There's also a two-hour guided boat trip along the canal system, with views back to Castiglione.

The best times to visit are autumn, when migrant birds from northern Europe come by the thousand, and in spring, when the summer residents arrive.

***Open** 1–7pm Thu–Sun Sep–May, 4–10pm Tue–Sun Jun–Aug. Boat trips 6pm Tue–Sun Jun–Aug, by arrangement only Sep–May (min. 4 people). **Adm** museum and marsh only €5, free under-12s; with boat trip €12, €5 children 2–12. **Amenities** picnic area.*

PARCO REGIONALE DELLA MAREMMA

The outstanding **Parco Regionale della Maremma** ★★★, with its unspoiled *macchia* coastline, miles of parasol pines and deserted beaches, is the number-one reason to base yourself in south-western Tuscany. The coastal hills of **Monti dell'Uccellina** form the park's core and got their name from the area's teeming bird life (an *uccello* is a bird), so pack the binoculars. Residents include goshawks, tawny owls and jays. The park is spectacular in autumn when thousands of wild ducks, geese and herons invade on their way south to the sun. The highest peak in the park is **Poggio Lecci** at just 415m, so much of the 100 square kilometres of park is accessible to an older primary-age child, and sections of it to anyone out of a pushchair.

Essentials

The park's main **visitor centre** (☏ *0564 407098.* ***www.parcomaremma.it***) is at Via Bersagliere 7–9 in Alberese. You can't miss it. It's open daily 8.30am–1.30pm October to March, 8am–5pm April to September. There are no

Casa Rossa Ximenes

Italian Cowboys

Real cowboys, the *butteri*, have herded longhorn cattle and horses on the marshes of the Maremma and Lazio for centuries. They still do, but now also organise 1½ hour **equestrian shows** (€18, free 4–12s, weekly in summer) for tourists and treks for experienced riders. Day trips start from €45, up to week-long Tuscan horseback tours from €1,600. For both, contact **Equinus** (☎ *0564 24988*. ***www.cavallomaremmano.it***).

roads inside the Parco: the **car park** charges €6 a day in season only. There's a **cashpoint** at the visitor's centre.

Entrance to the park's main **trails** is €9, €4.50 for children 6–14. The **Forestal and Faunal** trails (shorter and flatter for youngsters, and with **disabled access**) are €6, children €4. Between 15th June and 15th September entrance to the best park trails is by **guided group visits** only, because of brushfire risk. Trips leave at 8.30am, 9.30am, 4pm and 4.30pm. On Fridays the 4.30pm trek is guided in **English**. The bus fare from the visitor centre to the trailheads (hourly) is included.

Cycling and **canoeing** ★ trips are organised along the Ombrone river by the **Centro Turismo Equestre** (☎ *0564 407102*. ***ilrialto@katamail.com***), who also arrange riding trips. **Bike hire** is €3 per hour or €8 per day. Guided two-hour canoeing trips are €16, €8 for children 14 and under. **Night treks** are available all year for groups of 8–12 (€15 per person, ***info@parco-maremma.it***), if you book ahead.

Around the Park

There are **no services** whatsoever in the park. Pack a picnic, sunblock, basic first-aid kit and change of clothes. Make sure **footwear** is sturdy trainers *at least*. You'll struggle for mobile phone reception out there.

Several marked trails head out from **Pratini**, where the shuttle bus from the visitor centre drops you, right in the heart of the park. The deeper in you get, the more olive groves give way to Mediterranean woodland of cork, ilex and ash. Suddenly you're alone in a wilderness of butterflies, bird calls and (if you're very lucky) wild boar.

The best trail for families is **A2**, *Due Torri*. It takes in a couple of Medici-built **watchtowers**. Many were repeatedly sacked by Barbary pirates in the 1500s, and have lain abandoned since. The **view** ★★★ from the first of the two towers is up there with the best in Tuscany. At under 6km, the hike is manageable, though steep in parts. Leave at least 2½ hours.

Trails **A1**, **A3** and **A4** are equally rewarding, but longer. With older children, you'll want to tackle them too.

An alternative, popular route heads from Pratini straight for the park's **virgin beach** ★★, Cala di Forno. The flatter **Forestal and Faunal** trails, **A5** and **A6** ★, depart from close to the visitor centre. **A7** is the only cycle track.

Marina di Alberese ★ ALL AGES

Follow signs; 8km from Alberese

Along with the **Tombolo della Feniglia** (see below), this is the best Tuscan **beach** south of Elba. Its serene pine-backed sands and gentle dunes are blessed with fine views of **Isola Giglio** in the haze. It can get **busy** on summer weekends but if you come out of season, you might have no more than a fox for company. Look out for Maremman longhorn cattle by the road on the way down.

It's forbidden to picnic outside designated areas, or camp anywhere on the beach.

***Open** 8am–dusk daily. **Adm** free. **Amenities** picnic area, parking (€6 per day, €4 per half-day), restaurant.*

Acquario di Talamone FIND

AGES 5 AND UP

Via Nizza 12, Talamone. ☎ 0564 887173. 100m uphill from marina.

This slightly ramshackle little aquarium houses fish and crustaceans found in the Orbetello lagoon. The lagoon's waters vary from very salty to almost fresh, and the tanks here reflect those changing environments. There are marine sound effects to set the mood, and English signage to help you around. The aquarium also serves as a hospital for **sea turtles** caught in fishermen's nets, and they'll happily show you the recuperating patients. It makes an interesting ½ hour diversion for little ones.

***Open** 9am–1pm and 3–5pm Tue–Sun, sometimes until 10pm May–Sep. **Adm** €3, €2 children 6–16; combined ticket with Parco Regionale della Maremma (routes T1, T2, T3) €7.50, children 4.50. **Amenities** English, parking.*

INSIDER TIP

The wild boar salami and *spaghetti alla pescatora* (with seafood) in the non-descript **Bar Centrale** (Via Aurelia Vecchia 20. *☎ 0564 884914*), in Fonteblanda between the SS1 and Talamone, is extraordinary. If you're hungry after the aquarium....

AgroBiologica Le Tofane GREEN

☎ 0564 407110. Off SP59, 4km south of Alberese.

This unassuming little farm shop is a goldmine for devotees of **pecorino** cheese. They make a dozen of so different kinds on-site, all with milk from their own flock of organically raised sheep: truffle, shallot, chilli, and several kinds of classic pecorino. There's also home-made organic jams and honey.

***Open** daily.*

MONTE ARGENTARIO

This scrubby rock protruding from the Tyrrhenian Sea got itself a grand name: **Monte Argentario**, 'the silver mountain'.

On to Lazio

If you're carrying on towards Rome, make a detour to the Giardino dei Tarocchi ★ (☎ *0564 895122. www.nikidesaintphalle.com*), an outdoor wonderland of Gaudì-esque sculptures and paths, created on a tarot theme by artist Niki de Saint Phalle. It's signposted just outside Pescia Fiorentina. At €10.50 adults, €6 children (under-7s free), it's a bit pricey, but great fun: open 2.30–7.30pm daily, April to mid-October.

Once an island, it is now connected to the mainland by a forested isthmus guarded by **Orbetello**. The town's lagoon is a vital wetland **nature reserve**, another great place along this coast to **birdwatch ★**.

Monte Argentario itself is dominated by two fishing villages-turned-resorts, fashionable among Florentines and Romans: **Porto Santo Stefano** and **Porto Ercole**. They're pleasant but packed to the rafters on summer weekends. Either resort can eat into a carefully planned budget. Porto Ercole was where artist and errant genius **Caravaggio** dropped dead of fever in 1610 – right by a great **beach** (see below).

Porto Santo Stefano has clear water and a summer traffic problem. Both ports have **cashpoints** right on the harbour fronts. You'll need them.

Porto Santo Stefano is the jumping-off point for ferries to **Isola Giglio**, run by **Toremar** (☎ *081 0178. www.toremar.it*). Singles cost €5.30–6.30; there are 3–5 crossings daily, taking 1 hour. Porto Santo Stéfano's helpful **tourist office** (☎ *0564 814208. www.lamaremma.info*) provides trail maps and advice on **hiking ★** around Monte

Tombola della Feniglia – Monte Argentario

Argentario. It's just on your left as you drop down the hill into town, at Piazzale Sant Andrea 1, open 9am–1pm and 3.30–7.30pm May to September, 9am–1pm and 2–6pm October to March. It's closed Sundays.

There's more information on Monte Argentario at the town hall's **website**, ***www.comunemonteargentario.it***.

Tombola della Feniglia ★★

ALL AGES

Off SP2 3.5 km from Orbetello dir. Porto Ercole; park under pine canopy.

The long, flat expanse of sand stretching almost all the way from Monte Argentario to the mainland is an ideal **family beach**. It's serviced (in season), by **Mamma Licia Bar** (*☎ 0564 834187*) close to the parking, but farther along you're on your own. When the sun gets too much, there's shade under the **parasol pines** – and more solitude the farther you walk towards the mainland. Being the best beach on Monte Argentario by some distance, maybe the best on mainland Tuscany, it gets busy on summer weekends.

Open *always.* ***Adm*** *free.* ***Amenities*** *bar/restaurant, play area, parking.*

FAMILY-FRIENDLY ACCOMMODATION

For more accommodation ideas, see p. 28. **Eurocamp**, among others, offer great camping choices on Elba; see p. 245.

Duca del Mare

Piazza Dante Alighieri 1, Massa Marittima. ☎ 0566 902284. ***www.ducadelmare.it****.*

What this friendly hotel lacks in rustic charm it makes up for in amenities and value. Linked to the town centre (five minutes) by an illuminated pedestrian walkway, the Duca del Mare's large rooms have all recently been renovated and bathrooms are spacious. There's a shaded outdoor terrace for breakfasts *al fresco*. Only room 107 has a bath.

If you have small children, ask for the ground floor: you'll lose the panorama, but the hotel doesn't have a lift and the downstairs triples and quad are bigger.

Rooms *28.* ***Rates*** *Double €85–100. Extra bed €25–30. Breakfast included.* ***Credit*** *MC, V.* ***Amenities*** *disabled access, parking, pool (outdoor).* ***In room*** *A/C, sat TV, safe, shower only.*

Fattoria San Lorenzo ★★

Via Antica Aurelia 50, Grosseto. ☎ 0564 21562. ***www.fattoriasanlorenzo.it****. 4km south-west of Grosseto dir. Trappola.*

These tastefully restored **farm buildings** in the flat countryside between Grosseto and the sea suit young families, who make up most of their clientele. The two sites (across the road from each other) are ideal for the Parco Naturale della Maremma and Monte Argentario, trips down to the local beach, or simply utter relaxation down on the *fattoria*. Each **mini-house** is on two floors with bedrooms up and down, a lounge and (small) kitchenette plus a shower room and a bathroom. If you intend using the in-house restaurant, go for **Tenuta Livia** rather than **Le Capanne**.

The farm produces its own olive oil, and you can shop for veg and fruit from their orchard just down the road. In high season, it's week-long bookings (Sat–Sat) only, although in spring or autumn they'll take 3–4 days; that's the only catch.

They can arrange two-centre breaks with their other property, the **Borgo Antico Fattoria di Casalbosco**, just outside Pistoia.

Apartments *30 (2 sites). 2-bed €521–1,425 per week, 3-bed €638–1,800 per week. Cot €26 per week. Final cleaning €75–85.* ***Credit*** *AmEx, MC, V.* ***Amenities*** *bike hire (€10 per day), parking, pool (outdoor), restaurant, shop, WiFi.* ***In room*** *A/C, kitchenette, sat TV.*

Camping Valle Gaia

0586 681236. ***www.vallegaia.it****. SS1 exit Cecina centro; follow signs to Casale M.*

This friendly little **campsite** is ideally located away from the coast: perfect for mixing the beach and medieval sights in central Tuscany. From its pine-shaded patch just outside Casale Marittimo, Marina di Bibbona is 15 minutes, with Volterra 40 minutes in the opposite direction. Campsite services are standard; the on-site **pizzeria** deserves a medal (it also does take-away).

The adjacent apartments, **La Casetta**, are owned by the same people; prices €320–880 for weekly bookings only. Neither take credit cards.

Valle Gaia is used by **Keycamp** (see p. 245) and **Canvas** (see p. 244).

Pitches *150 (open Apr–Oct).* ***Rates*** *Adults €4.40–7.60, children 2–10 €3.18–5.50, pitch €8.10–13.70.* ***Amenities*** *bike hire (€7 per day), breakfast (€6.50), laundry (€3.50), parking, pool (outdoor), restaurants, shop, tennis.*

Hotel La Baia del Sorriso FIND

Via Aurelia 1023, Quercetano. 0586 752570. ***www.baiadelsorriso.com****. 1km north of Castiglioncello.*

What you really want along a busy coast is a stretch to yourself – well, the Baia del Sorriso's **private beach** is as close as you're going to get. Although their rocky little patch isn't stupendous, views from the rooms are: every one has an unimpeded **cliff-top panorama** of the boiling seas in Quercetano Bay. There isn't a better site this side of Elba.

Rooms are spacious and cool, with tiled floors and large bathrooms; a triple can comfortably accommodate a cot leaving room to swing a Teletubby. There are also three small apartments available for month-at-a-time rentals.

Rooms *33 (open Mar–Oct).* ***Rates*** *Double €95–130, triple €125–160, quad €155–190. Cot €15 per night. Breakfast included.* ***Credit*** *AmEx, MC, V.* ***Amenities*** *parking, private beach, restaurant.* ***In room*** *A/C (most), sat TV.*

Hotel Capo Sud ★ FIND

Lacona, Elba. 0565 964021. ***www.hotelcaposud.it****. Above Margidore beach.*

Set in a quiet corner of the island, east of Lacona, the Capo Sud's **clifftop views** and friendly staff make an awesome first impression. Rooms are set in small villa-blocks wedged into a steep slope down to Margidore's dark beach. **Il Sole** and **La Luna** offer the best combination of seclusion and beach access, but accommodate double-plus-cot combos only. The best 'proper' triples are in **Il Pino** and **L'Aleatico**. Inside, family rooms are cool and spacious, if a bit bland and needing a furniture update. Each room has its own outside space: invest a little extra to make it a **sea view**. It's worth eating in the **restaurant** at least once.

Like everywhere on Elba, **book well ahead** in summer; prices are keenest in quiet May.

Rooms *40 (open mid-Apr–Sep).* ***Rates*** *Double €72–158 (garden view), €84–168 (sea view). Cot €15. Extra bed €22–66. Breakfast included.* ***Credit*** *MC, V.* ***Amenities*** *parking, pool (outdoor), private beach, restaurant (menu €20).* ***In room*** *A/C (€12 per day), fridge, TV, safe.*

FAMILY-FRIENDLY DINING

La Gramola, Castagneto Carducci, see p. 145.

Il Beccafico ★ FIND

MAREMMAN/SEAFOOD

Via Montebello 7, Castiglione della Pescaia. ☎ 0564 939658. ***casedimoggino@tiscali.it****.*

At first sight this place looks a little grown-up, the music a bit intimate for a family lunch; but the **exuberant service** soon puts you at ease. The cellar-style dining room on the way up to the Borgo Medioevale welcomes children: they'll happily make up pasta with tomato or meat sauce or cook an escalope however the youngsters like it, whatever's on today. For adults, the menu changes monthly and rotating daily specials might include *tagliolini* with octopus, tagliatelle with venison or salt cod *alla Livornese*, all cooked to a high standard. Even the house white, a **Monteregio DOC**, goes down a treat.

If you need a **highchair**, reserve ahead: they only have one.

Open *12.30–2pm and 7.30–10pm Fri–Wed.* ***Main courses*** *€8–14.* ***Credit*** *MC, V.* ***Amenities*** *highchair, reservations accepted.*

Ristorante Taverna Nel Buco

MAREMMAN

Via del Recinto 11, Castiglione della Pescaia. ☎ 0564 934460.

This tiny eatery, almost *under* rather than *in* Castiglione's Borgo Medioevale, is certainly worth the climb for superb food and a cosy ambience. The menu is steadfastly local rather than 'Italian'. As well as **17 soups** to sample, main courses focus on seafood: octopus, cuttlefish and sardines all make an appearance. A real treat if you're blessed with adventurous little eaters. Note, it's open evenings only – book ahead to be sure.

***Open** 7–11.30pm Tue–Sun. Main courses €7–19. Credit MC, V. **Amenities** reservations accepted.*

Bar Centrale, Fonteblanda, see p. 161.

La Botteghina ★★ VALUE LIVORNESE

Via Roma 159, Livorno. ☎ 0586 805110.

You'd be hard pushed to find a more 'authentic' trattoria in Tuscany: well outside the centre of untouristy Livorno. Luckily, it's almost opposite the **Mediterranean Natural History Museum** (p. 141), too. There's no menu to speak of, just a daily rotating list of top Livornese *antipasti*, *primi* and *secondi*, bound to include some of cuttlefish, fresh anchovies, *baccalà* (salt cod) *alla Livornese* and/or a *frittura mista* of whatever's been landed today. If you're lucky, Livorno's signature dish, *cacciucco* (similar to Marseille's fishy *bouillabaisse*), will be on.

For tots, they'll cook up spaghetti with a tomato sauce or an escalope to their taste. Perhaps a place to **avoid with fussy eaters**; also the restaurant takes cash only.

***Open** 12.30–2.30pm and 7–9.30pm Mon–Sat. **Set menu** €11–13 inc.*

Il Beccafico, Castiglione della Pescaia

Vitabella Palazzetto strada provinciale SP 160

house wine and coffee. ***Amenities*** *highchairs, reservations accepted.*

Il Balestruzzo PIZZA/MAREMMAN

Via Albizzeschi 6, Massa Marittima. 0566 904105.

This charming, cellar-style eatery is bang in the *centro storico*. The menu is short, but manages to squeeze in something for everyone: local cuisine sits alongside **Pizza Margherita**. The Maremman classic wild boar with olives features, as does fish: the *ribollita maremmana* (fishy soup-stew) and mixed fish grill are both great. For the children, as well as two pages of pizzas, there's veal cooked however they fancy it. The wine list is distinctly average.

Open *midday–2.30pm and 6.30–10pm Tue–Sun (closed Fri lunch).* ***Main courses*** *€9–14.* ***Credit*** *MC, V.* ***Amenities*** *reservations accepted.*

Osteria Libertaria ★★ FIND ELBAN/SEAFOOD

Calata Matteotti 12, Portoferraio, Elba. 0565 914978.

It doesn't matter where you sit in this tiny, family-run eatery, you'll be dining with the pleasing din of **sizzling fish**. The usual suspects – including fried squid and grilled whatever-looked-good-at-this-morning's-market – are always joined by Elban specialities: maybe *riso nero* (risotto blackened with squid ink) or salt cod *all'Elbana* (with black olives and pine nuts). There's always a token grilled meat; for the children, they'll cook a simple pasta sauce or plain grill a white fish. They also do chips (*patate fritte*).

Despite its tranquil spot at the far end of the port, you'll need to **arrive early** to grab one of two prime quayside tables; there's more terrace seating out back. It's handy for the ferry: make it your first or last stop on Elba.

Open *midday–2.30pm and 7–11pm daily Apr–Nov.* ***Main courses*** *€7.50–13.* ***Credit*** *MC, V.* ***Amenities*** *highchairs, reservations accepted.*

La Barcaccina ★★ SEAFOOD

Via Tridentina 1, San Vincenzo. 0565 701911. ***www.terra-toscana.com/labarcaccina****. At southern end, next to Parco Comunale.*

There are a million places to eat seafood along the Etruscan Coast, but this one on San Vincenzo's beach is a **bit special**. Fish is fresh from the morning market. The menu changes accordingly but always features mixed fish grills and plenty of shellfish. Despite the serious attitude to food, the atmosphere is **informal**: children can run amok on the beach while you wait to eat; dress up or down as you please. To feed youngsters, they'll grill a white fish and serve it with **proper chips**.

A local alternative, with a loftier reputation but no beach-front, is **Gambero Rosso** (Piazza della Vittoria 13. *0565 701021*). It's closed Mondays and Tuesdays: in summer, book ahead for either restaurant.

Open *12.30–2.30pm and 7.30–10pm Thu–Tue, closed Nov–Easter.* ***Main courses*** *€8–20.* ***Credit*** *AmEx, MC, V.* ***Amenities*** *highchairs, parking, reservations accepted.*

7 The Val d'Orcia, Valdichiana & Pitigliano

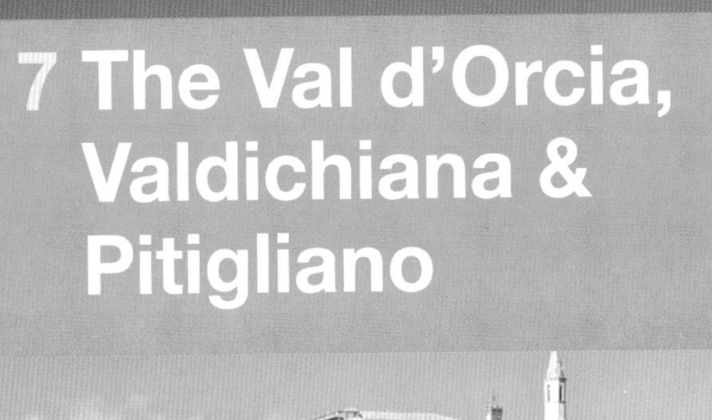

Vitabella Palazzetto, strada provinciale SP 160

SOUTHERN **TUSCANY**

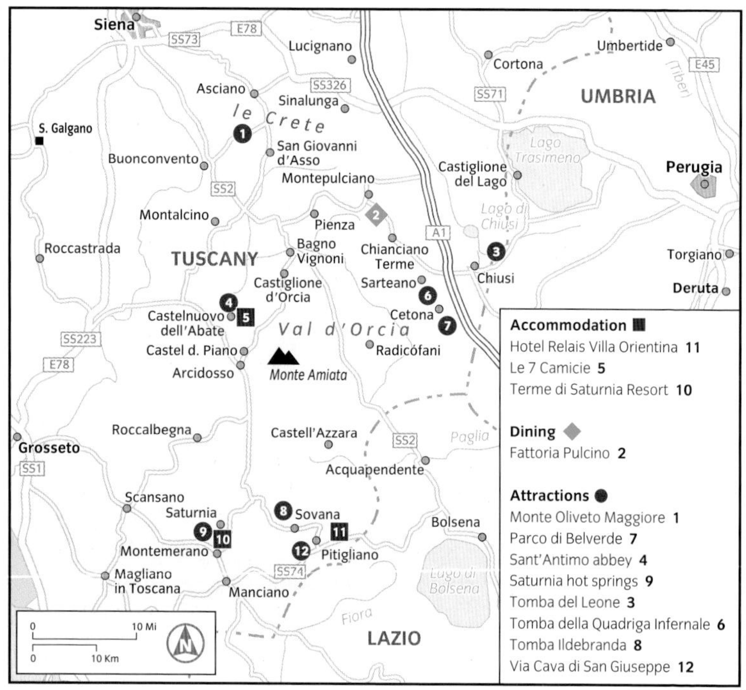

Italy's Etruscan heartland has a reputation among those in-the-know. It's sprinkled with attractions for over-18s only: sage nods in the illustrious *cantinas* of Montalcino and Montepulciano, furrowed brows among architecture buffs admiring Pienza's *palazzi*, and hushed tones in the abbeys of Monte Oliveto Maggiore and Sant'Antimo. This spectacular, manicured land of bleak farms, bright greens and limestone ridges, apparently lifted straight from the background of a Renaissance painting, is frequented by people on holidays who are *very serious indeed*.

Or at least, that's the stereotype – but don't give up yet! Montalcino's best spot for tasting its iconic wine, Brunello di Montalcino, is inside a cool castle. Pienza's little balcony has a view of the Val d'Orcia that'll knock youngsters dead – if the one over the Valdichiana from Cortona's keep hasn't wowed them already. You'll find local shops selling quality pecorino (sheep's milk cheese), extra virgin olive oils and fine wines round almost every corner in the area's hill-towns. Even gourmet Chiusi has enough underneath its streets to keep imaginative little minds ticking over. And we haven't even mentioned Pitigliano yet. This untouristy gem anchors a network of ancient subterranean walkways, wide open and free, with only your puff and a 9pm bedtime to limit you. Who said the Etruscans were boring?

x. strada statale SS323), km 14, Località Poggio al Leccio 58038 Seggiano (Grosseto)

Just don't forget the car-sickness pills: there's plenty of twisty-turny driving, too.

CORTONA

Despite its dramatic Valdichiana lookout, ancient **Cortona** ★ has a slightly stern look from a distance. Once inside the massive stone walls, its charm is revealed: a warren of paved streets and limestone palazzi, busy with swifts, swallows and stone staircases that disappear into blind alleys. Though the unwitting star of a publishing phenomenon, Frances Mayes' *Under the Tuscan Sun*, it remains a rustic hill-town with a real life beyond its artistic heritage. Both Luca Signorelli (1445–1523) and Sassetta (1392–1451) were Cortonese.

Essentials

Cortona is easily reached by **car**, 24km south of Arezzo off the SS71 and under an hour from Perugia and Lago Trasimeno's resorts. **Parking** is another matter: when the road divides just below Cortona, turn right and park for free in the lot on your right. From there, a new escalator flies you up the worst of the hill.

Roughly hourly **LFI buses** (*☎ 0575 39881. www.lfi.it*) from Arezzo (€2.80, 50 minutes) terminate in Piazzale Garibaldi, by the gate.

The **tourist office** (*☎ 0575 630352. infocortona@apt.arezzo.it*) is at Via Nazionale 42. Between Easter and September, it's open 9am–1pm and 3–7pm Monday to Saturday, mornings only on Sundays. It closes an hour earlier afternoons otherwise. The same building has a **cashpoint**. Mobile phone reception in Cortona is hopeless.

Around Town

Cortona is simply a great place to hang out. With young ones, though, we strongly advise you limit your wanderings to the bottom 'storey', running northwest from Piazzale Garibaldi to

Children's Top Attractions of Southern Tuscany

- Catching a first glimpse of Pitigliano growing from **living rock**, p. 179.
- Exploring the town's Jewish heritage and **ghetto**, p. 181.
- Basking in the warm **spa waters** at Saturnia, p. 182
- Hiking the Etruscan **Vie Cave**, p. 181.
- Scaling **Cortona** to the Fortezza Girifalco, p. 166.
- Braving the **labyrinth** under Chiusi, p. 177.
- Discovering ancient **wall art** in the Tomba della Quadriga Infernale, p. 178.
- Tucking into **Etruscan food** at Zaira, p. 185.

Piazza del Duomo and taking in the best two museums. The rest is major-league steep.

The illustrious **Museo dell'Accademia Etrusca e della Città** (☎ *0575 637235. www.cortonamaec.org*), or MAEC, has been renovated; the ground floor is now a well-signed multimedia trip to Cortona's Etruscan and Roman past. The sudden first-floor leap from Late Antiquity to 1920s Futurist Gino Severini marks the start of a chaotic but diverting procession through medieval Sienese altarpieces, Florentine heraldry and Egyptian mummies. It's open 10am–7pm daily April to October, closing two hours earlier and all-day Monday between November and March. Admission is a steep €7, €4 for anyone taking a child under 14.

Among some modest panels in the **Museo Diocesano** (☎ *0575 62830*), opposite the Duomo, are a pair of corkers. Fra' Angelico's **Annunciation** ★ rightly gets the plaudits, but Luca Signorelli's **Lamentation over the Dead Christ** ★★ is an outstanding example of his work, loaded with despair and surreal background detail. Hours are the same as MAEC; admission is €5, €3 for children 6–14.

The ice creams at **Gelateria Snoopy**, opposite MAEC in Piazza Signorelli, couldn't possibly live up to their hype but it's still the best place in town. The steps under the 13th-century **Palazzo Comunale** ★, round the corner in Piazza della Repubblica and right opposite some fine piazza cafes, are the ideal slurping spot.

Fortezza Medicea Girifalco ★★ AGE 10 AND UP

☎ *0575 637235*

If your children are old enough to climb, Cortona's major highlight is all uphill. The best route follows the wall from Piazza Garibaldi along Via Santa Margherita, the **Via Crucis** ★. This torturous, stepped ascent is enlivened by 15 mosaics depicting the **Stations of the Cross** by Cortonese Futurist Gino Severini. By the second time Christ falls, you'll feel like doing the same. The route is **impossible** with a buggy; don't attempt it with under-10s, asthma or a heart condition. Pause for a restorative drink at the bar by **Santuario Santa Margherita**.

Built in 1556 by a relative of Pope Pius IV, the four surviving bastions of the **Fortezza** have unmatched **views** ★★★ as far as Castiglione del Lago, Arezzo and the colossal Monte Amiata.

Open *10.30am–1.30pm and 2.30–6pm daily.* ***Adm*** *€3, €1.50 children 6–12.* ***Amenities*** *English, parking.*

FUN FACT **On the Level**

So rare are lanes without a slope, that Cortona's main street of Via Nazionale has earned the nickname '**flat street**'.

The Etruscans in 167 Words

Greek historian Herodotus reckoned that the Etruscans came from Turkey, but the more usual explanation is that they were simply the people who lived around here, and who gave their name to 'Tuscany'. From about 800 BC there are signs of Etruscan civilisation: they were farmers, seafarers and miners, with complex government structures, language and artistic forms. Fast forward to 100 AD and they've disappeared, assimilated by the rise of Rome. Their most important 12 cities were known as the **Dodecapoli**, and included *Velzna* (now Orvieto), *Arretium* (Arezzo), *Clevsin* (Chiusi) and *Curtun* (Cortona). Though each was largely autonomous, at their peak they controlled the territory between the Tiber and the Arno, with lands as far north as the Po and south to Salerno.

If you want to swot up before your trip, there's plenty more at ***http://en.wikipedia.org/wiki/Etruscans***. Should the Etruscan bug catch, the best places to head are the **Tomba della Quadriga Infernale** in Sarteano (p. 178) and the museums in **Orvieto** (p. 219) and **Cortona** (see above).

MONTEPULCIANO

Best known for its noble wine, **Vino Nobile di Montepulciano** ★, (see p. 169), Montepulciano is perched 664km up a volcanic ridge above the Valdichiana. It's the southern Tuscan hill-town par excellence, with emphasis firmly on the *hill* bit. Little legs and pushchair-pushers' will struggle: it's **seriously steep.** The narrow streets are full of fine Renaissance architecture, and shops offering wine tastings and *tipica* produce.

Essentials

Montepulciano is 72km southeast of Siena, on the SS146. **Parking** can be tricky: follow signs for '*centro storico/corso*' as you enter town; drive past the tourist office down the narrow hill: you can park there for free. **Pay parking** is right above, under the Porta al Prato (€1 per hour), but you'll need a fortune to bag a space. Opposite there's greenery, the **Giardino di Poggiofanti**, with **swings and a slide.** An alternative entry point is **car park 8** (also free): take the uphill left fork *immediately after* the Pienza/Chianciano junction. The route up from the car park alights adjacent to the **Fortezza** (closed), where there's a shady public garden with **swings and a slide.** You're far closer to Piazza Grande this way, but the climb is murder with a pushchair.

Between four and eight daily **TRA.IN buses** (*☎ 0577 204246. www.trainspa.it*) link **Siena** and Montepulciano, via Pienza. The 1½ hour journey costs €4.50.

The **tourist office** (*☎ 0578 757341.* ***www.prolocomontepulciano.it***) is now at Piazza Don

MONTEPULCIANO

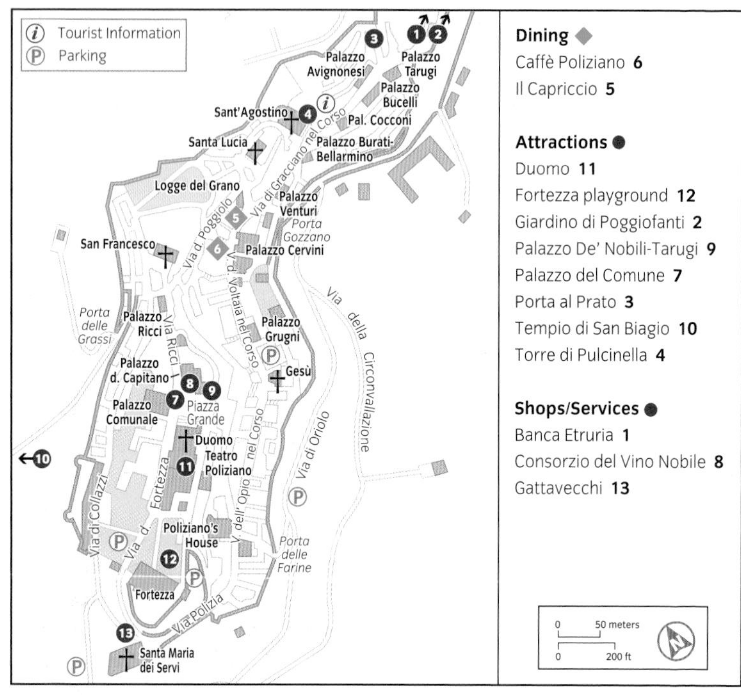

Minzoni 1, outside Porta al Prato (with a Banca Etruria **cashpoint** opposite). It's open 9am–12.30pm and 3–8pm daily between April and September; it closes an hour earlier and Sunday afternoons otherwise. If you don't fancy the uphill trek to Piazza Grande, orange hopper buses (**pollicini**) make the journey every 15–20 minutes. Buy **tickets** from the tourist office (90¢), good for an hour of travel. If you're with young children, we *strongly* recommend this method of getting to the top of town.

Montepulciano's major *festa* is the **Bravio delle Botti** ★ on the penultimate Sunday in August. Teams from the town's *contrade* race to push a wine barrel up the length of the main street, the Corso, wearing medieval costume.

Exploring the Town

There's no denying the sophisticated ambience lent to Montepulciano by its Renaissance *palazzi*. Antonio da Sangallo (the Elder) and Michelozzo were kept busy for years applying the architectural theories dreamt up by Pope Pius II and Rossellino in Pienza 50 years earlier (see below). They've lined the Corso with fine examples, but the highlight is Sangallo's **Palazzo De' Nobili-Tarugi**, in Piazza Grande.

FUN FACT Whose Side You on, Anyway?

It's easy to spot a hill-town's traditional protector and friend. The *marzocco* (heraldic lion), like the one in Montepulciano's Piazza Savonarola, symbolises **Florence**. **Siena** is represented by a she-wolf suckling two human children (Romulus and Remus). You can't miss it as you walk into nearby **Chiusi**'s Piazza Duomo.

For the youngsters, a couple of less refined sights may prove more memorable. The **Torre di Pulcinella**, in Piazza Michelozzo, is topped by a figure of **Punch** (*Pulcinella* in Italy), who strikes the hour. For endless **views** ★ into Umbria, scale the Gothic **Palazzo Comunale** (€1.60) in Piazza Grande. The roof terrace is open 10am–6pm daily; turn left up the stairs as you enter and pay on the second floor. Under-12s ascend for free.

Montepulciano's outstanding work of art, a dazzling **Assumption of the Virgin** ★ (1401) altarpiece by Sienese **Taddeo di Bartolo**, is inside the unfinished **Duomo**, also in Piazza Grande. The rather dark Renaissance interior also hides a painted terracotta frieze (c. 1512) by Andrea della Robbia known as the **Gigli altar**. It's in the Baptistery on your immediate left as you enter.

Right opposite, inside the **Palazzo del Capitano del Popolo**, is one for the wine buffs. Turn right from the corridor for the **Consorzio del Vino Nobile di Montepulciano** ★ (*0578 757812*. ***www.consorziovinonobile.it***). It offers a rotating menu of tastings of the town's renowned wine: €2 a glass, €5 for three. Local wineries without a shop in town also sell by the bottle here. It's open 11.30am–1.30pm and 2–6pm Monday to Friday (2–6pm only Saturday)

Punch on the Torre di Pulcinella

Montepulciano's Corso

from the week prior to Easter until the end of October. If you're heading into the country for some wine touring, they can provide maps and ideas, as can the **Strada del Vino Nobile** office (*0578 717484. **www.stradavinonobile.it***) across the corridor.

The best place in town to be seen sipping an (expensive) *cappuccino* is the Art Deco **Caffè Poliziano** (*0578 758615. **www.caffepoliziano.it***), at Via di Voltaia nel Corso 27. Forget their ice cream; across the street and just downhill at no. 14, **Il Capriccio** is better.

A steep 20-minute downhill walk from Porta dei Grassi takes you to the **Tempio di San Biagio**, a photogenic Renaissance church designed to a Greek cross plan, like St Peter's in Rome. Don't attempt the trek with a pushchair.

Gattavecchi ★ AGE 3 AND UP

*Via di Collazzi 74. 0578 757110. **www.gattavecchi.it**.*

A **child-friendly winery**? Not exactly, but Gattavecchi does have something to pique children's interest. Their cellars (you're free to poke around) have been in use since before 1200, originally by the friars of **Santa Maria dei Servi**. Older still is the tiny room at the bottom of the cellar chiselled from the rock; it was probably a chapel whose age can only be guessed. As you'd expect from one of Montepulciano's pioneering wine families, Gattavecchi **Vino Nobile** ★ (€12.50) is top-notch. The **Riserva** ★★ (€16), aged in oak *barriques* for a further six months, is superlative. They also sell wine for everyday drinking; tasting is free.

Open *9am–1pm and 2–7pm daily.* ***Credit*** *AmEx, MC, V.*

PIENZA

South of Siena in the heart of the Val d'Orcia, Pienza is one of

The Winemaker's Year

The busiest time of year for any winegrower is the **harvest**, usually in September. You might find some vineyards less than excited to see you if you turn up during the picking period: check first. That's not to say the rest of the year's quiet, mind you....

January/February: the vines are pruned and stakes mended, and the barrels from last year are kept topped up with wine to stop the air getting in.

March: new vines are planted; last year's young-drinking wine is bottled.

April/May: barrels are racked to separate the sediment, and vines are pruned to concentrate flavour in a few new shoots.

June/July: vines are trained so that they get as much sun as possible, and then sprayed against disease.

August: excess bunches of under-ripe grapes are cut away and the winery is prepared for harvest.

September/October: the winery is working at full-tilt on the *vendemmia*, the harvest, and starting the fermentation process that turns grape juice into wine.

November/December: it's time to take cuttings for the new year and make some early tastings of this year's young wine. And crack open a good bottle for Christmas dinner.

If you want to learn more about the region's reds, get Hugh Johnson and Andy Katz's **Tuscany and its Wines** (Mitchell Beazley, £12.99).

Tuscany's smaller gems. It was created in the mid-15th century by humanist Pope Pius II and architect Bernardo Rossellino as the ideal Renaissance town. If you think that the cost of the Millennium Dome or the London 2012 Olympics soared, Rossellino's budget was 10,000 florins and he spent 50,000. Still, Pius was so pleased he scrapped the old name of Corsignano and named it after himself. For Pi-enza read Blair-ville or Thatcher-ton.

In spite of being heavily frequented by tourists, it remains a delightful place, also famous for its delicious, locally produced sheep's cheese, 'pecorino di Pienza'.

Essentials

For **drivers**, Pienza is 14km west of Montepulciano, 55km south-east of Siena down the SS2 and then the SS146. You're certain to find a place in the (free) **car park** beside the Agip garage on the road to/from Montepulciano. It's five minutes to the centre. There are six daily **TRA.IN buses** (€3.60, 1¼ hours) from Siena.

The **tourist office** (✆ *0578 749071*) is inside the courtyard at Corso Rossellino 30. It's open 10am–1pm and 3–7pm daily,

FUN FACT UNESCO in Tuscany

Tuscany has more UNESCO World Heritage sites than any other Italian *regione*. As well as the historic centre of Pienza, and the surrounding emerald plains of the Val d'Orcia, there's:

- the Piazza del Duomo, Pisa: p. 113.
- the historic centre of Florence: p. 48.
- the historic centre of San Gimignano: p. 90.
- the historic centre of Siena: p. 81.

Poor old **Umbria** has just one such site: the Franciscan sights of Assisi, p. 202. For all 830 World Heritage sites, and what it takes to make the list, see ***http://whc.unesco.org/en/list***.

15th March to October; weekends only in winter. Another useful trip-planning resource, with a clickable map, is ***www.pienza.info***.

The first Sunday of every month sees Pienza's busy **organic food market**.

A Tour of the Town

Pienza is **flat**, and most sights are crammed into the splendid **Piazza Pio II** ★. This squashed Renaissance set-piece is as far as Pope Pius's town-planning dream reached. It's like a Matchbox version of architectural perfection. Of the standing follies, the highlight is the **Duomo** ★. Notice the light-drenched inside; that was part of Pius's brief to his builders. Alas, this fine monument is built on a precipice and is slowly cracking up. The piazza's other main 'sight', **Palazzo Piccolomini** (*0578 748392. **www.palazzopiccolominipienza.it***), is only accessible via a half-hour **guided**

Pienza

tour (regularly in English). Unless you and the youngsters have a particular interest in Renaissance *palazzi*, you'll be bored rigid. However, it's almost worth the €7 (€5 for children) to catch the devastating **view** ★★ south over the Val d'Orcia from the *palazzo*'s hanging garden and triple-decked *loggia*. Tours depart every half-hour, 10am–6pm, Tuesday to Sunday, from mid-March to mid-October; the last tour goes at 4pm otherwise. The palace is closed the second halves of February and November. You can get *almost* the same view for **free** anytime by walking down the steps between the Duomo and the Palazzo on to the old walls.

Among the dozens of friendly *tipico* shops lining Corso Rossellino, **Marusco e Maria** (*0578 748222*), at 15–21, stands out. It stocks 23 varieties of local sheep's milk **pecorino** cheese. You'll find the best ice cream away from the main drag: Snoopy's **Punto Gelato** ★ is across the road from Piazza Dante.

Monte Oliveto Maggiore

AGE 8 AND UP

8km north-east of Buonconvento. ***www.monteolivetomaggiore.it***

The most famous of Tuscany's rural **monasteries** is among the loveliest. Set in the scarred hills of the *Crete Senesi* (see p. 88) and with glorious views, Monte Oliveto Maggiore was founded in 1319 by a Sienese nobleman who renounced his wealth to live as a hermit. It owes its fame to the **Chiostro Grande** ★, painted with **frescoes** begun by Luca Signorelli in 1497 and completed by Sodoma in 1508. As frescoes go, these are easy to follow, recounting events in the life of **St Benedict**. Start in the back-left corner as you walk in and run clockwise. Sodoma painted the first and last of Benedict's deeds and miracles (a self-portrait with pet badger adorns panel 3); the change of style as Signorelli takes over, for 9 panels from God punishing Florenzo, is obvious.

The friars ask that you **dress appropriately** (no strappy tops or shorts) and respect their **silence**. This isn't a place to bring boisterous youngsters. The gatehouse restaurant, **La Torre** (*0577 707022*), has a shaded terrace – and positively encourages talking.

Open *9.15am–midday and 3.15–6pm daily (until 5pm winter).* ***Adm*** *free.* ***Amenities*** *bar/restaurant, English (audioguide €1), parking, picnic area.*

FUN FACT

Hollywood in Tuscany

If you want to see where the Oscar-winning film The English Patient was filmed, take the short drive from Pienza to **Sant'Anna in Campresa**. Pienza itself was the backdrop for much of Franco Zeffirelli's 1968 *Romeo and Juliet*.

MONTALCINO

If you know anything at all about wine, you don't need us to introduce **Montalcino**. The word comes with its own fanfare. There are few wines in the world to match the intensity of a fine **Brunello di Montalcino**. The origins of this delightful hill-top town go back to Etruscan times and life still ebbs and flows to the rhythm of its red grape. It isn't the obvious destination for children; there's *just* enough to keep them occupied while you knock back a few samples of the great red. And for all its pomp, Montalcino is still rustic at heart. Two streets back from the *tipico* food and wine shops, you'll find a ragged olive grove and someone's washing out to dry.

Essentials

Montalcino is easily reached by **car**, just 43km south-east of Siena. The best place to **park** (for free) is the town's western edge, along Viale Strozzi. From Siena, Montalcino is also served by regular **TRA.IN buses** (*0577 204246. www.trainspa.it*); it's a 1¼ hour journey (line 114). The bus drops you in Piazza Cavour, at the north end of town, or next to the Fortezza.

The **tourist office** is at Costa del Municipio 8 (*0577 849331. www.prolocomontalcino.it*), a ramp in the shadow of the bell tower. It's open 10am–1pm and 2–5.40pm Tuesday to Sunday between November and March; the same hours daily otherwise. There's a **cashpoint** around the other side of the tower.

Family-friendly Events

Montalcino's festivals revolve around hunting – and are inevitably food-and-wine affairs. Most interesting is the **Sagra del Tordo**, on the last Sunday in October: it 'celebrates' the thrush, spit-roasting them by the thousand. If you've ever wondered what songbirds taste like, this is the weekend to come.

Exploring the Town

Continue along the old walls from Viale Strozzi; the best spot to gulp down the panorama is the **Santuario della Madonna del Soccorso**. You'll know when you're there: there's **swings and a slide** next to it. Continue to Piazza Cavour and turn into Via Mazzini. From there walk the length of the *passeggiata* to the **Fortezza** (see below). Along the way, stop in at **Il Ranocchio** (*347 9527882*) for funky (if pricey) children's clothes. It's open daily 9.30am–1pm and 4.30–7.30pm. A sterner alternative is the **Museo d'Arte Sacra**, notable for four extraordinary carved **Crucifixions** ★ from the 1300s. It's in the cloisters of **Sant'Agostino** church, at Via Ricasoli 31, open 10am–1pm and 2–5.40pm Tuesday to Sunday; entry is €4.50, €3 for children aged 6–10. A joint ticket with the Fortezza saves €2.

La Fortezza ★ ALL AGES

Piazzale Fortezza. 📞 *0577 849211.* ***www.enotecalafortezza.it.***

Of the 1,001 places in Montalcino to taste wine, only one has ramparts: the **Fortezza**. Built in 1361, the castle's moment arrived when the Sienese holed up there for four years after their city's final defeat by Florence in 1555. You and the children can walk round the pentagonal walls and scale a ladder to the highest turret. On a clear day, you'll see Siena. Just don't look down.

Inside the keep, the **Enoteca La Fortezza** stocks a range of **Brunello di Montalcino ★★**, carefully selected from 208 registered producers in the DOCG (see p. 32). If you know Brunello, ask the knowledgeable, English-speaking staff to pour you something from the southern area; you'll get a fruitier surprise. Apart from 2002, every vintage since 2001 has been excellent or better. Two tasting samples cost €9, three €12 and five €19. A plate of salami or local cheese to complement costs €9. Youngsters tearing round the castle for free? Priceless.

If this is your only stop in Montalcino, you can **park** right outside (€1.50 per hour).

Open *9am–8pm Apr–Oct; 10am–6pm Nov–Mar.* ***Adm*** *€3.50, €1.50 under-12s (to walls).*

Abbazia di Sant'Antimo

AGE 5 AND UP

Castelnuovo dell'Abate. 📞 *0577 835659.* ***www.antimo.it.*** *9km south of Montalcino.*

Should the urge ever strike, it would be hard to find a better place to be a monk. The serene setting of Sant'Antimo, among vines at the foot of Castelnuovo dell'Abate, lends the exquisite Romanesque abbey a serenity rarely found on the tourist trail. The followers of St Augustine

Abbazia di Sant' Antimo

Bagno Vignoni

Signposted off the main road between Montalcino and Pienza is a pool like nothing your children have ever seen. For starters, you can't swim or splash in it. More remarkable is its Renaissance *loggia*, that it's where the village's **piazza** should be, and that it was frequented by **St Catherine of Siena** (see p. 87). Beware: Bagno Vignoni is a tour bus favourite, so arrive early; there's a café and *gelateria* opposite.

who reside here still worship in Gregorian chant – after a service (they're private and precede morning visiting hours), the smell of incense wafts across surrounding fields.

There's a well-marked **hiking trail** to the monastery from Montalcino for fit families. Ask about a map at the tourist office.

Open *10.30am–12.30pm and 3–6.30pm Mon–Sat.* ***Adm*** *free.* ***Amenities*** *parking.*

CHIUSI

The Etruscan city of Camars, or Clevsin, now known as **Chiusi**, doesn't leave quite the same aesthetic impression as its neighbours. Architecturally, it's a bit of a mish-mash; artistic highs are relatively lacking. There are, though, at least three things (mostly Etruscan) that make a short visit worthwhile: tunnels, towers and tucker. For the last, see p. 185; for the rest, read on.

Essentials

Chiusi is easily reached from just about anywhere in Italy: it's a major **rail** hub on the Florence–Rome line, with hourly direct trains to **Siena** (1¼ hours, €5.40) and **Arezzo** (45 minutes, €4.40), too.

By **car**, it's on the **A1**, 80km south-east of Siena and 50km from Perugia. The best spot to **park** (free) is off Via Pietriccia; if you approach from the west, follow the 'P' to the right as you enter the *centro storico*. There's a **playground** and **views** ★ to Umbria and Lazio in the Giardini Pubblici above the car park.

The **tourist office** is at Piazza Duomo 1 (*0578 227667. **prolocochiusi@bcc.tin.it***), opposite the campanile. It's open 10am–1pm and 3–6pm daily June to

'Montalcino's Fort'

TIP

Rome for the Day

You might be surprised how close you are to Rome. A day trip to Italy's capital is easy. From almost anywhere in southern Tuscany make for the railway station at **Chiusi–Chianciano Terme**. Trains to **Roma Termini** station (1 hour) run roughly hourly from 4am. A single costs from €8.20, depending on type of train, with 4–12-year-olds half price. Contact **Trenitalia** (*892021. www.trenitalia.it*) for timetables and tickets.

September, closing an hour earlier in May. It's open November to April 10am–midday, and until 2pm in October. They sell a **combined ticket** for all the sights for €11 (€9 for under-18s). There's a **cashpoint** uphill from the tourist office, on the corner of Via Porsenna and Via Petrozzi.

The Sights

The **Etruscans** (see p. 167) are almost the only game in town; Chiusi's major attractions revolve around them. Before you embark for Etruria, check out the town's Romanesque **Duomo** ★: dazzling mosaics including a giant *Assumption* appear to rise up behind the altar (50¢ for lights). In fact, these are **frescoes** painted in a 'mock-Byzantine' style between 1887 and 1894 by Arturo Viligiardi.

Chiusi's museum set-piece is its **Museo Archeologico Nazionale** (*0578 20177*), at Via Porsenna 93, housing local finds from the Bronze Age onwards. Most of the collection is Etruscan, including intricately painted ceramics and a 6th-century BC funerary **sphinx**. There's English signage all the way round; it's open daily 9am–8pm and costs €4, €2 for 18–25s. Your ticket is good for entry into two Etruscan tombs 3km north of Chiusi: the **Tomba del Leone** and **Tomba della Pellegrina**. Tell the staff when you leave the museum and they'll make sure someone's there to unlock the tombs for you. Hours are the same as the museum. The nearby frescoed **Tomba della Scimmia** ★ is visitable Tuesdays, Thursdays and Saturdays only, at 11am and 4pm (2pm winter). Book a place at the museum desk.

If the children are getting history-fatigue, carry on past the tombs for another 2km to **Lago di Chiusi**, for free swimming, rowing boats and a lakeside picnic area.

Labirinto di Porsenna ★

AGE 5 AND UP

Museo della Cattedrale, Piazza Duomo. 0578 226490.

Whether or not this labyrinth cut from the sandstone had anything to do with **Porsenna**, the Etruscan king who attacked Rome, isn't really the point. The 120m open to guided tours are part of a system of defensive tunnels and aqueducts that underpin the entire town. An atmospheric

half-hour tour leads you through the ancient Etruscan cave system before arriving at a giant Roman cistern, 6m high with a vaulted ceiling right under Chiusi's Piazza Duomo. The tunnel was once used by a private fire brigade who demanded payment before dousing your house.

To top the visit off, you're free to climb the 140 steps inside the **campanile of San Secondiano** for **views** ★ over Chiusi and 360° of Tuscan and Umbrian countryside.

Tours are in **Italian**, with an English handout.

***Guided tours** every 40 minutes. 10.10am–12.10pm and 4.10–6.10pm daily Jun–Oct; 10.10am–12.10pm Mon–Sat, also 4.10–6.10pm Sun, Nov–May. **Adm** €3 (€4 with Museo della Cattedrale). **Amenities** English.*

SARTEANO

For an escape from high-season hordes for the day, the walled town of **Sarteano**, 9km west of Chiusi, might just have what you're looking for. This serene little place hides a couple of under-visited gems. To catch the town's blockbuster (see below), visit on a **Saturday**. At other times, you'll have a pleasant little hill-town, dotted with post-Renaissance *palazzi*, mostly to yourself.

The **tourist office** (*☎ 0578 269204. **turismo@comune.sarteano.siena.it**.* Wed and weekends 10am–12.30pm) at Corso Garibaldi 9, close to **Piazza Giugno XXIV**, can supply a map and point you to 16th-century Palazzo Gabrielli for Sarteano's **Museo Civico** (€2.50; see below). This small collection features Etruscan finds from the area. It's open 10.30am–12.30pm and 4–7pm Tuesday to Sunday between May and October, weekends only otherwise.

Continue into Piazza San Martino for the **Chiesa di San Martino** ★. The boxy interior has three *Madonnas* from the 14th and 15th centuries. Best of the lot is Domenico Beccafumi's Mannerist 1546 **Annunciation** ★, swept by light and shadow with a stormy landscape out the window.

For youngsters, there's the **Castello** (€3 adults, €2 children), open weekends only 10.30am–12.30pm and 3–7pm April to September, 2–5pm the rest of the year. To cool down, you can all pay to use the large swimming pool at **Parco delle Piscine** (see p. 184), followed by a superlative *gelato* at **Bar I Diavoli** ★ (*☎ 0578 266754*), Via di Fuori 79. Try the mildly alcoholic, very authentic *zuppa inglese* (trifle) flavour.

Tomba della Quadriga Infernale ★★ FIND AGE 3 AND UP

*c/o Museo Civico, Via Roma 24. ☎ 0578 269261. **museo@comune.sarteano.siena.it**.*

Hands-down the best Etruscan attraction in the area, the **Tomb of the Chariot from Hell** is one part of a complex of at least 14 excavated in 2003. Inside, guarding the entrance to the Underworld, are four vivid

frescoes dating from around 330BC. The most striking shows a **demon charioteer** driving two lions and two griffins – the only time this image has been seen in Etruscan art.

After the tour is over, you're free to explore the other tombs on the necropolis, all open, which extend for 1km on a ridge with stupendous **views** ★★ over the Valdichiana.

Visits are limited to 40 people per week, on **Saturdays only**. In summer, email a few weeks in advance to book; otherwise a few days' notice usually suffices. It's in **Italian**, with an English handout. You'll also need a car to drive the 2km to the site. Even if it's not Saturday, ask at the museum desk for directions to the necropolis. There are 13 other tombs to scramble around.

Guided tours *Sat only.* ***Adm*** *€5, inc. Museo Civico.* ***Amenities*** *English.*

Parco Archeologico Naturalistico di Belverde FIND

AGE 5 AND UP

Belverde, Cetona. 0578 239219. ***www.ctnet.it/museo/cetona/parco/index.html****. 5km south of Sarteano, dir. San Casciano.*

Ready for some summer scrambling in the countryside? Cetona's '**archaeological nature park**' adds interest to a random roam by peppering the *percorso* with vaguely educational stuff related to the area's Paleolithic population. There's a reconstructed ancient dwelling, caves to explore and a Bronze Age cult cemetery – as well as **panoramas** over the Valdichiana.

An extra 50¢ on the ticket price gets you into Cetona's **Museo Civico**, with finds from the park's digs.

Open *9am–1pm and 4–7pm Tue–Sun Jun–Sep.* ***Adm*** *€2.50, children €2.* ***Amenities*** *café, parking.*

PITIGLIANO & THE DEEP SOUTH

It's a fair old diversion from the main sights of Tuscany to bag **Pitigliano** ★★★. You won't regret it, though. Even devoted beach-hounds and jaded hill-town veterans won't be quite prepared for the almost Transylvanian sight of a town growing out of a volcanic tufa perch. Look closely: it's impossible to see where rock ends and houses start. Silhouetted against a Tuscan sky, or even better illuminated against the inky night, it's unforgettable.

Essentials

Although a long haul from Florence and Siena, Pitigliano is an easy day trip from the coast. It's 80km from Grosseto, along the **SS74**. It's also easy if you're staying near **Orvieto** (p. 219) in southern Umbria. Wherever you come from, make sure you **enter the town from the west**, from Manciano, for that **view** ★★★. You can **park** for free just outside the centre: uphill from the arched viaduct over the road, take the right fork marked *cimitero*. Park anywhere on the left along there.

The **tourist office** (☎ *0564 617111. www.comune.pitigliano.gr.it*) is at Piazza Garibaldi 51, open 10.20am–1pm and 3–7pm Tuesday to Sunday between April and October, 2–6pm in March. Winter opening is limited. There's a **cashpoint** behind the ilex trees in Piazza della Repubblica, and a park with **swings and slides** outside the historic centre on Via Ugolini.

A Family-friendly Festival

The highlight of Pitigliano's festival year is the **Torciata di San Giuseppe** ★, on 19 March. This fire festival to welcome spring includes a torchlit procession along ancient *vie cave* (see below), climaxing in the burning of a wicker man, symbolic of winter, in Piazza Garibaldi. It's never too packed.

Exploring the Town

Pitigliano's twisted alleys and gnarled stone staircases make for pleasant strolling – mostly navigable with a pushchair. For local wine, ceramics or *Star Wars* figures, browse the shops along **Via Roma**. A little more offbeat is the **Studio of Adrian America Pio** (Via Zuccarelli 45. ☎ *0564 614430*), whose King Crimson-inspired insect art is about as far from the Uffizi as you'll find in Tuscany. Of course, it's open when it's open – he's an artist.

For a cheap lunch in town, the always-busy **La Magica Torre** ★ (☎ *0564 616260*) at Piazza Petruccioli 73 sells fab

Pitigliano

TIP Sweet as Cherry Wine

If you're in a wine shop around Pitigliano, you might spot a red you've never heard of, even if you're a buff. It's made from the **Ciliegiolo** ('cherry-like') grape grown only in the Maremma and areas of southern Umbria. **Ghiottornia** ★ (*0564 616907. **www.ghiottornia.com***) at Via Roma 111, stocks it. Doesn't taste much like cherries, though, fortunately.

pizza by the slice. Even better, you choose the size of the slice yourself.

Jewish Museum, Synagogue and Ghetto ★★

*Vicolo Marghera (off Via Zuccarelli). 0564 616006. **lapiccola gerusalemme@libero.it**.*

If your children have an interest in what happened to Europe's Jews, this will be the family highlight of Pitigliano. It was the Jewish community that gave Pitigliano its nickname **La Piccola Gerusalemme** ('little Jerusalem'). This maze-like museum, built into the ghetto where the town's Jews were banished by the Medici rulers, is fascinating. The ritual baths, *matzo* oven (last used for Passover in 1939) and kosher wine cellars are carved into the tufa that underpins the town. The synagogue was built in 1598, not long after Jews were banished from Rome, and by 1960 it was in disrepair. It's a sombre reminder of how first Christian Europe, then the Nazis and Fascists, treated our neighbours.

Bits of the trail are **steep**, so hold your children's hands – and no pushchairs. It also gets busy on Sundays. If you're interested in more Jewish sights in Tuscany, ask at the *biglietteria* for the free, English-language **Jewish Tours in Tuscany** guide.

***Open** 10am–12.30pm and 3–6pm Mar–Nov, until 6.30pm Jun–Sep, until 5.30pm Dec–Feb; closed Sat. **Adm** €2.50, €1.50 children 6–12. **Amenities** English, shop.*

Vie Cave

0564 617111. Between Pitigliano and Sovana.

You can just about imagine those Etruscans processing along *vie cave*, ancient subterranean walkways hollowed from volcanic rock. Or driving livestock along them. Or, well, infact, nobody knows what they did with them – maybe it was something to do with magic. But they're great: these hidden channels are up to 7m deep; you can walk for miles in them. You'll need a map (the Pitigliano tourist office has one), a decent pair of trainers, and plenty of puff. Even in summer you'll have the routes mostly to yourself. The best of the bunch is the **Via Cava di San Giuseppe** ★, 1km out of Pitigliano on the road to Sovana.

More structured for youngsters, the **Museo Archeologico all'Aperto 'Alberto Manzi'**

(☎ *0564 614067.* €4, children €2.50) on the SS74 just outside Pitigliano has real *vie cave* and reconstructions of Etruscan homes.

Open *always.* ***Adm*** *free.*

Tomba Ildebranda

☎ *0564 614074. 2km west of Sovana.*

The most important Etruscan site in southern Tuscany, **Hildebrand's Tomb** was (in its 3rd-century BC heyday) decorated with vivid pictures of vegetables. Weird. It's now an evocative ruin that your children are free to scramble on, over and underneath. The tomb is just one part of a network of Etruscan burial sites and *vie cave* that you could spend a few hours exploring. The English-language signage on the way round is so good that by the time you're all done, you'll know more about Etruscan funerary architecture than any human could ever need. Or, with appropriate footwear, you could just run around the place: the **Via Cava di Poggio Prisca** is especially cool.

The pretty little village of **Sovana**, nearby, is also worth a stop. There's a picnic area right at the village entrance under the ruined fortress. Otherwise, its pedestrian centre is an ideal spot for a family mooch.

Open *10am–7pm daily Mar–Nov.* ***Adm*** *€5, free under-12s.* ***Amenities*** *English, picnic area, shop.*

INSIDER TIP

If you're planning an Etruscan overdose, the **Etruscan Card** (€10) gets you into all 13 sites around Pitigliano and Sorano, museums and necropoli. It's also good for 10% off **Orvieto Underground** (p. 222). It's available from any of the sites. For information, email ***arethusa.parcotufo@virgilio.it***.

Saturnia Hot Springs ★

1km south of Saturnia; as road bends left 500m after Terme di Saturnia, park on dirt track and walk (1 minute).

There are more Etruscan remains at Saturnia, but the place is on the map for something different altogether: the waterfall of **thermal springs** just outside town off the road to Montemerano. This cascade of swirling, steaming, slightly stinky sulphur water at a constant 37°C is a surreal place for a family dip. It's free, it's an oddity – and it's stunning. On a sunny day, the cascade reflects an intense cobalt blue, looks like nothing so much as an oversized ornamental water feature and takes a great snap.

The springs get busy at weekends, even way out of season.

Adm *free.* ***Amenities*** *café/bar.*

FAMILY-FRIENDLY ACCOMMODATION

B&B Porta Castellana FIND

Via Santa Lucia 20, Montalcino. ☎ *0577 839001.* ***www.portacastellana.it.***

Two things you almost never find within the walls of a Tuscan hill-town are both here: **parking** and a **garden**. The Porta Castellana's former workshops have been converted to two fine rooms, with exposed stone, stylish antiques and new bathrooms. One can accommodate an extra bed; the other can be opened up into a separate adjoining room making a small 'apartment' for up to five. The constant gentle breeze keeps it all cool. From April to October, breakfast is served outside under the gazebo as the mists slowly lift from the Val d'Orcia below. It's magical. There are no cots (bring your own) and no TV – you'll just have to enjoy the silence.

Rooms *2.* ***Rates*** *Double €75, adjoining rooms for up to 5 €130. Extra bed in double €20. Breakfast included.* ***Credit*** *MC, V.* ***Amenities*** *parking.* ***In room*** *shower only.*

Le 7 Camicie ★★

Strada Provinciale di Sant'Antimo, km 10+200. *335 6363730.* ***www.le7camicie.it****. 1km south of Castelnuovo dell'Abate.*

If the vines grew any closer to Le 7 Camicie, they'd be in the swimming pool. The **converted farm complex** could hardly be better sited for some southern Tuscan wine tourism from a family-friendly base. The apartments are simply but stylishly decorated, with cool tile floors and exposed beams. Kitchenettes and bathrooms are adequate if unspectacular. The views back to Montalcino are something else.

For large groups, there is an apartment that sleeps 12. Note, the swimming pools (one of which is kept at an all-year 40°C by a thermal spring) aren't fenced; daily bookings accepted outside summer, Christmas and Easter (from €70 per night).

Apartments *15.* ***Rates*** *1-bed €350–650 per week, 2-bed €750–1200 per week, 3-bed €1000–1500 per week. Cot €20 per week.* ***Credit*** *MC, V.* ***Amenities*** *parking, pools (outdoor).* ***In room*** *A/C, kitchen, sat TV, shower only.*

Albergo Portole

Portole, Cortona. *0575 691008.* ***www.portole.it****. 8km north-east of Cortona.*

It's not every Tuscan hotel that has a **1960s fighter plane** parked across the road: the former pilot who runs the Portole parked it 12 years ago to amuse children who stay. Yours are welcome to explore at leisure. Inside, rooms are standard if unexciting; outside, a modern extension sucks some character from the rustic limestone inn. The real draw, though, is the setting: high in the hills above Cortona, you'll struggle to find a more peaceful spot in Tuscany. Dinner on the panoramic terrace with just the pine trees for company is magical.

Rooms *20.* ***Rates*** *Double €100, family room (for 4) €120. Cots free. Breakfast included.* ***Credit*** *AmEx, MC, V.* ***Amenities*** *parking, playground, restaurant.* ***In room*** *A/C, sat TV, shower only.*

Thermal Spa at Hotel Relais Villa Orientina

Parco delle Piscine

Via del Bagno Santo 29, Sarteano. 0578 26971. ***www.parcodelle piscine.it****. 9km from A1 Chiusi–Chianciano Terme exit.*

In a corner of Tuscany not blessed with many campsites or holiday parks, this place in Sarteano makes an ideal family base: Montepulciano, Chiusi and Lago Trasimeno are all within half an hour. Although the setting is a shade unspectacular, facilities certainly aren't: the usual ping-pong and playground are joined by tennis courts (€13 per hour), a floodlit five-a-side pitch (€50 per hour) and high-season child and adult entertainment programmes. The three swimming pools are heated by a **thermal spring**, and so never budge from 24°C.

Mobile homes are standard, well equipped, and sleep four or six without much room to spare. During July, there are discounts for stays of five nights and over.

Keycamp and **Eurocamp** use the site (see p. 245).

Pitches *509 (+ mobile homes) (open Apr–Sep).* ***Rates*** *adults €10–14, children 3–10 €6–8, pitch €10–14.* ***Mobile homes*** *for four €45 per night (€105 Jul–Aug), for six €60 per night (€130 Jul–Aug). Cot €1 per night.* ***Credit*** *MC, V.* ***Amenities*** *entertainment, Internet (€6 per hour), laundry (€4.50), parking, playground, pools (outdoor), restaurant, shop.* ***In mobile homes*** *kitchenette, shower only, WiFi (€6 per hour).*

Hotel Relais Villa Orientina ★

Via Valle Orientina, Pitigliano. 0564 616611. ***www.valleorientina.it****. 3km east of Pitigliano; signposted at Km 55+300 on SR74.*

Despite the unpromising drive up from the road, this modern, well-equipped hotel just outside Pitigliano fits the family bill. The Villa Orientina is set in its own little valley, with large gardens, archery lessons, bikes for the children, chirruping birds and a gurgling stream. The outdoor pool and **spa** are heated by thermal springs. Inside, the ingenious, though not huge, family rooms have bunks that fold from the wall to give you more daytime space. It's not quite the Terme di Saturnia (see below), but then it's nowhere near the price either.

They have a sister hotel in nearby Manciano, the **Borgo Nuovo** (*0564 620035.* ***www. ilborgonuovo.net***).

Rooms *20.* ***Rates*** *Double €80–150, triple €100–170, quad €120–190. Breakfast included. 10% discount for longer stays.* ***Credit*** *AmEx, MC, V.* ***Amenities*** *parking, pool (outdoor), spa (€5, children €3), tennis.* ***In room*** *shower only, sat TV.*

Terme di Saturnia Spa and Golf Resort ★★

*0564 600111. **www.termedisaturnia.it**. 1½ km south of Saturnia dir. Montemerano.*

The **luxury** choice among southern Tuscany's spa hotels, this is strictly for the flush. Although the ambience may be a little corporate for some, the quality of service on every level stands out – as you'd expect from a place that's won readers' awards from *Condé Nast Traveller* and *Spafinder*. Little touches like wireless Internet through the TV in every room give it an edge. Various stay-and-spa packages are available: check their website. A great place to treat older children – and so it should be at that price, I hear you say.

***Rooms** 140. **Rates** Double €400–620, triple €560–850. Breakfast included. Cot €30. **Credit** AmEx, MC, V. **Amenities** babysitting, bars, laundry service, parking, pools (indoor/outdoor), restaurants, spa, tennis. **In room** A/C, safe, sat TV, WiFi.*

FAMILY-FRIENDLY DINING

Ristorante Zaira ★★ SOUTHERN TUSCAN/ETRUSCAN

*Via Arunte 12, Chiusi. 0578 20260. **www.zaira.it**.*

In a town with a great reputation for eating, this traditional dining room stands out. Food is anything but standard: 'Etruscan' dishes feature alongside regular southern Tuscan food like house speciality *pasta del Lucumone* (baked in the oven with pecorino, parmesan and ham). For the children, they'll cook up pasta with a simple sauce; alternatively, the *coniglio* (rabbit) *al limone* is delicate enough not to offend, depending on what pets you have at home obviously... Make sure you pop down to see their **wine cellar**: 20,000 bottles are stored in Etruscan tunnels and wells.

A nearby alternative is **La Solita Zuppa** (*0578 21006*), at Via Porsenna 21.

***Open** midday–2.30pm and 7–9.30pm Tue–Sun (daily summer). **Main courses** €6–14.50. **Credit** MC, V. **Amenities** highchairs, reservations accepted.*

Re di Macchia MONTALCINESE

Via Saloni 21, Montalcino. 0577 846116.

This back-street restaurant popular with locals specialises in exquisitely cooked *cucina tipica Montalcinese*. Apart from loaded bruschetta, *tagliolini* with nettles and a soup or two, it's **meat** all the way; you're in hunting country, remember. The poor old **wild boar** in particular gets it: he's in the salami *antipasto*, served with *pinci* (squat, thick spaghetti) and even pops up in a goulash. Not a place to take vegetarians.

If that's a bit hardcore Tuscan, an alternative across the street, with many of the same dishes plus two pages of pizzas, is **Ristorante San Giorgio** (*0577 848507. **ristorantesangiorgio@prolocomontalcino.it***). It's open every day April to October.

Open** midday–2pm and 7–9pm Fri–Wed. **Main courses** €8–16. **Credit

MC, V. ***Amenities*** *reservations accepted.*

La Loggetta ★ TUSCAN

Piazza di Pescheria 3, Cortona. ☎ 0575 630575. ***www.locandanelloggiato.it.***

Okay, so it's touristy, but La Loggetta has the **best perch** in Cortona: above Piazza della Repubblica looking right at the Palazzo Comunale. Stop by as soon as you hit town to reserve a lunchtime seat under the *loggia* (€3 per person cover charge). The menu is solid rather than spectacular, but cooked much better than you might expect given the prime location. Pasta dishes are especially tasty, from basic ravioli with porcini mushrooms to inventive flourishes like *fettuccine* with cabbage and truffles. For youngsters, there's pizzas, plain grilled chicken and fried spuds.

For fewer tourists, better value but no view, head uphill to **Trattoria Dardano** ★ (☎ *0575 601944*) at Via Dardano 24.

Open *12.30–2.30pm and 7.30–9.30pm Thu–Tue.* ***Main courses*** *€7–15.* ***Credit*** *MC, V.* ***Amenities*** *highchairs, reservations accepted.*

Fattoria Pulcino ★ GREEN SOUTHERN TUSCAN/GRILL

☎ 0578 758711. ***www.pulcino.com.*** *1½ km south of Montepulciano on SS146, dir. Chianciano.*

If you could mark a spot for a perfect panorama of Montepulciano, your X would come down somewhere near the **terrace** at Pulcino. This former monastery is now the headquarters of a *tipico* empire selling Vino Nobile (€16), organic olive oil (€8 for 250ml) and salami *della casa* from their roadside farm. The large restaurant's cooking is almost beside the point, but a menu of pizza, pasta and grilled meats is perfectly executed, if limited. The 'local' choice is *pici di Montepulciano*, a thick, handmade spaghetti.

Smoking is still allowed on the panoramic terrace and ordering from the grill (free-range chicken, beef, veal) means a longer wait than pasta or pizza; it's cooked from scratch. Don't forget your camera for those views.

Open *midday–10pm daily, call ahead in winter as times vary.* ***Main courses*** *€8–16.* ***Credit*** *AmEx, MC, V.* ***Amenities*** *parking, reservations accepted.*

La Giara ITALIAN GRILL

Viale Europa 2, Sarteano. ☎ 0578 265511.

This large, modern and (it must be said) plain dining room on the edge of Sarteano ticks most of the boxes for a family bite on the move – especially for fussy eaters. There's pasta a million ways, roast chicken, salads and even chips, all cooked to perfection. Best of all, there's a proper **wood oven** for authentic pizzas at super-reasonable prices (dinner only), including a 'Baby Margherita' (€3.50). For something local, try **Valdichiana beef** cooked on the flame-grill or (if it's on) ravioli with a homemade nut pesto.

Open *midday–2pm and 7–10.30pm Tue–Sun.* ***Main courses*** *€5–18.* ***Credit*** *AmEx, MC, V.* ***Amenities*** *highchairs, parking, reservations accepted.*

8 Perugia, Assisi & Northern Umbria

NORTHERN UMBRIA

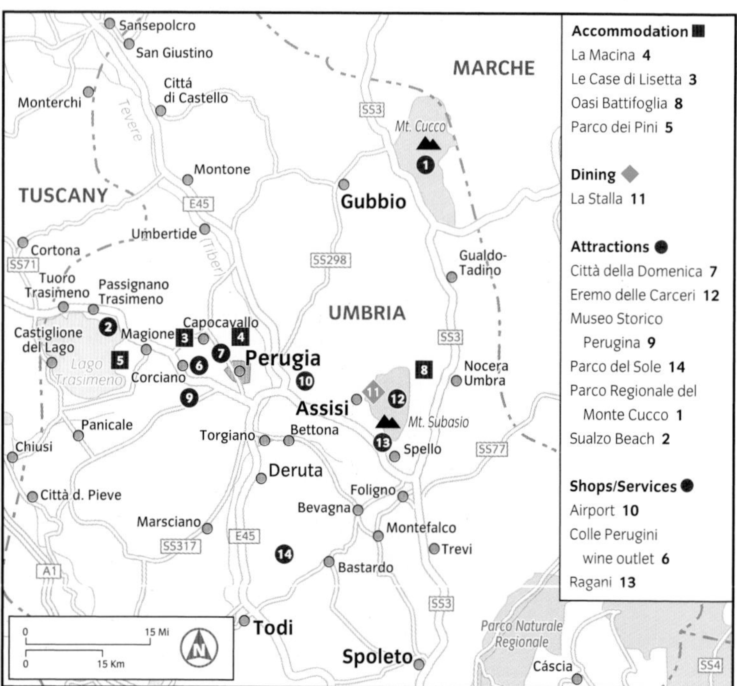

Umbria has the misfortune to sit beside Europe's most scenic patch of land. It doesn't have dramatic landscapes like the Tuscan Crete or the Val d'Orcia; there's no Florence or Siena, not even a San Gimignano. The balance of power between grape and olive swings to the less glamorous latter. What Umbria does have, though, is **peace**. A sense of itself that inhabits miles of unblighted, often empty, country dotted with hill-towns that still *work*. It's a place to get away from it all in a farmhouse or villa, if that's what takes your fancy. A place to eat well, relax by the pool and breathe deeply. It's an unshowy place in touch with its own soul, and Italy's: it's the only *regione* without an international border or coastline. Umbria is what it is, maybe even what Italy *was*.

At the spiritual heart is **Assisi**, a place of pilgrimage second only to Rome. Not just the birthplace of Italy's patron saint but also of Western art in the form of Giotto's frescoes covering the Basilica di San Francesco. **Perugia** is altogether different, young and fashionable, and quite un-Umbrian. There's art, of course, but the city is also at the centre of attractions designed to appeal to local and visiting families – with young, hip shopping options not to be found elsewhere in the region. Elsewhere in the north, Umbria's sort-of-seaside, **Lago**

Trasimeno, offers action on, in and above the water; pretty hill-towns like **Spello** and **Gubbio** cater for days when you just feel like a mosey. Relax, folks: we're in Umbria.

PERUGIA

Umbria's bright lights and big city isn't especially either. This medieval metropolis high above the River Tiber takes an ancient hill-town with a fine Corso and adds a dash of cosmopolitan youth. The shops that line Corso Vannucci are the height of Umbrian and international chic. The smell of outdoor living, the *caffè* lifestyle, is everywhere. Blame the **students** of the town's two universities, including 7,000 at the *Università per Stranieri* to learn Italian language and 'living', who keep the place jumping at night during term-time. Other notable residents (now former) are Renaissance artists **Pinturicchio** and **Perugino**, who as well as achieving acclaim in his own right, taught Raphael to paint. **Perugia** ★ also recorded the first **Flagellant**, a curious Christian sect who whipped their flesh to cleanse the spirit. They died out (alas, literally) just before everyone else discovered that flagellation wasn't a cure for the plague.

Essentials

Getting There

By Car Despite missing a motorway, Perugia is bisected by two fast, and **free**, roads. The east–west **SS75b** connects with the A1, Lago Trasimeno and Assisi; the **E45** *superstrada* heads north to Città di Castello and south to Todi and Terni. The best way into the town is the SS75b **Perugia Prepo** exit: to park, follow the 'P' signs for **Europa** or **Partigiani**, next to

Children's Top Attractions of Northern Umbria

- Feeling the **wow** in full effect at the Basilica di San Francesco, Assisi, p. 202.
- Meeting the art of **Giotto**, Cimabue, Lorenzetti and Martini, p. 202.
- Windsurfing and **canoeing** the placid waters of Lago Trasimeno, p. 196.
- Diving into the **art treasure** in the Collegio del Cambio, Perugia p. 193.
- Getting **enchanted** at the Botteghe Artigiani di Silvio Bambini, Città di Castello, p. 211.
- Scaling Monte Ingino in a **metal cage**, p. 209.
- Stocking up on cocoa and sugar at **Eurochocolate**, Perugia, p. 190.
- DIY **flamegrilling** at Assisi's La Stalla, p. 214.

each other south of the centre. The latter (€1.25 per hour) is handier for the escalators (*scale mobili*) up to Corso Vannucci; Europa is €1 per hour. If you want the 24-hour tourist '**day-pass**' (€8.90), ring the cashier's bell to pay in advance. The **bus station** is above Partigiani.

By Air Three weekly **Ryanair** (☎ *0871 246 0000. www.ryanair.com*) flights connect London Stansted with Perugia's **Aeroporto Internazionale dell'Umbria** (☎ *075 592141. www.airport.umbria.it*), 10km east of the city. It has four **car rental** desks: **Europcar** (☎ *075 5731704*), **Hertz** (☎ *075 5002439*), **Maggiore** (☎ *075 5007499*) and **Vis** (☎ *075 6929346*). The 30–40-minute bus from outside the terminal to **Piazza Italia** costs €3.50.

By Train Confusingly, two railways visit Perugia. The **state railway** (☎ *892021. www.trenitalia.it*) station serves **Rome** (change at Foligno, €10.50, 2–3 hours) and **Florence** (change at Terontola, €8.20, 2¼ hours) every couple of hours. There are also hourly trains to **Spello** (€2.30, 35 minutes) and **Spoleto** (change at Foligno, €3.70, 1½ hours). The station is a few kilometres south-west of the centre, although it's well connected with buses to/from Piazza Italia, at the foot of Corso Vannucci.

The station for the private **FCU railway** (☎ *075 575401. www.fcu.it*), Sant'Anna, is closer, in Piazzale Bellucci. These tiny trains serve **Città di Castello** (€3.05) and **Todi** (€2.55) every couple of hours.

Visitor Information & Festivals

Perugia's helpful **tourist office** (☎ *075 5736458. info@iat.perugia.it*) is at Piazza Matteotti 18, where it will stay until 2009 or 2010. It's open 8.30am–1.30pm and 3.30–6.30pm Monday to Saturday, 9am–1pm Sunday. Hours will soon change.

There are plenty of **web resources** for planning a trip to Umbria, even Perugia specifically. The best are ***www.umbria2000.it***, ***www.bellaumbria.net***, ***www.argoweb.it*** and, just on Perugia, ***www.perugiaonline.com***. Museum group **SistemaMuseo** (***www.sistemamuseo.it***) runs many museums in Umbria.

Pick up a copy of monthly listings magazine **Viva Perugia** ★ (80¢) at newsstands across the city. Inside every edition there are public-transport schedules for Perugia and elsewhere in Umbria.

The city's most famous *festa* is **Umbria Jazz** (***www.umbriajazz.it***), one of the world's pre-eminent jazz events. More family flavour is provided each October by **Eurochocolate** ★ (***www.eurochocolate.com***): 150 plus exhibitors pitch their tents on Corso Vannucci, the heart of Italy's cocoa capital. *Pesto alla cioccolata*, anyone?

INSIDER TIP

For events and services for children in Perugia and all over Umbria, bookmark ***www.infobambini.net***.

Fontana Maggiore

Fast Facts: Perugia

Car Rental See 'Getting There', above.

Cashpoint There are *bancomats* every few yards along Corso Vannucci.

Chemist **Farmacia Andreoli** (*075 5720915*), next to the Collegio del Cambio at Corso Vanucci 27, is open 9am–1pm and 4–8pm.

Hospital An accident and emergency service is provided by **Santa Maria della Misericordia** (or 'Silvestrini'. *075 5781*) in San Sisto. In an emergency, call *118.*

Internet The central choice is **Internet Corner** (*075 5720901. www.internetcorner.it*) at Piazza Danti 5/b, behind the Duomo; it's 5¢ per minute or €5 for three hours. They also have a **hotspot**.

Around Town

The best way into Perugia, via escalators from Partigiani's car park, drills you into a preserved subterranean street and the former **Rocca Paolina** ★ (*075 5725778*). This symbol of Papal authority was built after a brief war in 1531 between Pope Paul III and the Perugians over a tax on salt – to this day, Perugian bread is salt-free. After Italian unification in 1860, locals ripped the castle to pieces and built Piazza Italia on top.

The city's main drag is fairly **flat**, as long as you don't wander too far from the shops and bars along sophisticated **Corso Vannucci** ★. Follow it past the massive **Palazzo dei Priori** ★ to Piazza IV Novembre and the Gothic **Fontana Maggiore** ★★. The fountain's decorative sculpture was added in the late 1200s by the Pisanos. It serves as a

PERUGIA

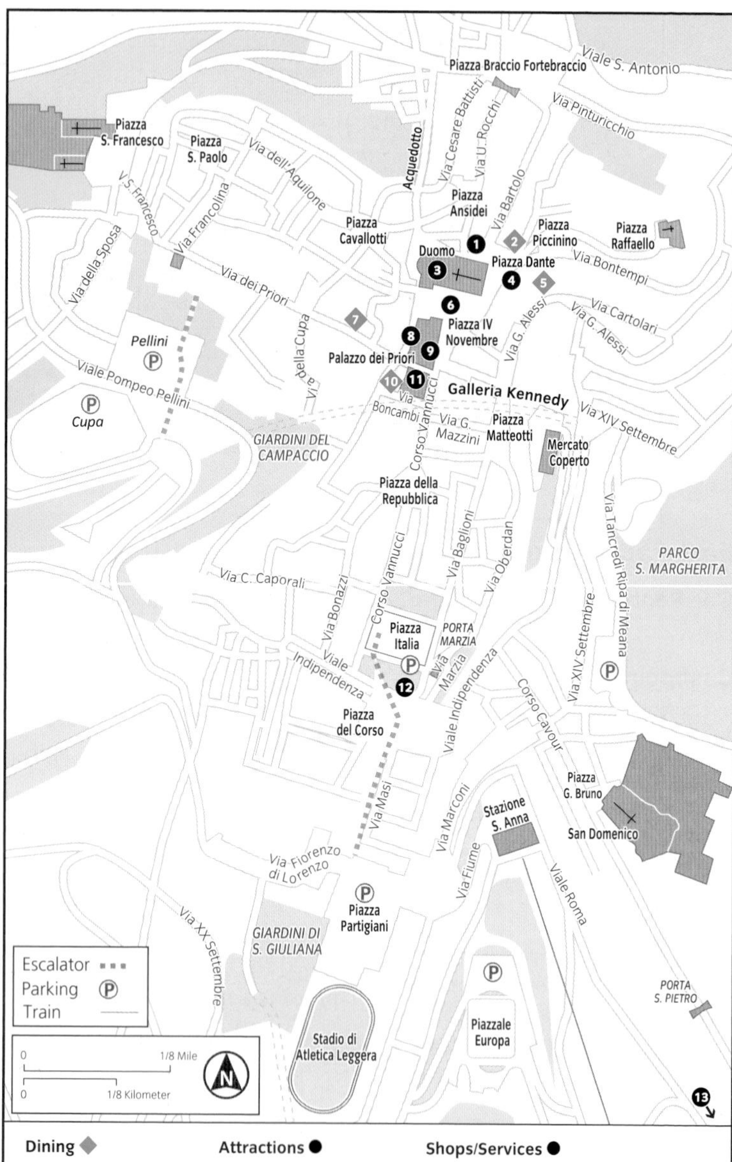

Dining
- La Botte **5**
- Lepri **7**
- Osteria del Turreno **2**
- Taj Mahal **10**

Attractions
- Collegio del Cambio **9**
- Duomo **3**
- Fontana Maggiore **6**
- Orto Medievale **13**
- Palazzo dei Priori **8**
- Pozzo Etrusco **4**
- Rocca Paolina **12**

Shops/Services
- Farmacia Andreoli **11**
- Internet Corner **1**

Palazzo dei Priori, Perugia

calendar of medieval Perugian life: panels showing the grape harvest and threshing of wheat mix with scenes of falconry and ritual slaughter, all interspersed with myth and zodiac symbols as well as the city's symbolic **Griffin**.

Beyond the piazza, the town's water supply came for hundreds of years from a 6th-century BC well, known as the **Pozzo Etrusco** (Piazza Dianti 18. *075 5733669*). If echoey, wet, 36m holes-in-the-ground appeal, it's open 10am–1.30pm and 2.30–6pm daily, opening an hour later and closing an hour earlier November–March; entry is €2 (€1 children 7–14).

There's a decent **playground** and a (free) **basketball court** in slightly scruffy **Parco Sant'Anna**, just downhill from Piazzale Europa. More pleasant is the leafy **Orto Medievale** ★ (*075 5856432*), a 10-minute walk south of town on Borgo XX Giugno, open 8am–5pm Monday–Friday.

Lepri (*075 5726353*) at Via dei Priori 21 is a reliable central choice for ice cream.

Collegio del Cambio ★★

AGES 6 AND UP

Corso Vannucci 25. 075 5728599.

Behind an unassuming door on the side of the Palazzo dei Priori is Perugia's greatest **art** treasure. The **Moneychanger's Guild** commissioned **Perugino** to fresco their **Sala delle Udienze** in 1496; the chosen subject was the supposed harmony between Christian faith and humanism that typified Renaissance thinking. Socrates, Cato and Pericles, by the entrance, share billing with a *Nativity* on the far wall, each figure sporting the blank serenity that was the Umbrian master's trademark.

TIP Pick up a Pass

The Città Museo (075 5734760) pass covers 10 of Perugia's cultural attractions, including **all** those reviewed here. Any four in a 24-hour period costs €7; €12 gets you as many as you like within 72 hours. Buy the pass from any participating sight.

Though mostly painted by his students rather than Perugino, the **ceiling** ★★ steals the show: a vibrant Apollo is flanked by allegories of the planets. Look closer: can you spot all 12 **zodiac** signs? And are those vaults carved masonry or a clever paint effect? (Answers: yes and it's point effect.)

Open *9am–12.30pm and 2.30–5.30pm Mon–Sat, 9am–1pm Sun.* ***Adm*** *€4.50, €5.50 with Collegio della Mercanzia, free under-12s.* ***Amenities*** *English.*

Galleria Nazionale dell'Umbria AGES 12 AND UP

Palazzo dei Priori. 075 5741410. www.gallerianazionaleumbria.it.

No doubt this is Umbria's premier art gallery: a catalogue of painters active in the region from the 13th to the 19th centuries, since late 2006 occupying two floors of the Palazzo dei Priori. Alas, you'll have to be blessed with **very patient children** to get the most out of it.

A highlights tour should take in a *Madonna* by Sienese master **Duccio di Buoninsegna** painted for Perugia's San Domenico church, in Room 2. By **Piero della Francesca**'s polyptych in Room 11 we've moved on 60 years: look at his precise command of perspective in the top panel, an **Annunciation** ★★. Room 15 houses Perugino's **Adoration of the Magi** ★★: Joseph is represented with intense feeling, and there was no better Renaissance **landscape painter**. The expansion downstairs has allowed the gallery to show a raft of his work to maximum effect. Among lesser-known yet outstanding paintings, look out for Taddeo di Bartolo's 1403 **Pentecost** ★ (Room 5) and Iacopo Salimbeni's monochrome 1416 **Crucifixion** ★, the first for its radical composition, the second for a display of facial emotion that wouldn't become the norm for decades.

Open *8.30am–6.30pm Tue–Sun.* ***Adm*** *€6.50, €3.25 18–25s.* ***Amenities*** *disabled access, English, shop.*

South and West of Perugia

If you have a car, or hire one (see above), there's plenty in the hills around Perugia to keep you busy. For doing nothin' somewhere pleasant, the walled village of **Corciano**, 10km west of Perugia, has a majestic location surrounded by olive groves, streets of jasmine and oleander, geraniums against pale yellow stone, and all the time in the world to wander. There's an *alimentari* (deli) and a couple of eating options in the village. Bus **87** from Piazza Italia will take you there.

Città della Domenica

OVERRATED **AGES 3-7**

*075 5054941. **www.cittadelladomenica.com**. 3km west of Perugia; SS75b exit Ferro di Cavallo.*

Every time you seek ideas for entertaining children in Umbria, the same answer comes back: Città della Domenica. What you'll find when you get to **Sunday City** are animals behind wire fences, a labyrinth that could use a lick of paint, torn wigwams and a 'Crazy Bridge' so slippy it ought to be re-christened 'Treacherous Bridge'. That said, youngsters aged 3–7 will have fun; ours did. Once you've ridden the mini-train and seen the animals, make for the '**Baby Area**' for a ball pool, inflatable slide, trampoline and plenty of other little people to meet and greet.

You'll find a lower-key but less scruffy **animal park** experience at **Parco del Sole** (*075 8707308. **www.parcodelsole.com***), in Pianelli 21km south of the city (E45 exit *Ripabianca*). It's open 9am–7.30pm February to mid-October; entry €8, children €6.

__Open__ 10am–6pm daily Apr–mid-Sep, 10am–6pm Sat–Sun mid-Sep–Oct. __Adm__ €12, €8 children 4–10. __Amenities__ bar/café, English, parking, picnic area, shop.

Museo Storico Perugina

AGES 3 AND UP

*San Sisto. 075 5276796. **www.perugina.it**. 3km south-west of Perugia; SS75b exit Madonna Alta.*

If we have to hard-sell a trip to Perugia's iconic **chocolate factory**, you've probably bought the wrong guidebook. The home of *Baci* (kisses) started in 1907 selling sugared almonds and now pumps out 120 tonnes of the brown stuff a day, including 1½ million Gianduja-and-hazelnut kisses. Unfortunately, it's a few Oompa-Loompas short of a tourist attraction. The educational video and exhaustively documented 20th-century ads are dull for children. The world's biggest chocolate, a BaciOne weighing **5,980kg**, might get a satisfying gasp.

On the upside, there's a **free tasting** selection and the best kind of souvenir shop: one you can eat. Dig in.

TIP

The Finest Plonk Money Can Buy

To stock the fridge with everyday wines, forget the supermarkets or *enotecas* and head for the local co-operative, **Colli Perugini** ★. Their handiest outlet is Via di Vittorio 14, on the right-hand-side heading out of Ellera towards Corciano. A bottle of zesty **Colli Perugini Bianco** will set you back €2; their robust **ColleRegio** red is €5. The shop is open 9am–1pm and 3.30–7.30pm, closed Monday mornings.

***Open** 8.30am–1pm and 2–5.30pm Mon–Fri. **Adm** free. **Amenities** English (video), shop.*

Museo del Vino AGES 10 AND UP

*Corso Vittorio Emanuele 31, Torgiano. 075 9880200. **museovino@lungarotti.it**.*

These 19 rooms dedicated to the grape eschew the usual 'here's a barrel, there's a label' approach; Italy's **best wine museum** looks at the history of winemaking, and its impact on Mediterranean civilisation. You need an audioguide (free), or the companion **guidebook** (€7.75), to get the most out of superb expositions of the importance of wine to the Etruscans, Romans and Christians. There is also an unrivalled collection of 13–17th century **Majolica** art. Photographic displays show how the technology of wine making hardly changed in Umbria from the 2nd century BC until four decades ago. In other words, this is a seriously good museum.

There's no actual wine here. For that, go next door to the **Lungarotti** tasting *osteria*. From basic, slightly fizzy white **Frezza** (€4.50) to **San Giorgio** (€21), it's all good.

The **Museo dell'Olivo e dell'Olio** (Via Garibaldi 10. *075 9880300*), in the next street, continues the land-life theme, including an illuminating collection of ancient olive oil lamps. It opens an hour later.

***Open** 9am–1pm and 3–7pm daily (closes 6pm winter). **Adm** €4.50, €2.50 children/students (€7 and €4.50 with Museo dell'Olivo). **Amenities** English (inc. audioguide), shop.*

LAGO TRASIMENO

Don't despair: even landlocked Umbria has got a **seaside**, sort of. The flat, calm expanses of **Lago Trasimeno** ★ are only interrupted by the reflections of rolling green hills or the occasional ferryboat plying between the shores and one of the pin-prick islands that float at its centre.

Sitting right on Umbria's Tuscan border, the lake has plenty of splash to get you through – for now. Its median depth of 6.3m is so shallow that dry summers in living memory have caused ferry cancellations. Discussions are under way to get more water into the lake. Its curious birth (from tectonic movements digging an enormous hole that filled with rainwater) means that no river causes regular top-ups. Still, it's unlikely to affect your numerous kayaking, windsurfing and kitesurfing opportunities in the near future. The centre of action-packed Umbrian camping holidays is right here.

Before the campsites and boat trips arrived, the lake was most famous as the site of a **battle** commemorated in a place name by the north shore, Sanguineto ('bloody'). 15,000 Romans under the command of Gaius Flaminius were slaughtered by Hannibal's army in 217 BC; the local stream ran red.

Lake Trasimeno

Thankfully, life by Italy's **fourth largest lake** is more genteel now. Blockbuster sights are thin on the ground, but the water's clean, the sun usually shines, and **Castiglione del Lago** has enough to burn a morning away. And there are always those boat trips....

Essentials

Getting There & Around

The **car** is your best bet: Lago Trasimeno is under an hour from Orvieto, Perugia, much of south-eastern Tuscany, and Todi and Assisi. By public transport, Perugia's regular **train** (☎ *892021. **www.trenitalia.it***) connection with Terontola runs along north shore to **Magione** (25 minutes), **Passignano** (30 minutes) and **Tuoro** (40 minutes). At a push, five to seven daily **APM buses** (☎ *075 506781. **www.apmperugia.it***) connect **Castiglione del Lago** with Perugia (1¼ hours)

Once you're there, the **ferry** service is also run by APM (☎ *075 827157*). Summer and winter schedules differ sharply; three main routes link Passignano (€5.90 return), Tuoro (€4.70) and Castiglione (€6.40) to **Isola Maggiore**, and San Feliciano to **Isola Polvese** (€4.70). All journeys take 10–30 minutes.

Visitor Information

The lake's main **tourist office** (☎ *075 9652484. **E: info@iat.castiglione-del-lago.pg.it***) is in Castiglione del Lago's Piazza Mazzini, no. 10. It's open daily: 8.30am–1pm and 3.30–7pm Monday to Friday, opening half an hour later on Saturday mornings and half an hour later morning and afternoon on Sundays. Between October and March it doesn't open at all on Saturday afternoon or Sunday. Don't leave without a copy of the monthly **Intorno al**

Trasimeno magazine: it contains ferry timetables, a festival diary and essentials like what food markets are on when. Further planning resources include ***www.lagotrasimeno.net*** and ***www.trasinet.com***.

Castiglione del Lago also hosts one of Umbria's most colourful festivals. At the end of April hundreds of kites and hot-air balloons ascend for **Coloriamo i Cieli** (Let's Colour the Skies) ★ (*075 9652484.* ***www.coloriamoicieli.com***).

INSIDER TIP

Don't pay to **park** for the ferry in Castiglione del Lago. The scrubland opposite the playground and dock is owned by the town – parking is free.

Around the Lake

Don't get too excited about some **beach-life**: Elba (see p. 147) it ain't. Best of a mediocre bunch is Passignano's public beach (*spiaggia comunale*), just east of town. It's serviced by **Sualzo Beach** (*329 2736840.* ***www.trasinet.net/sualzo***); two sunbeds and an umbrella are €10 for the day, a pedalo €7 per hour. The **playground** and sand are free; there's also a bar/café.

Castiglione del Lago ALL AGES

www.comune.castiglione-del-lago.pg.it.

The 'capital' of Lago Trasimeno wouldn't exist in its current form without tourism. From a **quaint piazza** flanked by *tipico* shops, to the fine views of Castiglione's promontory from the ferry, it's (almost) all here because you are. Once a wheat-growing area and defence outpost of the Duchy of Perugia, it's now the place to visit the tourist office (see above). While you're here, €3 (€2 for children aged 6–14) gets you a joint ticket for the **Palazzo della Corgna** (*075 951099*) and the 13th-century **Rocca del Leone** ★. Highlight of the spartan palace is the *Sala delle Gesta d'Asciano*, frescoed in 1575 by Nicoli with scenes of battles from Lepanto to Montalcino. It's linked by a 186m-covered walkway to the '**Lion Castle**'. From the pentagonal walls an entire lake is laid out below like a magnificent turquoise carpet. Hold little hands up there. It's open 10am–1.30pm and 4–7.30pm daily.

Isola Maggiore ALL AGES

Passignano: 20 minutes ferry; Castiglione: 30 minutes ferry.

There isn't a great deal to *do* on Isola Maggiore. Trasimeno's most-visited island is famous for St Francis spending Lent there in 1213 and for a lace-making reputation that stretches back 100 years. That vanishing craft is remembered in a one-room **Lace Museum** (*075 8254233*) opposite the quay. It's open 10am–1pm and 3–6pm daily; €3, children €2. Signposted outside is the island's historical trail, an occasionally steep track to Maggiore's **308m summit**, crowned by olive groves and the 12th-century church of **San Michele Arcangelo**. Check with the Lace Museum that it's open if you want to get inside: it has

'Isola Maggiore'

medieval frescoes by the Umbrian School. An alternative route down takes in the even-more-ancient **San Salvatore**, which is always closed.

The best thing to do before ferrying back is eat: **Sauro** ★ (*075 826168*) has a fine selection of lake fish (eel, perch, trout) at reasonable prices (€7–10) in a pleasant garden. Take the *filetto di persico* (perch), add *patate fritte*, squeeze a lemon and you've got...**fish and chips**. In summer, book ahead.

Isola Polvese ★ GREEN ALL AGES

*075 9659546. **www.polvese.it**. San Feliciano: 10 minutes ferry.*

While Maggiore looks back, Trasimeno's largest island thinks about the future: the whole place is an **environmental education centre** and **nature reserve**. It's not without history, though: there's evidence of habitation as far back as the Etruscans. In medieval times, 88 fishing families lived on the 70-hectare island, and they built the impressive **castle** to protect against constant raids. The last straw came with Tuscan incursions in 1643 and the island was abandoned for two centuries, before becoming a private hunting reserve.

Polvese's Aquatic Garden

Lakeside Action

The lakeside's largely gentle gradients are ideal for a family cycle. **Marinelli** (*075 953126*), at Via Buozzi 26 in Castiglione del Lago, has mountain bikes from age 6-ish upwards for €10 per day; across the lake, Passignano's **Sualzo Beach** (see above) has children's bikes from age 8 upwards at the same price. You'll find downloadable off-road route maps at ***www.lagotrasimeno.net/pagine.php?lang=en&id=26***. Upping the action ante a little, **Balneazione Tuoro** (*334 9794208. **www.laspiaggiadituoro.it***) rents **canoes** from Tuoro's beachfront: €5 per hour for a single, €7 per hour for a tandem. Children (8 and over) or adults can hire **windsurfs** (€8 per hour) from the same place, or take a five-lesson course for €200. Eight **kitesurfing** ★ (***www.kitecompany.it***) lessons at Tuoro are €250, but it's adults only. Both courses are always available in English. For the ultimate perspective on the lake, **Skydive Trasimeno** (*075 8350026. **www.skydivetrasimeno.com***) offers tandem jumps from 4,000m; ages 16 and up and weekends only. If you dare.

Traces of the past remain in a ruined Olivetan monastery and a church dedicated to the island's protector, San Giuliano. Pietro Porcinai's swimming pool of 1959 was built inside a sandstone quarry; it's now the island's **aquatic plant garden**. Alas, these best bits are only visitable with a **guide** (1 hour; hourly during Infopoint opening). It's a good tour (€2) and always available in English. Elsewhere on the island, there's room to roam along panoramic paths, through holm oak and olive groves – Polvese makes **organic oil** in its own *frantoio* (€8 for 500ml), for sale in the island's only (tiny) shop. If your children are into art, pick them up a pencil, too, and find a place to sit and draw. When the early summer poppies are out, it's divine.

If you fancy a quiet night, there are four basic family rooms (with bathrooms, no cots) at the island's former farmworkers' accommodation, now the 76-bed **Ostello Il Poggio** (*075 9659550. **www.fattoriaisolapolvese.com***). High season prices are €25 per person including breakfast; a three-course dinner with wine is another €10. Tots go free.

For information on Polvese's **educational and sustainability programmes** for groups, email ***plestina@tin.it***.

Infopoint** open 10am–1pm and 3–6pm daily Jul–Aug, Sun only Apr–Jun and Sep.* ***Amenities *bar/restaurant, English, picnic area.*

ASSISI

Driving up early in the morning, it's obvious that **Assisi** ★★★ is a special place. The rising sun behind Monte Subasio cuts massive silhouettes behind this medieval city of miracles. A peculiar blend of romance, architecture and devotion make it the quintessential Umbrian hill-town – *the* absolutely essential stop on any Umbrian tour. The region's most popular spot has a magic that isn't all about its most famous resident, **St Francis**. The biggest draw is the giant Basilica di San Francesco, built to honour him after his death and now almost as much a temple to pre-Renaissance painter Giotto. The rest is an ideally sited hill-town, hardly spoiled by its pesky traffic and tat shops, that absorbs its millions of tourists and pilgrims with a quiet ease. It's not hard to find a backstreet all to yourself. Though inevitably commercial (what place with this many visitors isn't?), Assisi has avoided an invasion of tack all too apparent in parts of Tuscany.

The town is essentially unmarked by the **earthquakes** of 26th September 1997 that killed four people inside the Basilica.

Essentials

Assisi is 18km east of Perugia (see p. 189), off the **SS75b**. Driving the centre's steep streets is forbidden for tourists. The best system with young children heads downhill all the way: park in **Piazza Matteotti** (€1.10 per hour), keep walking west and finish up at the basilica. Below there, in **Piazza Unità d'Italia**, catch the half-hourly minibus (90¢) back to Piazza Matteotti. The adjacent *tabacchi* sells tickets. If you're only here for the basilica, or don't mind uphill walks, there's a small car park in Piazza Unità d'Italia itself (€1.05 per hour); get in early.

INSIDER TIP

There's a map of Assisi's car parks at ***www.assisi.com/parcheggi.htm***.

Alternatively, the regular (six a day) **APM bus** (*075 506781*. ***www.apmperugia.it***) from Perugia (€3) stops in Piazza Matteotti.

The **tourist office** (*075 812534*. ***info@iat.assisi.pg.it***) is at the western end of Piazza del Comune, no. 22. It's open 8am–2pm and 3–6pm Monday to Saturday, 10am–1pm on Sunday. Request their **InfoAssisi** booklet, full of nuts-and-bolts information; there's a Banca dell'Umbria **cashpoint** across the piazza. There's a dedicated resource for disabled visitors: ***www.assisiaccessibile.com***. Further local information is at ***www.assisionline.com***.

Unless you have a religious motive, with children in tow the big dates in Assisi's calendar are best avoided. The **Festa di San Francesco** (3rd–4th October) and **Easter Week** are packed.

Assisi is missing a playground, but there's some green space in the **Parco Regina Margherita** behind Piazza Matteotti.

Around the Town

In a **UNESCO World Heritage** town dominated by one man and his story (see 'Saint Francis', below), you don't have to look too hard for secular interest. The geographical and civic heart is **Piazza del Comune**, with its 13th-century **Palazzo del Capitano** and the smart Corinthian columns of the Roman **Tempio di Minerva** ★ guarding its northern fringe. The most atmospheric route to the basilica goes downhill along medieval **Via Portica** ★, which becomes Via Fortini and Via San Francesco before arriving at the main event. En route, poke your head into the tiny **Oratorio dei Pellegrini**, at no. 13, the frescoed chapel of a pilgrims' hostel built in 1457.

Basilica di San Francesco ★★★ AGES 6 AND UP

Piazza di San Francesco. ☎ *075 819001.* ***www.sanfrancescoassisi.org.***

Though Assisi's basilica is known for its **art**, it's first a masterpiece of medieval **architecture**. The almost simultaneous construction

Basilica di San Francesco, Assisi

of huge Lower (1228) and Upper (1230) Churches in contrasting Romanesque and Gothic styles had no peer or precedent. Franciscan **Brother Elias**, the probable architect, invites contemplation downstairs while upstairs the grand Gothic vaults set up a gawp at **Giotto**.

It was in the Basilica's **Upper Church** that Giotto became the greatest single influence on Western art, though the attribution of his most famous frescoes is challenged by some modern scholars. His (possibly) 28-part fresco cycle on the **Life of St Francis** ★★★ was painted in the 1290s, pre-dating what is certainly his work in Florence's **Santa Croce** (p. 55) and Padova's **Cappella Scrovegni**. Start in the nave's far right, with

FUN FACT **Say It So**

While you're here, remember: it's *a-see-zee* not *a-see-see*.

FUN FACT Another Virgin

Like the place of worship behind Piazza del Comune's Roman façade, Santa Maria sopra Minerva was a common name for early Christian churches: they tended to be built on temples to the Roman goddess Minerva (the Greek Athena), like the Virgin Mary another incorruptible virgin. Hence '**Saint Mary on top of Minerva**'.

the Homage of a Simple Man, and read clockwise. The famous Sermon to the Birds is behind you on your left as you enter, but the next two panels show what Giotto (or whoever) was about; both are full of tension, emotion, narrative detail and an attempt at perspective that had never been seen before. At a time when plain representation of devotional icons was the norm, he painted people with real faces.

'Tempio di Menerva, Assisi'

Downstairs in the **Lower Church**, pause especially for Simone Martini's 1317 **Cappella di San Martino** ★★ (first chapel on the left) and Pietro Lorenzetti's 1315 **Crucifixion** ★★ and 1320 **Deposition** ★★★ in the left transept. The crypt houses the chokingly atmospheric **Tomb of St Francis** ★ and four of his followers, so well hidden it wasn't rediscovered until 1818. The reverence inside is likely to impress even a primary-age child.

INSIDER TIP

We can only scratch the surface here. Head to the basilica's bookshop and buy a copy of non-intimidating **Assisi: where to find...** ★ (€9.30) and your appreciation will increase dramatically.

Some planning hints. First, the basilica's **dress code** is enforced: no short skirts, shorts, sleeveless tops or low-cut dresses. Ditto the *silenzio*: don't bring a mid-tantrum toddler. While access to the churches is fine for **buggies**, you won't be able to get to the cloister or shop. Finally, if you need to change nappies, make for the toilets in the plaza below the Lower Church: the desk downstairs will direct you to a proper **baby change**.

***Open** Lower: 6am–6.45pm daily. Upper: 8.30am–6.45pm daily. **Adm** free. **Amenities** disabled access, English (audioguides).*

Foro Romano & Rocca Maggiore AGES 7 AND UP

*075 813053/812033. **assisi@sistemamuseo.it**.*

Assisi's two secular highlights can be seen on a single ticket by the **Pinacoteca Comunale** (Via San Francesco 10). Archaeology-wise, the **Foro Romano** ★ is a bit of a work-in-progress. An entrance room houses inscribed tablets and headless statues, but head down the tunnel and you're at the heart of 2nd-century BC **Asisium** – right below 21st-century Piazza del Comune. The echoes of life above make an intriguing juxtaposition.

At Assisi's other extreme, the semi-ruined 14th-century **Rocca Maggiore** crowns a *very* steep hill behind the town. Don't attempt the relentless climb with a pushchair or young children. When you get up, the geometric rhythms of olive groves flanking the Vale of Spoleto make for a stunning **view** ★. Relentless renovations make the Rocca's entrance a bit scruffy; **claustrophobes** and **vertigo-sufferers** shouldn't go inside.

***Foro open** 10am–1pm and 2.30–7pm daily Jun–Aug, closes 4pm Mar–May and Sep–Oct, 10.30am–1pm and 2–5pm daily Nov–Feb. **Rocca open** 10am–sunset daily. **Adm** €4.50, €2.50 children 9–18. **Amenities** bar (Rocca), English, parking (Rocca), shop.*

Eremo delle Carceri

AGES 4 AND UP

*075 812301. **eremo.carceri@tiscali.it**. 4½km north-east of Assisi; drive or taxi (075 813100).*

In theory, St Francis's mountain retreat is a place of sanctuary and **silence** – a spot for contemplation wedged into a ravine on the wooded slopes of Monte Subasio. Despite the polite signs, though, there isn't much chance of quiet. The tiny rooms of the hermitage itself remain atmospheric, despite being overrun with tourists, especially the rock 'bed' where St Francis slept. Remember to duck.

You'll find more peace and plenty of shade in the tracked **woodlands** ★ behind the monastery, where Francis preached to the birds.

***Open** 6.30am–6.45pm daily (6pm Nov–Easter). **Adm** free. **Amenities** parking.*

SPELLO

From its little balcony above the checkerboard plains of the Vale of Spoleto, the warm-pink glow of **Spello** is visible for miles. The former Roman retirement town of Hispellum caught the tourism bug late – even in high season you'll find a quiet backwater or a corner with a measure of peace. It's an essential half day for **art-lovers**, with the best Pinturicchio you can see for free, and home to one of Umbria's most charming festivals. Each Corpus Christi, 60 days after Easter, the streets are

The Life of Saint Francis

1182 Francis is born in Assisi, the son of a wealthy businessman and his French wife
1201 An increasingly disillusioned Francis is captured in battle by the Perugians
1206 He claims that a vision in San Damiano commands him to rebuild the church
1209 Pope Innocent III approves Francis's religious order, the Frati Minori, after seeing him in a dream
1211 He receives Clare of Assisi, and the Order of the Poor Dames is founded
1219 Francis appears before Sultan Melek-el-Kamel and proposes trial-by-fire to test the true religion
1220 He builds the first Christmas crib in Greccio
1226 Francis dies in the Porziuncola, on 3rd October
1228 Pope Gregory IX canonises St Francis and lays the first stone of the Basilica di San Francesco
1939 St Francis is named Italy's patron saint

carpeted in fresh petals for the **Infiorate** ★ (***www.infioratespello.it***). Come by train.

Spello isn't easy with a **pushchair**: streets are steep and mostly cobbled, and there are no pavements, making car-dodging a full-time job.

The pro-loco **tourist office** (☎ *0742 301009*. ***prospello@libero.it***) is at Piazza Matteotti 3. It's open 9.30am–12.30pm and 3.30–5.30pm daily all year. The town's website has trip-planning information: ***www.comune.spello.pg.it***.

Essentials

Spello is 28km south-east of Perugia (see p. 189), on the SS75 just short of Foligno. The **parking** spaces immediately on your right as you drive in may well be taken; make for three signposted (and free) car parks on the other side of town as you approach from the SS75. **Trains** (☎ *892021*. ***www.trenitalia.it***) run hourly from Perugia (€2.30, 35 minutes). It's a 10-minute walk from the station into town.

A Quick Tour

The best route for a cobblestoned mooch is up Via San Severino to the foot of the ruined **Rocca**. You can't get in, but the **views** ★ over the pancake-flat Vale of Spoleto, back to Assisi and what's left of a Roman amphitheatre, are worth the climb. It's **nigh impossible** with a pushchair.

Spello is a treat for fans of **religious art** (see below), but the renovated **Pinacoteca Civica** (☎ *0742 301497*) next to

TIP A Bite on the Go

It looks a bit ordinary from the outside, but the large panoramic garden at **Bar Bonci** (*0742 651397*), Via Garibaldi 10, is an ideal spot to take a break with children. Forget the pizza and pasta dishes; share plates of local salami (€6), cheeses (€6), mixed bruschetta (€3) and *torta al testo* (flatbread; €2).

Santa Maria Maggiore is strictly for hardcore fans only. It's open 10.30am–1pm and 3–6.30pm April to October, 10.30am–12.30pm and 3.30–5.30pm otherwise. Admission is €2.60, €1 for children 7–14; closed Mondays. Continue downhill to the corner of Via Sant'Angelo and peek through the arch window into the remains of the **Cappella Tega**. It was frescoed in 1461 by Nicolò Alunno.

Finish your tour at the excellent **playground** wedged between Piazza Kennedy and the main road, Via Centrale Umbria.

Santa Maria Maggiore

AGES 5 AND UP

Piazza Matteotti

Don't be distracted by the showy Baroque interior; Santa Maria Maggiore is a major spot for Umbrian **Renaissance** painting. To the left and right of the altar a *Madonna and Child* and a *Pietà* by Perugino neatly book-end the life of Christ. The highlight is the **Cappella Baglioni** ★, frescoed like Siena's **Piccolomini Library** (p. 83) by Pinturicchio. It's on the left as you walk in; take €1 for lights.

The vaulted ceiling depicts four sibyls (pre-Christian prophetesses). The three main panels read left to right: an *Annunciation* (see p. 194), followed by a *Nativity* and *Christ's Dispute with the Doctors*. At the far end of the first panel, a Pinturicchio self-portrait 'hangs' on the wall. When the lights run out, you'll get a better view of the **ceramic floor** laid by craftsmen from Deruta, just south of Perugia.

***Open** 8.30am–midday and 3–6.30pm daily. **Adm** free. **Amenities** shop.*

Ragani ★ ALL AGES

*Via degli Ulivi 8. 0742 301156. **www.olioragani.com**. 2km from Spello dir. Assisi; follow sign by Ristorante Astro.*

For *degustazione* with a difference that everyone can get into, stop in at this family *frantoio* (olive press). Conditions 350m up the slopes of Monte Subasio ensure that their **first cold-pressed olive oil** from November's harvest is among Umbria's best. The regular *extra vergine* (€10 for 750ml) is smooth and slightly sweet; strictly regulated **DOP Umbria** ★★ (€13 for 750ml), made with at least 70% green fruit, has a distinct olive aroma and a peppery bite. For the full flavour experience, **drink** the oil when you taste instead of dipping bread. It sounds a bit grim, but you'll notice the difference.

***Open** 9.30am–7pm daily.*

THE FAR NORTH

The hazy hills of the Umbrian north stretch from Perugia's suburbs to Sansepolcro, just over the Tuscan border. Aside from flurries of industry in the Tiber Valley, it appears a land where nothing happens. The major town is **Gubbio**; its medieval limestone buildings overlook a picturesque, undulating valley. It's the only place up here that ever seems busy.

Thousands pile in every 15th May for the **Festa dei Ceri** ★. Giant candles (*ceri*), bearing images of St Ubaldo, St George and St Anthony, are raced from the town to the Basilica di Sant'Ubaldo on the mountain above.

Elsewhere, the Alta Valle del Tevere's main point of interest is **Città di Castello**, an artisan, working place quite unlike the hill-towns elsewhere on the tourist trail.

Essentials

Northern Umbria is sliced in two by the E45 *superstrada*, making the two main towns easy by **car**. To park in **Gubbio**, follow the 'P' signs on the road from Perugia: left at the second mini-roundabout, right at the next two, to the **Teatro Romano** free car park; there's a great **playground** ★ behind. Marginally closer, at **Piazza 40 Martiri**, there's pay parking (80¢ per hour).

Città is even easier: exit the E45 at '*Città di Castello nord*', turn right at the first major roundabout and you'll eventually pass **Parcheggio Ferri**. It's free and three minutes from the Duomo, up the *scala mobile* over the road.

If you're using public transport, for Gubbio there are eight daily **APM buses** (✆ *075 506781. www.apmperugia.it*) from Perugia (€4.30). For Città, the hourly

Loggia dei Tiratori, Gubbio

FUN FACT **Crazy World**

Gubbio's Fontana dei Matti, the 'fountain of madmen', is in the tiny piazza known as Largo del Bargello. Run round it three times, get yourself baptised with its water, and you're officially entitled to hold a 'nutter of Gubbio' licence.

FCU train (☎ *075 5754034. www.fcu.it*) takes 1¼ hours and costs €3.05. Forget the wilds farther north, east or west without a car.

The **tourist office** (☎ *075 9220693. www.gubbio-altochiascio.umbria2000.it*) in Gubbio is at Via della Repubblica 15. Morning hours are 8.30am–1.45pm Monday to Friday, 9am–1pm Saturday, 9.30am–12.30pm Sunday; in afternoons, it's open 3–6pm October to March and 3.30–6.30pm March to October. The office is closed Sunday afternoons in January and February.

In **Città** (☎ *075 8554922. www.cittadicastello.regioneumbria.eu*), it's under the Logge Bufalini in Piazza Matteotti. The helpful office is open 8.30am–1.30pm and 3.30–6.30pm Monday to Friday, 9.30am–12.30pm and 3.30–6.30pm Saturday, 9.30am–12.30pm only Sunday. There are **cashpoints** almost opposite both offices.

For online trip-planning, Città's *comune* website is useful: *www.cdcnet.net*.

Gubbio & its Wilderness

Being stuck out on its own all these years has done funny things to Gubbio. Its preserved medieval centre and Roman street plan are the most visited spot in the north, but a feeling of **isolation** remains. Poor roads, pine woods and historical links with Urbino and Le Marche as strong as those with its own region, make Gubbio an Umbria apart.

Your likely entry point is **Piazza 40 Martiri**, named after 40 locals murdered by the Nazis for assisting partisans; they're remembered every 22nd June. Stretched out above the giant **Loggia dei Tiratori**, used by woolworkers to stretch yarn, is a photogenic panorama of the medieval city.

The best route uphill follows **Via dei Consoli**, terminating in **Piazza Grande** ★. This three-sided balcony is dominated by the fortress-like **Palazzo dei Consoli** ★★, built in the 1330s. It houses the **Museo Comunale** (☎ *075 9274298*), home to the 3rd-century BC **Eugubine Tablets** – the only existing record of the Umbri language transposed in Etruscan and Latin letters: ancient Umbria's **Rosetta Stone**. It's more fun exploring the old palace than examining the exhibits: don't miss the **secret corridor** ★ from the back of the Majolica ceramics room to the Pinacoteca upstairs. And don't let tots run up the main staircase: it has an **extremely dangerous** low handrail. Entry is €5 (€2.50 for children aged 7–25); daily morning hours are 10am–1pm, afternoons 3–6pm (2–5pm November to March).

Elsewhere, fans of Umbrian painting shouldn't miss **Ottaviano Nelli**'s outstanding 1420 **Life of St Augustine** ★ covering the apse of **Sant'Agostino** (*075 9273814. **www.santagostino.net***), outside the Porta Romana. There's an explanatory leaflet and light switch left of the altar; drop in a coin and you're away. It's often open all day, but get there before noon or after 3.30pm to be sure.

Gubbio's tourist office (see above) should also be your first stop if you plan to trek, spelunk (cave) or mountain-bike in the wildernesses of the **Parco Regionale del Monte Cucco** ★ (*075 9170400. **www.cens.it***); there's generally a list of guided excursions you can join between May and September. For more information on these, or the park in general, email ***parco.montecucco@libero.it*** or see ***www.parks.it/parco.monte.cucco***.

INSIDER TIP

If you're after **crafts**, there's a permanent display by local artisans halfway up the steps to Piazza Grande from the top of Via della Repubblica. You'll find brochures and business cards for each. It's open daily, 10am–1pm and 3–6pm.

Funivia Colle Eletto ★

AGE 3 AND UP

Via San Girolamo. 075 9273881

The most fun you can have in an Umbrian cage is this metal boneshaker to the top of **Monte Ingino**. The trip lasts five minutes (no room for pushchairs). As well as **views** ★ of the valley spread below, as far east as Monte Cucco, the top station has shady tables for a panoramic picnic. Five minutes farther up the path is the **Basilica di Sant'Ubaldo**, dedicated to a 12th-century bishop who saved the town from marauding German 'Holy Roman' Emperor Barbarossa. Aside from his desiccated (and venerated) remains, check out the huge 'Ceri' carried up here during Gubbio's iconic *festa* (see p. 207).

***Open** daily. **Adm** €5, €4 children 4–14. **Amenities** bar/restaurant, shop.*

Città di Castello

There's a lot to like about **Città di Castello**. In the Middle Ages it was known as *Castrum Felicitatis*, the 'Town of Happiness'. More recently, as a tobacco, printing and textile centre, it developed an **artisan** aura that's only reluctantly fading. You'll still see signs of it clinging on in backstreet workshops and unique gift outlets all over town. Chain stores aren't welcome here. There's no distinguished piazza, little medieval masonry, and few foreign visitors. You'll have to settle for enough

Città of Art

The town's **galleries** are all of the serious variety. Most well-known is the **Pinacoteca Comunale** (☎ *075 8520656. **www.cdcnet.net/pinacoteca***), Umbria's second gallery after Perugia, on Via della Cannoniera. 30 rooms trace the development of Umbrian art from its roots to the 1900s. Sadly, despite **Raphael** and **Luca Signorelli** both being active in Città, only one work from each remains: a damaged *Holy Trinity* by Raphael and Signorelli's 1498 *Martyrdom of St Sebastian*, not one of his classics. Best of the rest is Room 16, dedicated to **Raffaellino dal Colle** ★. It's open 10am–1pm and 2.30–6.30pm (3–6pm November to March). Make sure to ask for the English-language handout: explanations are the most detailed and academic anywhere in Umbria.

An otherwise dry **Museo del Duomo** in Piazza Gabriotti (☎ *075 8554705*) is livened up by an embossed, 12th century **silver altar front** ★ illustrating scenes from the *New Testament* and **Rosso Fiorentino**'s oh-so-dark *Christ in Glory*. It's open 10am–1pm and 3–7pm; afternoon hours are 2.30–6.30pm October to March.

Completing the trinity is (shock, horror) a modern art museum, the **Collezione Burri** (☎ *075 8554649. **burriart@tiscalinet.it***), in the Palazzo Albizzini on Via Albizzini. Burri's home town has an unmatched collection of his textured, abstract art. His 1963 *Grande Plastica* isn't something Raphael could have dreamed up. Hours are 9am–12.30pm and 2.30–6pm Tuesday to Saturday, 10.30am–12.30pm and 3–6pm Sunday. **Admission** to any of the three galleries is €5, children €3. All galleries are closed Mondays.

art treasures to satisfy an expert, a little infant magic and perhaps the **ugliest cathedral** in Umbria – it's a magnificent sight that has to be seen to be believed. The town is untainted, authentic and best of all flat: pushchair-pushers can give weary forearms a time-out.

Strolling Città

It's a feature of Città that most of its medieval buildings were fitted with later **façades**. At the **Palazzo del Podestà**, facing the tourist office across Piazza Matteotti, spot the obvious 'new' (1687) front stuck on an old (1368) palace. Keep walking for an unmissable **duomo**. The cylindrical campanile seems lifted from a Breton *château* and grafted onto an architectural mess.

If your Italian's up to it, the best way to pass 45 minutes is a guided tour of **Tipografia Grifani-Donati** ★ (☎ *075 8554349. **grifanidonati@libero.it***) on Corso Cavour. This family printer has occupied the former church of San Paolo since 1799; you'll see lithographs and engravings printed in the original workshops, still in use. It's available Monday to Friday 9am–12.30pm and 3–7pm, plus Saturday mornings, and costs €10. Your souvenir is made in front of you on 19th-century printing machines. If time doesn't allow, pop into the **shop** across the street (no. 4) and buy a postcard (€1) with a difference, *ex-libris* images designed by Grifani over the centuries.

There's a **playground** opposite the duomo, and another behind Parcheggio Ferri, which sometimes has **trampolines**.

Botteghe Artigiane di Silvio Bambini ★ FIND AGE 1-8

Logge Bufalini, Piazza Matteotti. ☎ 075 8554384.

Down an unlikely spiral staircase outside the tourist office is a world of **magic** for little ones: a room alive with intricate models of Città's pre-war high street: knife-grinders, masons, barrel-makers and weavers at work. It's the lights and sounds of a town in miniature. Silvio Bambini's work is fantastic popular art, every piece handcrafted from olive and oak over 22 years. At **Christmas**, he shows a collection of cribs and Nativity models, with festive decoration and music.

Open *10am–12.30pm Thu and Sat.* ***Adm*** *free.*

FAMILY-FRIENDLY ACCOMMODATION

For more accommodation ideas, see p. 213.

Oasi Battifoglia ★ FIND

Loc. Paradiso 33, Assisi. ☎ 075 802320. ***www.oasibattifoglia.com****. 10km north of Assisi off SS444.*

If it's **rural** you're after, this *agriturismo* 15 minutes from Assisi and twice that from Gubbio and Spello, has sticks to spare. The individually named apartments differ widely, but all are simply decorated. **Sabrina** ★★ is ideal for families of four or more, with two large bedrooms (one en suite), a compact, modern kitchen and a large living area with a sofa bed and wood-burning stove. They're all part of the original farmhouse, at the centre of what is still a **working family farm**. Don't neglect the restaurant run by *Signora*: veal, chicken, bread, veg, wine and honey are all *della casa*. If they buy it in, they buy it locally. They don't take credit cards. In summer, stays must be three nights or more.

Apartments *6.* ***Rates*** *adult €30–40 per night, children 3–8 €15–20 per night. Cot €10 per night. Breakfast included.* ***Amenities*** *parking,*

TIP Back to HQ

To find the best bases for discovering as much of Umbria as you can in a limited time, follow **two simple rules**. First, stick to the north-central belt: don't go south of Todi (Chapter 9) or too far north of Perugia. Second, stay near one of the two fast roads, the SS75b and E45 *superstrada*. Follow those and you're an hour from just about anywhere.

Le Case di Lisetta

playground, pool (outdoor), restaurant. ***In apartment*** *disabled access (1 apt.), highchair, kitchen, sat TV, shower only.*

Hotel Subasio ★

Via Frate Elia 2, Assisi. ☎ 075 812206. ***www.hotelsubasio.com****.*

The **queue-dodger's** choice in Assisi: you could hardly sleep any closer to the Basilica, as this historic hotel's long list of famous guests would testify. Make no mistake, you're paying for the **location** these days. Outside the public areas, the hotel's 1860s grandeur has a faded edge. Rooms vary widely in size, décor and layout: ask for a view of the valley, a large bathroom, and room 22 or 25 if possible – both have huge private terraces. Otherwise, you'll have to settle for a small balcony and *aperitivi* downstairs with the Vale of Spoleto spread below. Don't accept a room on the street side.

Rooms *70.* ***Rates*** *Double €185, triple €210, suite €235. Cots free. Breakfast included.* ***Credit*** *AmEx, MC, V.* ***Amenities*** *babysitting, bar/restaurant, Internet (free), laundry service. parking (€10 per night).* ***In room*** *A/C, fridge, sat TV.*

Ostello Il Poggio, Isola Polvese, see p. 200.

Le Case di Lisetta ★ VALUE

Migiana di Corciano. ☎ 075 6978568. ***www.lecasedilisetta.com****. 3km north of Corciano.*

If your sums say you can't afford a **private villa** with a pool, this place might make you recalculate. Of the four houses located in a forest close to Perugia, Corciano and Lago Trasimeno, two are suited to travelling families. The old granary, known as

Cicala, is the best. Downstairs is a large bedroom, living room and bathroom, with a tight kitchen/diner; a separate apartment upstairs has two bedrooms and a bathroom. Décor is simple and tasteful, with beams, whitewash and terracotta tiles.

At this price, there are obviously **frustrations**: linen isn't even what we'd call matching, let alone stylish; cooks will want to chuck a decent pan and a sharp knife in the car. Although it doesn't chime with generally swish conversions and pool area, much of the kit is bargain-basement stuff. But outside high summer, the **price** is outstanding. It's week-long bookings and cash only.

Houses *4.* ***Rates*** *€420–1300 per week.* ***Amenities*** *parking, pool (outdoor).* ***In house*** *kitchen, shower only.*

La Macina FIND

Oscano. ☎ *075 584371.* ***www.oscano.com****. 6km north of Perugia.*

Set among lush agricultural hills, these apartments put a twist on the typical '**farm holiday**': they're on the edge of 250 hectares belonging to the 4-star **Castello d'Oscano**. Guests are free to use the castle-hotel's facilities, including a €10 buffet breakfast. The features of the former stables have been maintained, so there's loads of character outside but a touch of gloom within: living rooms and windows are small and terraces haven't been inauthentically

Your Own Umbrian Retreat

It could only be Umbria: empty hill-towns and epic views under the midday sun, long lunches of the finest ingredients cooked simply, a flash of sunflower yellow and the aroma of olives. Just don't limit yourselves to spectating: renting a secluded villa, *agriturismo* or farmhouse enables you to *take part* in Umbria. Buy ham cured and hung on a local farm, pan-fry a lake fish picked up at the morning market, barbecue a *bistecca alla Fiorentina* (T-bone) and wash it down with a neighbour's robust red. Eat seasonally and sustainably: asparagus in late spring, wild *porcini* mushrooms as summer turns to autumn. All the time, you're putting something back to the countryside. You're **living local** – it's what Umbria does best.

More prosaically, a farmhouse or villa rental is also a **practical** choice for families. It supplies the flexibility to come and go as you please, and to feed little ones at times that suit. Splash around in your own pool, rent some bikes, take long walks in the early evening before dinner together on the terrace. In addition to a selection in the 'Family-friendly Accommodation' sections here and in Chapter 9, you'll find details of villa specialists and **tour operators** covering Umbria on p. 244. For more on *agriturismo* holidays, see p. 30.

bolted on. Kitchenettes are well-equipped but bedrooms could use new soft furnishings. Ground floor apartments 1 and 3 are coolest in mid-summer; 9 and 10 are the biggest.

The full **castle experience**, complete with Scarlett O'Hara staircase and antique library, will set you back €290–310 a night for a junior suite.

Apartments *13.* ***Rates*** *Apt. for four €375–650 per week, apt. for five €450–775. Cots free.* ***Credit*** *AmEx, MC, V.* ***Amenities*** *parking, pool (outdoor).* ***In apartment*** *kitchenette, safe, sat TV, shower only.*

Parco dei Pini

Via Gandhi 1, San Feliciano. ☎ 075 8476270. ***www.villaggioparcodeipini.it****.*

This intimate little **campsite** offers something different to the 400-pitch super-sites that circle Lago Trasimeno. Its roadside location under the pines just north of San Feliciano looks right at Isola Polvese and Castiglione in the distance; some pitches, the common area and pool are on the **lakeside**. Inside, mobile homes are the usual compact design (apparently for five/six, but in reality four max); they're newly refitted and well kitted out, but a little close together. Best of all, they're rentable by the night year-round: the site never closes.

Pitches *75 (+ 7 mobile homes).* ***Rates*** *adults €6–7, children 4–10 €4–5, pitch €6–7.* ***Mobile homes*** *€45–85 per night, €12 final cleaning charge.* ***Credit*** *MC, V.* ***Amenities*** *bar/restaurant, bike hire, Internet, laundry, parking, pool (outdoor).* ***In mobile home*** *kitchen, shower only.*

FAMILY-FRIENDLY DINING

La Stalla ★★★ VALUE

SELF-SERVICE GRILL

Via Eremo delle Carceri 24, Assisi. ☎ 075 812317. ***www.fontemaggio.it****. 1½ km from centre, dir. Eremo.*

There aren't many restaurants where you can feed the whole family healthily for **under** €20: four huge bowls of spaghetti plus a litre of water and a ¼ of

TIP Lunch Alternatives in Perugia

Where better than a student city to find a half-decent curry house? Taj Mahal (☎ *075 5722894*), off Via dei Priori at Via dei Vermiglioli 10, has a choice of set lunches (€10 veggie, €12 meat, €13 fish) and full *à la carte* at dinner. There's even Cobra and Kingfisher lager. It's open daily 12.30–3.30pm and 7.30–11.30pm.

La Botte (☎ *075 5722679.* ***www.ristorantelabotte.com***), at Via Volte della Pace 31, is rather more local, with a good reputation and a vast menu that includes pizzas. Their €11.50 *turistico* has a long list of options; closed Sundays.

house red will leave you change. The outdoor flamegrill has more if you're stocking up: steak, pork and sausage skewers, chicken, even barbecued potatoes. You'll need to be ready for some **DIY**. Grab a tablecloth and cutlery, find a spot under the large pergola and order at the till; whatever happy chaos your youngsters create won't match what's already going on. While you're waiting (it's all cooked from scratch), don't miss the world's best *bruschetta al pomodoro*. How do they get so much flavour into tomatoes on toast? Answers on a postcard.

Open *12.30–2.30pm and 7.30–10pm Tue–Sun.* ***Main courses*** *€3.50–9.* ***Amenities*** *highchairs.*

Pallotta ★ UMBRIAN/CLASSIC ITALIAN

Vicolo della Volta Pinta, Assisi. 075 812649. www.pallottaassisi.it.

You don't have to veer far from the **tourist traps** ringing Piazza del Comune to find good food; this much recommended trattoria is through the medieval arch on the south side. The exposed-beams-and-stone dining room works well with a **traditional menu** and old-fashioned dessert cabinet. Food is simple, seasonal and well cooked: Umbrian *antipasti*, local and classic Italian pastas, and plain grills served without fuss. The family carnivore is sure to enjoy an all-meat *arrosto misto* (mixed roast). For children, there are veal escalopes or plain pasta'n'sauce, which they're happy to cook right away and serve first. There are also tasting menus for vegetarians (€24) and gourmets (€25), and 14 wines by the glass, ¼ or ½ a litre.

It's rightly popular: **book ahead** or arrive promptly.

Open *12.30–2.30pm and 7.30–9.30pm Wed–Mon.* ***Main courses*** *€6–15.* ***Credit*** *AmEx, MC, V.* ***Amenities*** *highchairs, reservations accepted.*

La Cantina UMBRIA/PIZZA

Via Piccotti 3, Gubbio. 075 9220583.

There's plenty of gourmet choice in town, but this noisy, vaulted cellar is a reasonable **compromise** with young children. Local food is complemented with a range of well-priced pizzas (€4–7) and a value *menù turistico*: pasta, grilled pork or roast beef *all'inglese*, salad and dessert for €13. For the daring, there's *frittata al tartufo* (thick omelette with truffles) and pretty much anything with local *porcini* wild mushrooms. The semi-subterranean spot and slightly wonky air-conditioner ensures that even on a hot day, you all keep your cool – as long as you get into the spirit of the chaotic, but cheery, service.

Hardcore foodies should book ahead for the medieval basement at **Osteria del Re** (*075 9222504*), Piazza Busone 17: expect tripe, salt cod, truffled cheese and *polenta* (maize slop).

Open *12.15–2.30pm and 7.30–10pm Tue–Sun.* ***Main courses*** *€6–13.* ***Credit*** *AmEx, MC, V.* ***Amenities*** *A/C, highchairs, reservations accepted.*

Sauro, Isola Maggiore, see p. 199.

Corso Vannucci, Perugia

Al Coccio ★★ FIND UMBRIAN

Via del Quadrifoglio 12/a, Magione. ☎ *075 841829.* ***www.alcoccio.it****.*

This isn't the kind of place you find on your own (we didn't either); a **local hangout** in a plain side-street outside Magione. The ambience is typical *ristorante*, with ceiling fans blowing strong, hams hanging and walls decked with red wines, heavy on the **Montefalco DOC**. It's all *tipico Umbra* in the true sense, where a serious attitude to food doesn't crowd out the family welcome. Children can eat pasta and plain grills, or join a tour of Umbrian specialities. Pecorino cheese cooked in the oven for starters, followed by *umbrichelli* pasta with truffles and juicy rabbit *della Nonna* (roasted with rosemary and leeks, like granny used to make). Even the soufflé's local: the chocolate is **Perugina**, made down the road.

Open *12.15–3.30pm and 7.30–11pm Tue–Sun.* ***Main courses*** *€7–16.* ***Credit*** *AmEx, MC, V.* ***Amenities*** *highchairs, reservations accepted.*

Osteria del Turreno ★ VALUE SELF-SERVICE

Piazza Danti 16, Perugia. ☎ *075 5721976.*

This self-service (*tavola calda*) diner opposite the duomo has been serving **basic lunches** with a Perugian twist for decades. The day's dishes are displayed in a glass cabinet; pick what you fancy, pay at the till and take it to your table (inside or out), canteen-style. Options always include simple pasta (like *lasagne*, €3.60), grilled meats and plenty of salad and veg. Sometimes even sort-of chips. Desserts are a bit scarce – but beer and wine aren't.

There are no highchairs, but (just) enough room inside and out for a buggy.

Open *12.15–3pm Sun–Fri.* ***Main courses*** *€3.10–6.20.*

Bar Bonci, Spello, see p. 206.

9 Orvieto & Southern Umbria

CENTRAL & SOUTHERN UMBRIA

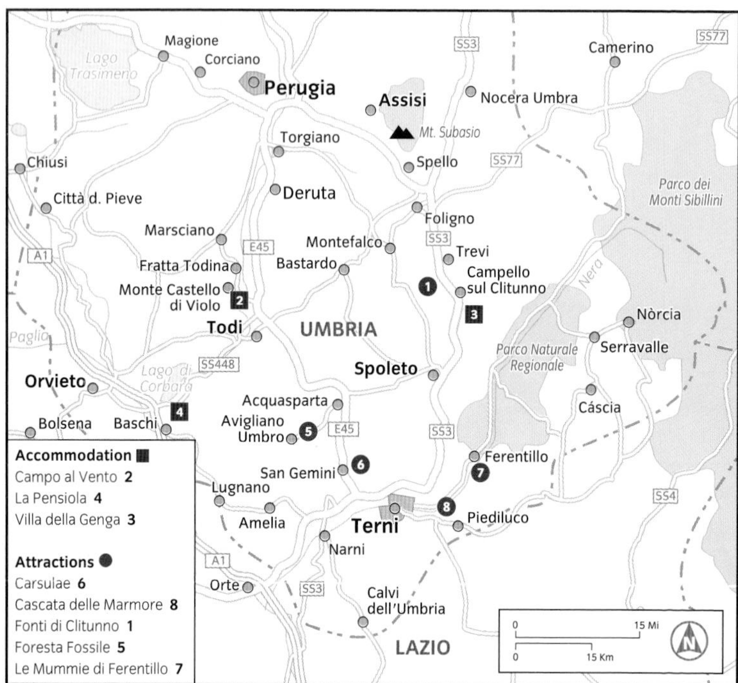

No sign lets you know that you've arrived in 'southern' Umbria. In fact, it barely registers: the bottom half of the region is an extension of the **green hills** and pastoral countryside that covers the north. Like its mirror image, the country becomes wilder and less tainted the farther you move from the (ahem) 'busy' central belt. It's the ideal terrain for escaping to a secluded villa or farmhouse. A place to find a quiet niche all of your own, among breezy hilltop villages and rolling agricultural views where the onset of international tourism has hardly left a scratch on the pace of daily life. More than anywhere in Tuscany and Umbria, existence around here remains governed by the rhythms of the sun and the path of the seasons.

From a sightseeing point of view, though, it is a little trickier. Etruscan **Orvieto** – the pearl of the south and Umbria's magnificent cathedral *città* and wine centre at the meeting point of Lazio and Tuscany – isn't a place you'd fancy day-tripping from **Norcia**; it's too far, and roads round here don't oblige if you want to get anywhere fast. Plan to stay around the centre if you can; the sleepy, laid-back towns of **Todi** and **Montefalco**, at the core of Italy's 'Green Heart', are quintessential Umbria with sights and views the children will love. You could say the same about **Spoleto** 11 months out of 12, but for a few weeks in June and July when its festival is the centre of the arts world. As a bonus, all three towns are within reach of the white waters of the **Valnerina**, the ruins at **Carsulae** and the hidden world of the Dominican Inquisition below **Narni**; each a great spot for burning off the distinctly calorific local food. It's considered among Italy's best **cuisine** – as long as you like truffles.

ORVIETO

The defining feature of southern Umbria's most touristy town is its cathedral, with its sparkling façade fronting on the massive piazza. Day-trippers come to **Orvieto** ★★ from as far as Florence and Rome to see it. You'll have to get here early if you prefer your holiday snaps without added tourists. The rest of town looks much like it did 500 years ago, a preserved medieval centre stuck high on a **volcanic plug**, visible for miles in every direction. This impenetrable perch ensured that *Velzna* was among the most powerful members of the *dodecapoli* (see p. 167); its Etruscan heritage has left an **underground** world that's just as much fun to explore as the one up above.

It's quaint, sure, but these days Orvieto's cobbled alleys and streets still have a lived-in feel: even along Corso Cavour there are butchers and barbers besides the wine tasting, ceramics and *tipico* shops.

Essentials

Orvieto is straightforward by **car**, especially from southern Tuscany: it's right by the **A1**. The main road link to the rest of Umbria is the **SS448** to Todi (40 minutes). There's free and pay (€1 per hour) **parking** in Piazza Cahen; follow the yellow signs for '*pozzo san patrizio*' as you enter Orvieto. An alternative is the multi-storey west of town, **Ex-Campo della Fiera** (70¢ per hour). From there, take an escalator up to the old centre on its rock.

Orvieto Scalo is on the fast Rome–Florence train (✆ *892021. www.trenitalia.it*) line. **Chiusi–Chianciano Terme** (see p. 177), the main station for southern

Children's Top Attractions in Southern Umbria

- Riding the **rapids** on an inflatable raft in the Valnerina, p. 229.
- Getting grisly with the **gruesome mummies** of Ferentillo, p. 231.
- Meeting the **Etruscans** at Orvieto's Museo Claudio Faina, p. 221.
- **Exploring** another world, below Orvieto, p. 222.
- Digging in to **Umbria's tastiest ice cream** at Colder, p. 229.
- **Hanging out** at the Hotel Gattapone in Spoleto, p. 234.
- Sampling quality **cuisine** in a laid-back setting at Coccorone, p. 235.

Tuscany, is 25–35 minutes. **Perugia** (1½ hours) requires a change at Terontola. From Orvieto Scalo take the 100-year-old **funicular** (90¢) to Piazza Cahen. For the *centro storico*, either walk 10 minutes uphill on cobblestones or take **Bus A** (every 10 minutes, 7am–8pm) for the Duomo. Tickets are 90¢, and your funicular ticket is valid for a further hour. Accompanied under-10s ride free.

Next to the funicular terminal, Orvieto's semi-ruined 14th-century **Rocca** houses the **Giardino Comunale**, with a small **playground**. The mighty ramparts afford the best **view** ★ of Orvieto Scalo below – one from a distance. It's open 8am–7.30pm between May and September, but closes 4.30pm otherwise.

Orvieto's **tourist office** (*0763 341772. www.orvieto.umbria2000.it*) is at Piazza del Duomo 24. It's open 8.15am–1.50pm and 4–7pm Monday to Friday, 10am–1pm and 3–6pm at weekends. **Pasqualetti** (*0763 341034*), Piazza del Duomo 14, is the best *gelato* stop.

Around the City

Nothing you've yet seen in Tuscany or Umbria prepares you for a first encounter with Orvieto's **Duomo** ★. The 'Golden Lily of Cathedrals' is either the height of garish ostentation or a masterpiece. The attention-grabbing **façade** ★★, restored and glowing in Gothic glory, is grafted on to a Romanesque body originally planned in 1290 – the whole thing took 300 years to complete. Of Lorenzo Maitani's four **reliefs** ★★★ carved on exterior columns, look out for a brutal *Last Judgement* on the lower right: as the dead rise from their graves, demonic torturers look delighted and the damned a touch concerned. Inside, as well as the Cappella San Brizio (see below), check out Ugolino's frescoes in the **Cappella del Corporale** ★ (left of the altar) which tell the story of the **Miracle of Bolsena**: a young German priest was saying Mass nearby when blood dripped from the Host on to the altar cloth (the *corporale*). The cloth is kept inside, and memory lives on in the annual festival of **Corpus Domini** (or 'Corpus Christi') declared by Pope Urban IV in 1264, the following year. Along with Spello's **Infiorate** (p. 205), Orvieto's parade is the best place to experience the festival.

More likely to appeal to children are the fine **views** ★ to be had from the top of the **Torre del Moro** (*0763 344567.* €2.80) at Corso Cavour 87, Orvieto's clock tower whose bell has been

FUN FACT **4 x 4**

Orvieto is divided into four ancient *quartiere*: Corsica, Olmo, Stella, and Serancia. See if you can spot signs marking all four as you walk round.

TIP A Super Saver

The best cumulative ticket in Umbria is the Orvieto Unica Card (*www.cartaunica.it*). €18 (€15 students) gets you into **everything** mentioned below, as well as the **Museo Archeologico Nazionale**. There's five hours' parking at Ex-Campo della Fiera, a return trip on the funicular and bus, and discounts at hotels, shops and restaurants. Buy the ticket from the **funicular car park** (*0763 302378*) in Orvieto Scalo, any participating sight, or the **Carta Unica office** (10am–6pm summer, shorter hours winter) next to Orvieto's tourist office. It's valid for a year. We've listed individual prices for each attraction to help you calculate whether the card makes sense.

ringing since 1313. If you don't fancy all **236** steps, a lift whizzes up the first hundred or so. It's open 10am–8pm daily May to August, closing an hour earlier during March, April, September and October. November to February, hours are 10.30am–1pm and 2.30–5pm. Under-10s go free.

Cappella di San Brizio ★★

AGE 7 AND UP

Inside Duomo

If you've come to Orvieto to see the frescoes in the duomo, you're in good company: **Michelangelo** made sketches on his way south to paint the Sistine Chapel. Luca Signorelli's **Last Judgement** is considered a masterpiece of the early Renaissance, on a subject clearly close to Orvietan hearts. The main action is in the lunettes. There's no real order; all depict our anticipated final reckoning with varying degrees of gore. Compare the faces of **The Saved** and **The Damned** on either side of the altar; above your head, **The End of the World** ★ drips with blood. Easily the most striking image in the chapel is the glazed preacher and his demonic companion in **The Rule of the Antichrist** ★★★. The two robed figures on the far left are Signorelli and Fra' Angelico (see p. 57), who painted **Christ Judge** and **The Prophets** on the ceiling vaults.

Open *9am–12.45pm and 2.30–7.15pm Mon–Sat Apr–Sep, closes 6.15pm Mar and Oct, 5.15pm Nov–Feb; 2.30–6.45pm Sun Jul–Sep, until 5.45pm Sun otherwise.* ***Adm*** *€5, €4 children 7–18; includes Museo dell'Opera del Duomo (0763 343592.* ***www.opsm.it****).*

Museo Claudio Faina e Civico ★ AGE 7 AND UP

Piazza Duomo 29. 0763 341511. ***www.museofaina.it***

Two cheers for the only museum in Etruria that make the Etruscans come alive for **children**, including English-speaking ones. There are some rare finds on display, mainly from digs around Orvieto (*Velzna* in Etruscan). Notable are the striking 6th-century BC black-figure vases painted in Attic style by renowned Ancient

TIP Stick to the Classics

Just like in Chianti, the *classico* in Orvieto Classico signifies that white grapes come from the original growing area only (see p. 32). Look out for uncommon Orvietan versions, like off-dry (neither dry nor sweet) *abboccato*.

Greek vase-painter Exekias, and Room XVI's **tiny bronze warriors**, horses and goddesses from 100 years earlier. Star of the show is the **Museo dei Ragazzi** ★; displays that help youngsters interact with the exhibits by prompting 20 questions (and answers) in English and Italian. What did Etruscans eat? How does an archaeologist work? What is a sarcophagus? And so on. Each room has its own discussion point to help you round.

***Open** 9.30am–6pm daily Apr–Sep, 10am–5pm Oct–Mar, closed Mon Nov–Feb. **Adm** €4.50, €3 children 7–12, with bus/funicular ticket, or anyone with family. **Amenities** disabled access, English.*

Pozzo di San Patrizio

AGE 4 AND UP

Viale Sangallo. ☎ 0763 343768.

As a feat of Renaissance engineering, there's no doubting **St Patrick's Well** is impressive. Designed by Antonio da Sangallo the Younger in 1527, it took 10 years of digging, a 62m hole, and the destroying of an Etruscan tomb to strike water. Just as well no one was thirsty. The **double-helix** stairways never intersect; donkeys bringing water up avoided donkey down-traffic. Whether any ever admired the dizzy view through one of the 72 internal windows isn't documented.

Take a jumper – it's always cool and damp – and hold little hands. The well is **overpriced** – one for the Carta Unica (see above).

***Open** 9am–7.45pm daily May–Aug, until 6.45pm Mar–Apr and Sep–Oct; 10.45am–4.45pm Nov–Feb. **Adm** €4.50, €3.50 anyone in full-time education.*

Orvieto Underground ★

AGE 8 AND UP

*c/o Piazza Duomo 23. ☎ 0763 340688. **www.orvietounderground.it.***

The real history of Orvieto is the almost 3,000-year story of its

Pozza di San Patrizio

caves: over 1,200 artificial and natural caverns have been found in the pozzolana and tufa that the city sits on. Regular guided tours take in just two, under Santa Chiara convent, which have variously been used as Etruscan houses, water wells, ceramic ovens, pigeon coops, quarries and natural fridges. Most recently they were unwise shelters from Allied bombing of Orvieto Scalo station; a direct hit would have annihilated the soft rock.

The tour is fine for children who can climb a few steep steps (**no pushchairs**, obviously); take sweatshirts, it's always 15°C down there.

Dipping your toe in subterranean Orvieto, the **Pozzo della Cava** ★ (☏ *0763 342373. www.pozzodellacava.it*), at Via della Cava 28, is a better set-up for impatient youngsters. It's open 8am–8pm Tuesday to Sunday, costs €3 (€2 children, free under-6s), involves less walking and takes about 10 minutes to get round.

Guided tours *(1 hour) 11am, 12.15pm, 4pm, 5.15pm.* ***Adm*** *€5.50, €3.50 anyone in full-time education.* ***Amenities*** *English (2–3 times a day).*

TODI

It may be a concept that your children struggle with, but **Todi** ★ is a great place just to *be*, not necessarily to *see*. One of a group of 33 Italian 'Slow Cities', its sedate rhythm was hardly dented by the waves of publicity it received when it was voted the planet's supposedly '**Ideal City**'. In reality, it's a small hilltop town perched perfectly above the Tiber Valley, with a modest reputation for sustainability and woodcarving, a history that stretches back beyond Rome, superb 360° views, the best piazza in Umbria – and not an Internet café to be had for love or euros.

Essentials

Todi is 40km south of Perugia, off the E45 *superstrada*. For the quickest route into town, take the 'Todi-Orvieto' exit and turn right by the orange building immediately after Ponterio; it heads straight up to Todi's Porta Perugiana. **Don't park** here: turn right again for the **Porta Orvietana** car park (55¢ per hour). A glass lift whizzes you up to Via Ciuffelli.

The **APM bus** (☏ *075 506781. www.apmperugia.it*) stops in the centre, on Piazza Jacopone; the only useful connection is with **Perugia** (1½ hours, €4.30).

The **tourist office** (☏ *075 8945416. info@iat.todi.pg.it*) is at Piazza del Popolo 38. It's open 9.30am–1pm and 3–6pm Monday to Saturday, 10am–1pm Sundays in winter. Summer afternoon hours (May to September) are 3.30–6.30pm.

Around the Town

Built on top of a Roman temple, Todi's **Piazza del Popolo** ★★ is Umbria's most majestic medieval square. Its subtle grandeur derives from several buildings

Todi

preserved in harmony. The south side of the square is enclosed by the **Palazzo dei Priori**, with its curious trapezoidal tower. To the east stands the **Palazzo del Popolo**, above the tourist office, and **Palazzo del Capitano**, built within 30 years of each other in the 13th century. Best of the lot, Todi's **duomo** ★★ is a study in classy simplicity. A square bell tower and plain façade draw the eye towards the rose window, added to the 12th-century structure in 1500.

Art pilgrims should make for the **Purgatorio di San Patrizio**, at the Monastero di San Francesco, Via Borgo Nuovo 20. This 14th-century fresco was among the first depictions of the circles of Hell envisaged by Dante's *Divine Comedy*. Alas, it isn't possible to get really close. It's open 9–11am daily, except Saturdays.

Signposted opposite the tourist office are the **Cisterne Romane** (*075 8944148*), old water cisterns that form part of 5km of tunnels under Todi. Admission is €2 (€1.50 6–25s). It's open 10am–1.30pm and 3–6pm Tuesday to Sunday between April and October; 10.30am–1pm and 2.30–5pm weekends only otherwise.

Uphill and right of San Fortunato (see below) is Todi's **Parco della Rocca**, a ruined fort with far-reaching views and a better-than-average **playground**.

San Fortunato AGE 3 AND UP

Piazza Umberto I. 075 8945311. ***todi@sistemamuseo.it.***

Not *another* church, surely? Yes, but we're not here for (what's left of) the art. Climb the 153 stairs of the bell tower for the best **views** ★ in town: into Piazza del Popolo, over the agricultural plains of the Tiber Valley and best of all to **Santa Maria della Consolazione** ★, a monumental Renaissance church built to a Greek cross plan in perfect proportion.

On the way out, stop in at San Jacopone's simple **tomb**, downstairs. If you've been to San Gimignano, see who can spot **St Sebastian** (p. 91) first.

Open *10am–1pm and 3–6.30pm Tue–Sun Apr–Oct; 10.30am–1pm and 2.30–5pm Tue–Sun Nov–Mar.* ***Adm*** *€1.50, €1 6–25s.*

Foresta Fossile FIND

AGE 10 AND UP

Dunarobba. ☎ 0744 940348. ***www.forestafossile.it****. 14km south of Todi.*

A pleasant 20-minute drive from Todi, through an almost English rural idyll, is a curious phenomenon commonly (and wrongly) called a '**petrified forest**'. In fact these are the preserved, *not* fossilised, remains of an ancient Sequoia forest on what was once the shore of Lago Tiberino. It's **wood** of 3,000,000-year vintage, mummified in grey clay and only found when the brickyard next door was digging raw materials for its ovens. The 50 giant stumps, some over 4m in diameter, are all inclined at a 30° angle to the east, resulting from tectonic movements in prehistory. A weird sight.

Take **hats** for the children: the temperature reaches 40°C in summer. The site isn't navigable with a pushchair, and becomes a clay bog in the rain. And brace yourselves: although it's an intriguing tour, the place is deeply **un-picturesque**.

Guided tours *(1 hour) hourly 10am–1pm and 4–7pm Tue–Sun Jul–Aug; 10am–1pm and 3.30–6.30pm Fri–Sun mid-Apr–Jun and Sep; 10.30am–3.30pm Fri–Sun Oct–mid-Apr.* ***Adm*** *€5, €3 children 6–14.* ***Amenities*** *English, parking, shop.*

MONTEFALCO

The journey is almost as much fun as the arriving in **Montefalco**. The 475m 'Balcony of Umbria' surveys a 360° scene of wine trellises, olive groves and arable fields east to Spoleto and west to Todi. It's the home to the big exception among Umbria's unheralded wines. The town's **Sagrantino di Montefalco ★★**, made from an indigenous grape, qualifies as a DOCG (see p. 32) and must be matured for 2½ years before release. Great years, like **2003**, can improve in the bottle for a further 15, leaving a rich, velvety wine quite unlike neighbouring Tuscany's *robusto* reds.

The town is anchored by the fine hexagonal **Piazza del Comune**, whose 13th-century **Palazzo** is tastefully embellished with a simple *loggia*. Down the

Montefalco's Need-to-Know

Parking is plentiful and free around the walls; just follow them when you drive up. The **Strada del Sagrantino** wine trail office doubles as **tourist information** (☎ *0742 378490.* ***www.montefalcodoc.it***). It's in Piazza del Comune, on the Palazzo's left.

Corso at **Sant'Agostino**, the once-extensive **frescoes** have long been knobbled by damp, but children with a grisly streak should check out the illuminated body of the 'Holy Pilgrim' in the right wall. This **mummified corpse** was an anonymous Spaniard who came to venerate the holy bones of Beata Chiarella and Beata Illuminata in the adjacent casket; he reclined on a pew and died. On a lighter note, the church has an all-year singing and dancing **Nativity** scene carved from chalk and wood, complete with a medieval market, water feature and flying angels. Drop a coin in the box and press the button to get it going. If that doesn't satisfy youngsters, there's a shady **playground** round the back.

Back uphill in Piazza Domenico Mustafa, the nameless bar serves yummy **ice cream** ★.

Museo Civico di San Francesco ★ AGE 5 AND UP

Via Ringhiera Umbra. ☎ 0742 379598. ***www.benozzogozzoli.it***

Seeing first-class art in an environment that isn't crammed with visitors is a circle that can't often be squared. Here's an exception. **Benozzo Gozzoli** is an artist who'd have a higher profile if his masterpiece, Pisa's Campo Santo (p. 113), hadn't been razed by Allied firebombs in World War II. His frescoed apse of this former church was his first major commission, completed in 1452; it saw him step from the shadows of Lorenzo Ghiberti (p. 50) and Fra' Angelico (p. 57), with whom he'd long collaborated. **The Life of St Francis** ★★ will be familiar to people with Assisi already under their belt (see p. 201). To follow the story, start at his birth (lower-left), basically a *Nativity*, and work clockwise; return to the left and work clockwise again, before starting on the upper-left lunette and clockwise again to Francis's death.

Elsewhere in the cavernous church, Perugino's 1503 **Nativity** ★, as much an Umbrian landscape as a devotional work, shows his mastery of skin tone and composition. Downstairs houses the archaeological collection, including a reconstructed traditional wine *cantina*.

Open *10.30am–1pm and 3–7pm daily Jun–Aug, afternoon hours 2–6pm Mar–May and Sep–Oct, 10am–1pm and 2.30–5pm Tue–Sun Nov–Feb.* ***Adm*** *€5.* ***Amenities*** *disabled access, English (audioguide €3), shop.*

Brizi GREEN ALL AGES

Via Verdi 60. ☎ 0742 379165. ***www.frantoiobrizi.it.***

Occupying almost one side of Via Verdi, opposite Santa Chiara, Brizi is a **one-stop-shop** for what Montefalco is all about. At the centre of things is an **olive oil** ★ business that's been run with passion since before World War I. The *frantoio* still uses traditional granite wheels to get a complete cold press and retain the olives' vitamins. Don't be fooled by the price (€6.50 for 500ml): this is a serious oil, made only from hand-picked fruit, more labour of love than commercial venture. Brizio also selects small **Sagrantino** wine producers to sell in their *cantina*; only those whose grapes poke above the spring mists that make pesticides necessary farther downhill. If you find a **2003 Sagrantino** ★★, grab it.

There's also a family **trattoria** ★, where the commitment to seasonal food and simple Umbrian cooking is apparent the second you walk through the door; the **bed-and-breakfast** upstairs has five individually named rooms, three with private facilities, and a panoramic communal terrace. It's the perfect spot to experience 24 hours of life in a working hill-town. Cash only.

***Open** daily.*

Fonti del Clitunno FIND ALL AGES

*☎ 0743 521141. **www.fontidelclitunno.it**. 1km north of Campello sul Clitunno.*

The source of the river Clitunno has been a site of ancient pilgrimage and gladiator fights, admired by Pliny and rocked by a massive earthquake in 444 AD, which reshaped the terrain. Since the 1860s it's been a small **Romantic garden**; a little patch of England on a sunbaked Umbrian plain, complete with weeping willows, poplars, babbling brook and a couple of swans. Even Byron liked it here. As a peaceful respite, it's only slightly marred by traffic noise and a plastic wire fence. Don't forget your **duck-food** (50¢) on the way in.

***Open** 8.30am–8pm May–Aug, until 7.30pm Apr and Sep; long lunch closures Oct–Mar. **Adm** €2, free under-11s. **Amenities** bar, parking, picnic area (outside garden), restaurant (☎ 0743 275057. main courses €6–13), shop.*

SPOLETO

Provincial backwater for 11 months of the year, centre of the Italian arts world for the other, **Spoleto** ★ is a contradictory place. Though largely without the medieval air that wafts about Assisi and Todi, it was once the seat of a Duchy that ruled central Italy as far south as Naples. The **duomo** is the equal of Todi's, and the town trumps anywhere in Umbria for **Roman heritage**. Although arty, it has a welcoming feel and a fair degree of accessibility, even for young families. The town's crooked streets and hidden corners are ideal for getting pleasantly lost or stopping for a *caffè* with the locals. It's also well sited: the wilds of the Valnerina (see p. 231) are over the hill, and the sophisticated central Umbrian belt, notably Assisi and Perugia, is just a short drive or train trip.

If it's culture you're after, come in late June: the **Spoleto Festival** (***www.spoletofestival.it***) has been gaining profile since its inauguration in 1958. It's now one of Europe's leading arts and music festivals – hosting classical music, dance and opera in some unique settings around the town. Remember, if you're coming then, book months in advance

Rocca Albnoroziana, Spoleto

and expect to pay... well, more than you'd expect. Hotels here have three seasons: low, high and Festival.

Essentials

If you're based close to a station, Spoleto is a great place to visit by **train** (*892021. www.trenitalia.it*). Hourly services from **Perugia** (via Foligno; 1¼ hours, €3.70) stop here. From outside the station, take any bus for '*Piazza Carducci/Piazza della Libertà*' into the Old Town (plenty of room for pushchairs). Don't try to walk up (20–30 minutes) with young children. Bus tickets (90¢) are sold at the **Centro Servizi Stazione** on the platform.

By road, the town sits on top of the old Roman Via Flaminia, now the **SS3**, 26km north of Terni. There's usually plenty of **parking**; if the Festival is jamming spaces, **Spoletosfera** car park signed from the SS3 '*Spoleto sud*' exit will probably have some (50¢ per hour). It's a 5–10 minute (flat) walk to Piazza della Libertà.

Spoleto treats its guests well: the huge, helpful **tourist office** (*0743 238920. info@iat.spoleto.pg.it*) in Piazza della Libertà (no. 7) is open every day except Christmas. Summer hours are 8.30am–1.30pm and 4–7pm Monday to Friday, 10am–1pm and 4–7pm weekends. Between October and March, afternoon hours are 3.30–6.30pm. Independent *www.prospoleto.it* is also handy for information and events.

Once school's out (mid-June), Spoleto's annual **Summer Camp** kicks off: a succession of treks, sports events, mountain bike trails and bouncy castles to fill the long, hot months until September. Visitors' children are welcome: look out for posters around town.

Around the Town

A ramp down into Piazza del Duomo is a suitably grand prelude to Spoleto's architectural highlight, the **Cattedrale di Santa Maria Assunta** ★★ (*0743 231063*). Although obviously built in stages, it retains a harmony equalled only by Todi's duomo (see p. 224). Even the addition of a Renaissance balcony and portico to the 12th-century structure managed not to mess up the façade. It's open 8.30am–12.30pm and 3.30–6pm daily. Inside the apse is covered with **frescoes** ★ tracing the life of the Virgin Mary begun by **Filippo Lippi** (see p. 62) and completed by assistants after he died.

Children might prefer the spooky crypt of **San Isacco** ★ underneath 11th-century **Sant'Ansano**, open 8.30am–midday and 3.30–5.30pm (6.30pm in summer). The sarcophagus allegedly contains the body of San Isacco, who died in 552. The church is by the Roman **Arco del Druso**: look how much the street level has risen since that was built. Nearby **Via Fontesecco** is an atmospheric street with window-shopping potential.

Its location at the Piazza Vittoria end of Viale Trento e Trieste (no. 29) isn't exactly convenient, but don't miss **Colder Gelateria** ★★. Their ice cream (notably 'bread and chocolate' flavour) is the best we found in Umbria.

Casa Romana AGE 3 AND UP

Via di Visiale. 0743 234250. spoleto@sistemamuseo.it.

Spoletium had a strong Roman heritage, and an especially brutal reputation for martyring Christians – its amphitheatre needed an ingenious drainage system to whisk away the blood. This fantastically preserved **Roman House** under Piazza del Comune obviously belonged to

Wild Rides

Just over the hills from Spoleto, the Valnerina is Umbria's **white-water rafting** ★★ capital. **Pangea** (*348 7711170. www.pangea-italia.com*), based in Scheggino, caters for children aged 3 and up: it's €30 for adults, €20 for little ones. It's the same prices and age range at **Gaia** (*338 7678308. www.asgaia.it*) for 1½-hour trips from their base 6km outside Norcia. **Rafting Umbria** (*348 3511798. www.raftingumbria.it*) run two-hour trips along the Corno from Serravalle di Norcia; it's €35 adults, €25 children 4–14. Each outfit runs three to four trips a day; book ahead and take clothes that you don't mind getting wet. There's no need for special skills (or even to understand Italian). A two-bedroom wooden chalet at **Campeggio Il Drago** (*0743 751070. www.campeggioildrago.it*) makes a suitably adventurous base for budding rafters. Prices €40–80 per night.

someone rich, though there's little evidence that someone was Emperor Vespasian's *mamma* as previously claimed. What's left of the frescoed plaster gives an idea of how it was decorated 2,000 years ago. Although it feels sacrilegious to walk on the original mosaic floor, the experience certainly brings Roman life to, er, life.

***Open** 10am–8pm daily (closes 6pm mid-Oct–mid-Mar). **Adm** €2.50, €2 15–25s, €1 children 7–14. **Amenities** English, shop.*

A Walk in the Woods ★

AGE 8 AND UP

There's plenty to explore on foot or mountain bike on the wooded slopes of **Monteluco**, but it's just as easy to dip your toe in with a one-hour circuit starting by the gatehouse of the **Rocca Albornoziana** in Piazza Campello (*0743 46434*). So-so guided tours of the 1359 castle are available for the fort-mad; in summer they usually leave on the hour, 10am–7pm. It's €6.50, €5 for 15–25s, €2 for 7–14s.

From the piazza walk up Via del Ponte. Buy water from **Bar La Portella** as you pass – it's your last chance. Round the bend you'll catch a first (and best – snap now) view of the 14th-century **Ponte delle Torri** ★, 236m long, with nine pillars, standing 90m above the Tessino river below. It has become the emblem of Spoleto. Unbelievably, it was built on top of a Roman aqueduct. Exactly how *that* was engineered remains a mystery.

Once you're over the bridge, drink in the silence, birdsong and views back to Spoleto from the woods. **Michelangelo** came here to chill out, too. Continue parallel to the town until **San Pietro** church, whose façade **reliefs** ★ rank second only to Orvieto's (see p. 220). They narrate obscure medieval allegories, although (as in Orvieto) demons torturing sinners are rendered with particular relish. From the church, cross the busy road and take the second right. Straight ahead (five minutes) is **Piazza della Libertà**; the park on your left has a shaded **playground** if youngsters need more action.

There is a *possibility* (this is Italy, after all) that works closing the Ponte delle Torri won't have finished by 2008. Check.

THE FAR SOUTH

Economically, the south of Umbria is dominated by **Terni**. This industrial town, in a bowl of rolling agricultural plains, isn't somewhere you'll want to linger.

TIP **Need Info?**

The only reason to go to Terni is to collect information from the province's **tourist information service** (*0744 423047. **www.provincia.terni.it/turismo***) at Via Cassian Bon 7. It's open 9am–1pm and 3–6pm Monday to Saturday.

But it's at the centre of some attractions that escape the art-heavy bias. The rugged terrain of the **Valnerina** is Umbria's action-holiday capital – with white water, quiet campsites and remote hillsides ideal for family outdoor fun. Archaeological sites at Narni and Carsulae are intriguing enough to be accessible for all bar the very youngest. We wouldn't recommend basing yourselves right at the region's extremes – it's too awkward for too much of Umbria – but the best bits make cracking day trips from Spoleto and Todi, or even Perugia if you don't mind a long day in the car. Head south: you won't regret it.

Le Mummie di Ferentillo ★

AGE 10 AND UP

Chiesa di Santo Stefano, Ferentillo. 0743 54395. 17km north-east of Terni on SS209.

In the jagged shadows of the Valnerina (the valley of the Nera river) is a phenomenon usually linked with the Egyptian desert: **mummies**. For centuries, the dusty crypt of Santo Stefano was also Ferentillo's graveyard. Dry air, porous soil and a fungus that ate organisms causing putrefaction mummified several corpses. It's a **gruesome** roll-call of desiccated death: French soldiers tortured and hanged during the Napoleonic wars; Chinese honeymooners dead from cholera; a lawyer stabbed 27 times; even a bell-ringer who fell from his tower. All died here, and each remains frozen in a final agony: this ghoulish sight **absolutely isn't** a place to bring young or sensitive children.

Repeated thefts mean visits are by **guided tour** only, but they run regularly and are pretty loose. You may be given an English handout and left to it.

***Open** 9am–12.30pm and 2.30–7.30pm daily Apr–Sep, closed 6pm Mar and Oct; 10am–12.30pm and 2.30–5pm daily Nov–Feb; regular guided tours (15 minutes). **Adm** €3. **Amenities** English (handout).*

Cascata delle Marmore

ALL AGES

0744 62982. cascata@micanet.net. 6km east of Terni on SS209.

You don't come across a waterfall that runs to a timetable very often, but the 165m **Marmore Falls** aren't quite what they seem. The problem of what to do about regular flooding on the Rieti plain above was first tackled by the Romans in 271 BC: they cut a channel to create an **artificial cascade** into the River Nera. Patchy

Cascata delle Marmore

success was followed by inevitable local squabbles until the falls took their current shape in 1786.

The whole area is now a **landscaped park**, with four marked trails up and around the roaring water of varying degrees of difficulty; with a **buggy**, you're limited to standing at the bottom getting sprayed. Because the water now powers a hydroelectric station, it isn't always going when you want it to, but the **timetable** (see ***www.marmore.it*** or any Umbrian tourist office) accommodates visitor demands – more action Saturdays, Sundays and summertime. If they'd just do *something* with the concrete plaza that welcomes you (like bulldoze it), you'd have a thoroughly spectacular visit.

Open *daily Mar–Sep, Fri–Sun Oct, Sat–Sun Nov–Feb.* ***Adm*** *€4, €2 children 6–12.* ***Amenities*** *bar, English, parking, picnic area, restaurant, shop.*

Carsulae ★ ALL AGES

San Gémini Fonte. ☎ 0744 334133.

Tourists have been coming to this windswept hill for over 2,000 years: Umbria's largest **Roman** site was once a popular resort with the Imperial wealthy. Although some of the monumental blocks were recycled to build the 11th-century church of **San Gemini**, much of what remains is easily identifiable. You can walk right into the **Amphitheatre**, just as gladiators did when Carsulae was an important town in the 3rd century BC. Best of all, stroll along the ancient high street, on the limestone flagstones of the **Via Flaminia**, past the Forum, Temple of Gemini and out of the main gate to the necropolis. One circuit is an easy hour.

Strictly speaking, there's **no picnicking**. However, if you sneak in a sarnie for the children and dispose of litter properly, you'll probably escape jail.

Open *8.30am–7.30pm daily (closes 5.30pm Oct–Mar).* ***Adm*** *€4.40, €3.30 under-18s.* ***Amenities*** *bar, English, parking, shop.*

Narni Sotterranea AGE 12 AND UP

Via San Bernardo 12, Narni. ☎ 0744 722292. ***www.narnisotterranea.it****.*

When the Romans arrived here, they scrapped the town's ancient name and gave it 'Narnia', perhaps later nicked by **C.S. Lewis**. The highlights of its eerie 'underground' tour have a more recent vintage. The tiny frescoed church of **Sant'Angelo**, carved from rock and hidden until 1979, was already here when the Dominicans arrived in 1303. They found a more sinister use for other passageways and cellars: the **torture** room used by their Holy Inquisition is right under the abbey altar. An adjacent cell, covered in 18th-century **graffiti**, is one for the family cryptographer: spot masonic and Jesuit symbols, the 14 Stations of the Cross, and the repetitive number palindrome '07 24 42 70'. Weird.

It's a fascinating historical tour, but without concessions to young ones. There's a **playground** by the entrance if you want to operate split-shifts.

Guided tours *hourly (1 hour) 10am–1pm and 3–6pm Sun, 3pm*

TIP Noshing in Norcia

Worth a visit if you have time, Norcia (*www.comune.norcia.pg.it*) **is the** birthplace of St Benedict and Italy's **black truffle** capital. It also gave its name to a shop: *Norcineria* is a word used across central Italy to mean 'quality pork butcher'. Seek one out if you like salami or cured ham.

and 6pm only Sat, Apr–Oct; 11am–1pm and 3–5pm Sun Nov–Mar. ***Adm*** *€5, free under-14s.* ***Amenities*** *English (handout).*

FAMILY-FRIENDLY ACCOMMODATION

The **Spoleto Festival** skews prices and availability across Umbria's central belt from mid-June into July: book ahead. For more ideas on hotels and accommodation, see Chapter 2.

Villa della Genga ★ GREEN

0743 521186. ***www.leterrediporeta.it****. 2km south of Campello del Clitunno.*

At the centre of a sustainable, organic olive oil estate, this 18th-century estate is a grand base within 20 minutes of Spoleto, Spello and Montefalco. Inside and out, the feel is of a farmhouse *designed*, not just *converted*. Spacious, well-equipped country kitchens match in with terracotta-tiled living areas and cool bedrooms – even the pool is **stylish**. Outside, manicured grounds look out over the Vale of Spoleto without even the sound of a Vespa to disturb your slumber. If the mood grabs you, there are truffle-hunting and horse-riding treks to keep you busy.

Apartments *7.* ***Rates*** *€710–1890 per week.* ***Credit*** *MC, V.* ***Amenities*** *parking, pool (outdoor), tennis.* ***In apartment*** *A/C, cots, highchairs, kitchen, sat TV.*

Campeggio Il Drago, Cascia, see p. 229.

La Pensiola

0744 950521. On SS448, loc. Lago di Corbara. ***www.albergolapenisola.it****.*

This roadside, **motel-style** inn right on the lakefront makes an ideal overnight stop on a tour of southern Umbria: it's half an hour from Orvieto and the same from Todi. Somehow they've managed to squeeze some character into the three modern blocks.

Villa della Genga

Rooms are straightforward, no-nonsense affairs, some with baths, but can only accommodate triples (no quads). All rooms face the lake and share a communal terrace with four others. The garden is big and flat enough for children to stretch their limbs.

For local wine tasting, one of the famous names in Orvieto Classico, **Barberani**, is just across the road.

Rooms *19.* ***Rates*** *Double €80–130, triple €104–165. Cot €10. Breakfast included.* ***Credit*** *MC, V.* ***Amenities*** *parking, playground, pool (outdoor), restaurant, tennis.* ***In room*** *A/C, fridge, sat TV.*

Campo al Vento ★★ FIND

075 8796044. ***www.campoalvento.it.*** *3km south of Monte Castello di Vibio.*

You're never far from the middle of nowhere in Umbria and this *agriturismo*'s breezy hillside 20 minutes from Todi certainly qualifies. It's taken four years to convert an **18th-century stone farmhouse** into three apartments and four double/twin rooms in keeping with the original building. New wooden furniture in sympathy with the exposed-beams-and-tiled interiors was added. The effect is airy, stylish but still rustic, and brand new: it opened in 2007. The owner can sort excursions with a local riding school, and produces his own olive oil, chicken and wine to organic principles. During August, it's Saturday to Saturday bookings only.

Apartments *3.* ***Rooms*** *4.* ***Rates*** *Double €35–60, apartment €70–120. Breakfast included (rooms only).* ***Credit*** *MC, V.* ***Amenities*** *bike hire (free), parking, pool (outdoor), restaurant.* ***In room*** *cot, highchair, kitchen, sat TV, shower only.*

Brizi, Montefalco, see p. 226.

Hotel Gattapone ★★★

Via del Ponte 6, Spoleto. 0743 223447. ***www.hotelgattapone.it.***

If you don't pay €200 a night very often, this is one place to do so. Terraced into the precipice below Spoleto's castle, the Gattapone's silent spot gives the impression of **countryside serenity** just two minutes uphill from the Duomo. It's simultaneously a chic rural retreat and modern, stylish urban hotel. The three family rooms are all suites: a simple, tasteful but compact main room has a raised double-bed area; extra sleeping is with the TV in the annex. Each has a spectacular panorama of the Ponte dei Torri, as well as a bath.

There's no pool (but watch this space...) or cots (so, older children only). If your budget stretches to three nights or more, a small discount will be forthcoming. Always **book ahead**.

Rooms *15.* ***Rates*** *Double €140–170, suite €170–230. Breakfast included.* ***Credit*** *AmEx, MC, V.* ***Amenities*** *babysitting, bar, laundry service, parking.* ***In room*** *A/C, fridge, safe, sat TV.*

TIP

An Alternative in Spoleto

If the Gattapone's full, or a bit pricey, 21-room Hotel Charleston ★ by San Domenico (☎ *0743 220052. **www.hotelcharleston.it***) is a great second choice. Triples and quads from €99 and €105. Parking in their garage costs €10 per night.

FAMILY-FRIENDLY DINING

Brizi, Montefalco, see p. 226.

Coccorone ★★ VALUE UMBRIAN

*Largo Tempestivi, Montefalco. ☎ 0742 379535. **www.coccorone.com**. Behind Palazzo del Comune.*

We dread to think how much a dining experience of this **quality** would cost back home. The Umbrian and local dishes are cooked and presented perfectly; the service is attentive without hovering; the wine list would make a Michelin-starred restaurant proud. At no point are you made to feel unwelcome or intimidated, even with noisy children. For all this the going rate in Montefalco is €6–8 for pasta and €8–18 for a main course. Little ones can play it safe with pasta *al pomodoro* (tomato sauce) or veal cutlets. For the daring there's beef in Sagrantino wine, lamb with truffles or snail kebabs. Although the outdoor cover charge is a bit steep (€3), the best spot is under the parasols on the terrace: book ahead or arrive early.

***Open** 12.30–3pm and 7–10pm Thu–Tue (daily in summer). **Main courses** €8–18. **Credit** MC, V. **Amenities** highchairs, reservations accepted.*

La Loggia dei Priori ★★

SOUTHERN UMBRIAN

*Vicolo del Comune 4, Narni. ☎ 0744 726843. **www.loggiadeipriori.it**.*

The **oldest restaurant** in Narni's old town is also the best. The vaulted, dark interior is complemented by a rear terrace that makes up in cool shade for what it lacks in panorama. The short, classy menu screams 'proper restaurant'. Adventurous eaters might fancy start-to-finish black truffles: *crostini* to *tagliolini* or *gnocchi* to fillet steak with shavings on top. There are **no half-portions**, but they're happy for you all to order a selection of pasta and meat and split it up. If you go that route, note that *secondi* portions aren't huge. The extensive wine list has plenty of Sagrantino to ponder.

***Open** 12.30–3pm and 7.30–9.30pm daily. **Main courses** €8–18. **Credit** MC, V. **Amenities** reservations accepted.*

Trattoria Tipica Etrusca ★

ORVIETAN

*Via Maitani 10, Orvieto. ☎ 0763 344016. **tipica.tratt.etrusca@tiscali.it**.*

In a town full of self-service joints, the Etrusca offers a bite with a bit of **class**. Its spot within sight of the Duomo hasn't diminished a commitment to quality food and attentive service – and the air conditioning sure helps in summer. Tuscan classics like hare and boar, local pasta *umbrichelli* (thick spaghetti like Montepulciano's *pici*) and lashings of truffles (even in the ice cream) are served with a smile, especially to picky youngsters.

For something quicker, the oft-recommended self-service **Al San Francesco** (*0763 343302. www.cramst.it*) opposite does fine, as long as there isn't a tour bus in and you don't expect staff to be polite.

Open *midday–3pm and 7.15–10pm daily (closed Mon winter).* ***Main courses*** *€8–15.* ***Credit*** *AmEx, MC, V.* ***Amenities*** *reservations accepted.*

Trattoria Pecchiarda

BASIC UMBRIAN

Vicolo San Giovanni 1, Spoleto. 0743 221009. Down steps from Piazza Torre dell'Olio and follow sign.

It's worth the trek down steep streets and steps for this taste of lunch in a proper Umbrian trattoria. There's **no fuss** on the menu or the set-up: eat in or out, as you please, and pick from simple country soups, pasta, grilled meat and salad. *Stringozzi* (spaghetti by any other name) *alla spoletina* (tomato, parsley and chilli) is the local choice, but the *gnocchi* and *bistecca* are just as good. The atmosphere is chatty, the service smiley and the eating experience as real as you'll find in gourmet Spoleto.

Open *12.30–2.30pm and 7.30–9.30pm Fri–Wed.* ***Main courses*** *€8–28 (truffles).* ***Credit*** *AmEx, MC, V.* ***Amenities*** *reservations accepted.*

Cavour VALUE PIZZA & PASTA

Via Cavour 21–23, Todi. 075 8943730.

For value among Todi's fine range of restaurants, it's still hard to beat Cavour. The fare is **straightforward** – extra-cheesy pizza, pasta, grilled meat – with an Umbrian twist (i.e. truffles with everything, except the chips). The inside is a bit tatty, but the triple-decker **panoramic terrace** out back lives up to its billing; to grab the best table under the pergola by the precipice, get there early. If it's busy, you'll need patience: service is haphazard.

For a more serious eating experience, pay a little more (pasta €10–13) at **Umbria** (*075 8942737*), behind the tourist office.

Open *midday–2.30pm and 7.30–10pm Thu–Tue.* ***Main courses*** *€3.50–12.* ***Credit*** *MC, V.*

The Insider

1

Unlike large areas of Italy, there isn't much dialect spoken in Tuscany or Umbria. Essentially, the Tuscan dialect became what we now call Italian, so you'll see, hear and be using the same words as everyone else. We recommend that you pack a compact dictionary: **Collins Italian Express Edition** (£8.99) fits hand luggage and has some extra help with those tricky irregular verbs.

To delve a little deeper with the children, the BBC's award-winning language course, **Muzzy** (£149.95), has a revolutionary learning-by-cartoon method that works. It's available from ***www.bbcshop.com***, and always at ***www.ebay.co.uk***.

USEFUL WORDS & PHRASES

The Basics

English	Italian	English	Italian
Yes/No	Si/No	Goodbye	Arrivederci
Please	Per favore	Good night	Buona notte
Thank you	Grazie	Hi	Ciao
You're welcome	Prego	How are you?	Come va?
Hello (daytime)	Buongiorno	I'm sorry / Excuse me	Mi scusi
Hello (afternoon/evening)	Buonasera		

Getting Around

English	Italian
Do you speak English?	Parla italiano?
I don't speak Italian	Non parlo Italiano
I don't understand	Non capisco
Could you speak more slowly?	Può parlare più adagio?
What is it?	Che cos'è
What time is it?	Che ora è
What?	Cosa?
How?	Come?
When?	Quando?
Where is...?	Dov'è
Who?	Chi?
Why?	Perché?
Here/There	Qui/là.

English	Italian
Left/Right	A sinistra/ A destra
Straight on	Sempre diritto
Fill the car, please	Il pieno, per favore.
When does ... leave?	A che ora parte...?
bus (local)	l'autobus
bus (long-distance)	il pullman
ferry	il traghetto
ship	la nave
train	il treno
I want to get off at...	Voglio scendere a...
the airport	l'aeroporto
a bank	una banca

English	Italian
the beach	la spiaggia
the bridge	il ponte
the bus station	la stazione dell'autobus
the cathedral	il duomo la Cattedrale
the church	la chiesa
the hospital	l'ospedale
the museum	il museo
broken down	guastato il motore
bus stop	la fermata
by car	in macchina
diesel	gasolio
driver's licence	patente
entrance	entrata
exit	uscita
first floor	primo piano
ground floor	piano terreno
left luggage	guarda bagagli
lift	ascensore
no smoking	vietato fumare
one-day ticket	biglietto giornaliero
one-way ticket	(biglietto) solo andata
passport	passaporto
petrol	benzina
police	polizia
return ticket	(biglietto) andata e ritorno
slow down	rallentare
street	via
telephone	telefono
ticket	biglietto
toilets	bagni/servizi

Shopping

English	Italian
How much does it cost?	Quanto viene?
That's expensive	È caro
Do you take credit cards	Accetta carte di credito?
This one	questo
That one	quello
Do you have...?	Ha...?
I'd like...	Vorrei...
Aspirin	aspirina
boots	stivali
colouring book	libro da colorare
gift	un regalo
hat	un cappello
map	una mappa/ guida
newspaper	un giornale
pay-as-you-go top-up	una ricarica
phonecard	una scheda telefonica
postcard	una cartolina
raincoat	un impermeabile
shoes	scarpe
soap	sapone
stamp	un francobollo
sweets	caramelle
swimming costume	costume da bagno
suntan cream	crema per il sole
toothpaste	deatifricio

English	Italian
Is there a ... near here?	C'è un/a... qui vicino?
bakery	un fornaio
butcher	un macellaio
cake shop	una pasticceria
fishmonger	un pescivendolo
grocer	un drogheria
Highchair	seggiolino
launderette	una lavanderia automatica
market	un mercato
supermarket	un supermercato
wine shop	un'enoteca

Children's Stuff

English	Italian
Baby equipment	cose per bambini
Bottle warmer	riscalda biberon
Buggy/pushchair	passeggino
Chemist	una farmacia
Child seat	sedile per bambini
Dummy	ciuccio
Formula	latte in polvere
Follow-on milk	per proseguire
Nappies	pannolini
Playground	un parco giochi
Swings	altalena
Slide	scivolo
Steriliser	sterilizzatore
My child has...	Il mio bimbo ha...
a cold	un raffreddore
a sore throat	mal di gola
a headache	mal di testa
stomach ache	mal di pancia

Making Friends

English	Italian
What's your name?	Come ti chiami?
My name is...	Mi chiamo...
Do you want to play?	Vuoi giocare?
Let's play hide-and-seek!	Giochiamo a nascondino!
Who do you support?	Per chi fai il tifo?
I'm...	Sono...
English	Inglese
Scottish	Scozzese
Welsh	Gallese
Irish	Irlandese
a Liverpool fan	un tifoso del Liverpool
My mummy	la mia mamma
My daddy	il mio papà
My sister	Mia sorella
My brother	Mio fratello
My grandparents	I miei nonni

TIP In an Emergency

Aiuto!	help!
Può aiutarmi, per favore?	Could you please help me?
Pronto soccorso	first aid
Ambulanza	ambulance
Ospedale	hospital
Un medico	doctor
Mi fa male qui	It hurts here
Una ricevuta, per favore	an invoice/receipt please
C'è una farmacia qui vicino?	Is there a pharmacy near here?
Al fuoco!	fire!
Ferma! Al ladro!	stop! thief!

Your Hotel

English	Italian	English	Italian
We're staying for ... days	Restiamo per ... giorni	Extra bed	un letto in più
Is breakfast included?	È inclusa il prima colazione?	Cot	una culla
Are taxes included?	Le tasse sono incluse?	Shower	una doccia
Room	una camera	Sink	un lavandino
Double room	una camera doppia/ matrimoniale	Bath	una vasca
Twin room	camera a due letti	Key	una chiave
Triple room	camera a tre letti	Air conditioning	aria condizionata
Quad room	camera a quattro letti	Balcony	un balcone
Family room	camera per famiglie	Bathroom	un bagno
		Hot water	acqua calda
		Babysitting	il babysitting
		Swimming pool (heated)	una piscina (riscaldata)

Numbers

English	Italian	English	Italian
Zero	zero	Five	cinque
One	uno	Six	sei
Two	due	Seven	sette
Three	tre	Eight	otto
Four	quattro	Nine	nove

English	Italian	English	Italian
Ten	dieci	Eighty	ottanta
Eleven	undici	Ninety	novanta
Twelve	dodici	One hundred	cento
Thirteen	tredici	One hundred and one	centoeuno
Fourteen	quattordici	One thousand	mille
Fifteen	quindici	Two thousand	duemila
Sixteen	sedici	One million	un millione
Seventeen	diciasette	First	primo
Eighteen	diciotto	Second	secondo
Nineteen	diciannove	Third	terzo
Twenty	venti	Fourth	quarto
Twenty-one	ventuno	Fifth	quinto
Twenty-two	ventidue	Sixth	sesto
Thirty	trenta	Seventh	settimo
Forty	quaranta	Eighth	ottavo
Fifty	cinquanta	Ninth	nono
Sixty	sessanta	Tenth	decimo
Seventy	settanta		

Days & Months

English	Italian	English	Italian
Monday	lunedì	January	gennaio
Tuesday	martedì	February	febbraio
Wednesday	mercoledì	March	marzo
Thursday	giovedì	April	aprile
Friday	venerdì	May	maggio
Saturday	sabato	June	giugno
Sunday	domenica	July	luglio
Yesterday	ieri	August	agosto
Today	oggi	September	settembre
Tomorrow	domani	October	ottobre
Tonight	stasera	November	novembre
Morning	mattino	December	dicembre
Afternoon	pomeriggio	New Year	Capodanno
Evening	sera	Easter	Pasqua
Night	notte	All Saints' Day	Ognissanti
one hour	un'ora	Christmas	Natale

Restaurants & Food

English	Italian
I would like...	Vorrei...
something to eat	qualcosa da mangiare
a bottle of...	una bottiglia di...
a cup of...	una tazza di...
a glass of...	un bicchiere di...
breakfast	(prima) colazione
lunch	pranzo
dinner	cena
the bill	il conto
a knife	un coltello
a fork	una forchetta
a spoon	un cucchiaio
a napkin	un tovagliolo
Cheers!	Salute!
fixed price menu	menù a prezzo fisso
menu	menù/carta
children's menu	menù per bambini
extra plate	un piatto in più
small portion	una porzione piccola
waiter/waitress	cameriere/a
vegetarian	vegetariano/a
wine list	carta dei vini
salt/(black) pepper	sale/pepe (nero)
oil	olio
bread	pane
ice	ghiaccio
sugar	zucchero
rare	poco cotto/ al sangue

English	Italian
medium	medio
well done	ben cotto
appetiser	antipasto
starter	primo
main course	secondo
side dish	contorno
(red/white) wine	vino (rosso/ bianco)
beer	birra
water (still/sparkling)	acqua (naturale/ frizzante)
home-made	fatto in casa
Special of the day	specialità del giorno
Is service included?	È incluso il servizio?
Are there highchairs?	Avete un seggiolino?
Do you take reservations?	Accettate prenotazioni?
My child is a fussy eater, can you cook something simple?	Il bambino è un po esigente. Potete cucinare qualcosa di semplice?
I'm allergic to...	Sono allergico a...
nuts	noci
shellfish	crostacei
chicken	pollo
cod (salted)	merluzzo (baccalà)
fish	pesce
lamb	agnello
sausage	salsiccia
steak	bistecca

Eating *tipico*: Tuscan & Umbrian Food

Bistecca alla Fiorentina – grilled Valdichiana steak on the bone
Cacciucco – Livornese fish stew
Cantuccini – hard almond-flour Tuscan biscuits
Cervo/capriolo – deer
Cinghiale – wild boar
Fagioli – beans
Fritto misto – mixed fry-up (often seafood)
Lepre – hare
Panforte – gloopy fruit, nut and honey cake from Siena
Pecorino – sheep's milk cheese
Persico – perch
Polpo – octopus
Porcini – wild bolete mushroom
Ragù – meat sauce for pasta (what we call 'Bolognese')
Ribollita – a cross between soup and stew, usually vegetables but fishy in the Maremma
Seppia – cuttlefish
Tartufo – truffle
Testaroli – pancake-like pasta from the Lunigiana
Torta al testo – salted Umbrian flatbread
Vin santo – fortified dessert wine
Zucca – pumpkin (a common pasta filling)

ITALIAN TOUR OPERATORS

Abercrombie & Kent

0845 0700600. ***www.abercrombiekent.co.uk***

From small hotels to large villas, across Tuscany and Umbria – all with a luxury price tag.

Canvas Holidays

0870 1921154. ***www.canvasholidays.co.uk***

Award-winning mobile homes, chalets and tents, with children's clubs for all ages and early-booking offers galore.

Citalia

0870 9014014. ***www.citalia.com***

Italy specialist with villas and hotels in Tuscany and Umbria, including the Tuscan seaside.

Cottages to Castles

01622 775236. ***www.cottagestocastles.com***

Small, hand-picked selection of villas, apartments, farmhouses and urban hotels in Tuscany and Umbria.

CV Travel

0870 0623427. ***www.cvtravel.co.uk***

Quality villas and hotels in Tuscany and Umbria from a 35-year veteran of the business.

Discovery Travel

01889 882170. ***www.discovery-travel.co.uk***

Hand-picked hotels and villas, and activity holidays including golf, sailing and horse riding.

Eurocamp

08703 338338. ***www.eurocamp.co.uk***

European camping giant with tents and mobile homes in seven locations across Tuscany.

Great Rail Journeys

01904 521936. ***www.greatrail.co.uk***

Their 'Colours of Tuscany and Umbria' tour includes 1st-class travel to Perugia, Gubbio, Florence and Assisi, as well as a ride through the Val d'Orcia on the Trenonatura (see p. 86).

Hello Italy

01483 419964. ***www.helloit.co.uk***

Self-catering and hotel accommodation across both regions, with the widest selection out there on the Lunigiana.

Homelidays

www.homelidays.com

Web-based, pan-European direct rental network with some astonishing villa and farmhouse bargains – strictly for those with the energy to search a massive catalogue.

Inghams

020 87804433. ***www.inghams.co.uk***

Mass market lakes-and-mountains specialist with six hotels on Lago Trasimeno and discounts for children in parents' rooms.

Inntravel

01653 617949. ***www.inntravel.co.uk***

Three all-inclusive cycling itineraries in rural Tuscany, to suit families with teens and up.

Invitation to Tuscany

020 86002522. ***www.invitationtotuscany.com***

Tuscan specialist with some properties in Umbria, and a search facility for families on their website.

Keycamp

0870 7000123. ***www.keycamp.co.uk***

Perfect family operator, with campsite holidays built for youngsters: children's clubs, babysitting, single-parent discounts, even discounts at ***www.tinytotsaway.com*** (see p. 18). Four sites in Tuscany.

Kuoni

01306 747746. ***www.kuoni.co.uk***

Top-rank hotels and high-end properties throughout the region, including the sands of Versilia and Elba.

MyTravel

0870 2387777. ***www.mytravel.com***

Hotel packages to Florence at mass-market prices.

Owners Direct

www.ownersdirect.co.uk

The original rent-it-direct-from-the-owner website with properties across Tuscany and Umbria.

Owners' Syndicate

020 73817490.
www.ownerssyndicate.com

Luxury villas and quaint cottages all over Tuscany and Umbria.

Real Holidays

020 73593938.
www.realholidays.co.uk

Hand-picked villas with pools, boutique hotels and farmhouses converted into apartments in the quietest corners of Umbria.

Siblu

0870 2427777. *www.siblu.com*

Flexible camp specialist whose family-focused offering includes the giant Norcenni Girasole campsite south of Florence.

Simply Travel

0870 1664979.
www.simplytravel.co.uk

Apartments, villas and farmhouses with character across Tuscany and Umbria, to suit sizeable budgets.

Sovereign Villas

0871 6640011.
www.sovereignvillas.co.uk

Eight quality Tuscan villas in rural locations, all with pools.

Summer's Leases

0845 2302223.
www.summersleases.com

High-end villas for families of all sizes.

Thomson

0870 1652602.
www.thomson.co.uk

From on-a-budget to à la carte – sightseeing, spa and city breaks with a holiday giant.

Traditional Tuscany

01553 810003.
www.traditionaltuscany.co.uk

Castles, cottages, villas and apartments – even B&Bs – for 'the interested and independent traveller'. Includes Umbria, too.

Travel Matters

020 86757878.
www.travelmatters.co.uk

Family specialists with a few top-quality self-catering properties in Tuscany.

Vacansoleil

08700 778779.
www.vacansoleil.co.uk

Camp operator with a site to fit all families.

Villa Centre

01223 513593.
www.villacentre.com

Affordable villas of all shapes and sizes, spread throughout both regions.

Vintage Travel

0845 3440460.
www.vintagetravel.co.uk

Villas that sleep 2 to 22, all with private pools.

Index

See also Accommodations and Restaurant indexes, below.

General

A

B

C

L

M

N

O

P

Q

R

S

T

U

V

W

Z

Accommodations

Restaurants